"Many things I like about the book: it describes social development in ways that every parent should understand; it focuses on the parensultant role has expanded to include both hands-on help apossibility for parents to send short clips of interactions w, where they can be viewed by the therapist. All in all at that RDI expand to other countries...The most important breakthrough would be how to clone Steve 12 or 15 times, teach the clones various languages and send them on their way. And be sure to send one to Kentucky while you are at it."

PETER TANGUAY, MD, FACP
Spafford Ackerly Endowed Professor of Child and Adolescent Psychiatry (Emeritus)
Department of Psychiatry and Behavioral Sciences, School of Medicine, University of Louisville

"I really like the way you break down the research so that both parents and professionals can use it. I am going to recommend this book as required reading."

IVOR WEINER, PH.D.
Acting Director, Teaching, Learning and Counseling (TLC) Consortium
California State University, Northridge

"In *The RDI Book*, Dr Steven Gutstein offers a vision of the interpersonal grounding for communication and mental development – development that he relates to the functioning of our 'dynamic brains' – and moves with ease between an account of typical early development and a subtle yet powerful analysis of the difficulties faced, but also the opportunities presented, in fostering development among children with autism. Through the committed and rigorous application of developmental principles underpinning guided participation to 'forge new pathways' for individuals on the autism spectrum, the author not only provides an invaluable guide to parents and other caregivers or professionals seeking to help affected children, but also enables us all to appreciate what 'autism' really means...This is a wonderful and often moving book about a hugely significant approach to parent-led intervention for children with autism."

R.PETER HOBSON
Tavistock Professor of Developmental Psychopathology, University of London

The major contribution of this book for working with people diagnosed with ASD is the focus on dynamic intelligence as distinct from static skills. The review of dynamic processes is well grounded in current research and clearly points to the promotion of quality of life and the building of family strengths and supports as the primary treatment goal. The book also integrates relationship development models showing the importance of co-regulation and bridging as dynamic processes that foster and sustain dynamically adaptive ways of relating to the world.

ALAN FOGEL, PH.D.
Professor - Developmental Area, Department of Psychology, University of Utah

The RDI Book

ALSO BY STEVEN GUTSTEIN

My Baby Can Dance: Stories of Autism, Asperger's and Success Through the Relationship Development Intervention Program

Relationship Development Intervention with Young Children: Social and Emotional Development Activities for Asperger's Syndrome, Autism, PDD and NLD

Relationship Development Intervention with Adolescents and Adults: Social and Emotional Development Activities for Asperger's Syndrome, Autism, PDD & NLD

Solving the Relationship Puzzle

The Relationship Development Intervention Program and Education

All titles available from www.rdiconnect.com.

The RDI Book:

Forging New Pathways for Autism, Asperger's and PDD
with the Relationship Development Intervention® Program

by Steven E. Gutstein, Ph.D.

CONNECTIONS CENTER PUBLISHING
HOUSTON, TEXAS USA

For information on ordering from Connections Center Publishing, please contact us by phone, 713-838-1362, fax 713-838-1447 or e-mail: rdibook@rdiconnect.com.

www.rdiconnect.com

ISBN: 978-0-9777186-3-4

Cover graphic: ©iStockphoto.com/Illustrious
Credits for graphic elements used in illustrations are listed in Graphics Index.

Cover design and book layout by Carlotta Baird.

ACKOWLEDGEMENTS

Thanks are due to the scores of consultants, consultants-in-training and families who contributed in uncounted ways to the contents of this book. Special thanks are due to RDIconnect staff, especially Ana Hermosilla, Claudia Andreessen and Melanie Smith, for their endless efforts to improve what we do. Jessica and Peter Hobson, as well as their son Matthew, have acted as essential sounding boards for many of the ideas within. Special thanks to Maisie Soetantyo and Peter Dunlavey for supplying so much excellent footage of typical development with their daughter Emma. Hannah Gutstein and Carlotta Baird have worked tirelessly, as always, to organize, edit and revise. Thanks go to Hannah for listening to so many of my lectures and seminars, trying to separate wheat from chaff. Carlotta provided the incredibly helpful graphics that illuminate otherwise difficult concepts. Finally, endless gratitude goes to my wife Rachelle, for wearing so many hats, ranging from manuscript editing, to loving me unconditionally (no easy task).

*This book is dedicated to my adopted mother, Rachel,
who, for almost 30 years has never failed to fill my stomach
and guide my soul. —S.G.*

TABLE OF CONTENTS

APPENDICIES

PREFACE

First, you know, a new theory is attacked as absurd; then it is admitted to be true, but obvious and insignificant; finally it is seen to be so important that its adversaries claim that they themselves discovered it.

—WILLIAM JAMES

Over the years, I have talked at length with many adults on the autism spectrum about their lives and their dreams. They recount their desire to have an opportunity for the same quality of life you and I take for granted. They are not so different from us, just human beings who have gone through life in a state of perpetual confusion. They constantly experience feeling as if at any moment they might be swallowed up by stepping into a chasm. They feel discouraged and hopeless of attaining many of the things we take for granted: true friendship, a comfortable work environment and a loving intimate relationship. If you can, imagine trying to navigate this world all day, every day, then you will understand why even the most successful person on the spectrum feels like he or she is always at the edge of a precipice.

In 1996 my wife, Dr. Rachelle Sheely and I set off on a scientific journey to determine whether we could remediate the universal learning problems that define Autism Spectrum Disorders (ASD).[1] We hoped to shift the perception of what is possible, to raise the bar for people on the autism spectrum, their families and those

---

1   I intend to follow the current custom of including Autism, Asperger's Disorder and Pervasive Developmental Disorders under the single Autism Spectrum Disorders label. Research has concluded that there is little if any reason to continue making these diagnostic distinctions and these groups are typically placed together in modern studies of the condition. Hereafter I will use the "ASD" abbreviation to describe these conditions.

who work with them. Rachelle and I committed to finding a way to provide opportunities for the majority of ASD people to attain a quality of life as independent, emotionally connected, responsible adults. This book represents a waypoint in what has become a lifelong task.

The RDI Book is designed for two specific audiences: readers wishing to learn about the possibilities for remediating the core deficits that define Autism Spectrum Disorders (ASD) will find this book valuable, as will those who simply want to learn more about ASD.

I believe that RDI provides a first step in constructing a comprehensive, remedial approach to this complex disorder. The book is divided into two main sections. In the initial section, I present background and theory, an innovative view of what we now understand about ASD. I also describe a new, testable model, which I believe has great potential to alter the way intervention is provided. The second section describes our most current methods. It roughly corresponds to the parent training stages in the RDI® Curriculum: Education, Readiness, Apprenticeship, Guiding and Internalizing, and serves as a guide for family members and professionals interested in obtaining a comprehensive, up-to-date understanding of the workings of the Relationship Development Intervention® (RDI®) Program.

RDI has been a continually evolving methodology since its inception in 2000. The current volume replaces earlier works such as *Solving the Relationship Puzzle* and our two RDI® activity books. Due to the evolution of the program since their publication, we consider this a better representation of our current model of intervention.

The book provides a good introduction for professionals considering becoming RDI® Program Consultants as well as those already in the training process. Similarly, it serves as a resource for parents who are considering or are in the early stages of the RDI process as well as those more experienced with RDI who wish to provide greater understanding of the program to others.[2]

---

2   Readers who are currently involved with the RDI® Learning System should note that the staging of curriculum objectives is taken from the 2009 revision of the curriculum and may not be fully implemented at the time of the book's publication.

This work is not meant to be a comprehensive manual and does not claim to provide the expertise needed to function as an RDI® Consultant. Nor is it meant to contain *how to* techniques and methods. We strongly recommend that parents interested in RDI seek guidance from a Certified RDI® Consultant. We do not recommend that you employ RDI methodology in a piecemeal fashion. Consultant information is available on our website—www.rdiconnect.com.

Readers who, after completing this book, are interested in specific application of RDI in educational settings, should obtain **RDI and Education**. Those interested in first-hand experiences of families going through the RDI process will benefit from **My Baby Can Dance**, also available on our website. Readers who wish to gain more understanding of the key theoretical and research underpinnings of RDI should particularly review the works of Barbara Rogoff, Alan Sroufe, Peter Hobson and Alan Fogel.

Additional practical information concerning RDI is available on our website. This includes consultant listings, more detailed description of the RDI® Learning System (RDILS), announcements of workshops and information about the Professional Certification Program.

Those of us who are fortunate to be guides in the development of someone with ASD face both challenges and opportunities. The challenges include fully understanding the complexity of the hundreds of developmental pieces missing for even the highest functioning persons with this disorder. It has been a Herculean task to document and developmentally sequence a meaningful curriculum. It has taken a number of years to construct the hundreds of small, gradually more complex steps that allow persons with ASD to attain the competencies most of us learn intuitively and seemingly effortlessly. The opportunity is the thrill obtained when we slow down, remain in the moment and mindfully participate in each of the thousands of small steps in the day-by-day psychological re-birth of a fully functioning human being.

It is said that a journey of a thousand miles begins with a single step. While we haven't traversed the entire distance, I believe this book represents the many steps we have taken in the past ten years to provide a quality of life for persons on the autism spectrum. Started a little less than a decade ago, RDI provides a first attempt at constructing a comprehensive, remedial approach to this complex disorder. Thank you for walking alongside us on our journey.

Introduction

When you come to a fork in the road, take it. —YOGI BERRA

EMILY

Emily at age seven is a non-stop talker. This symptom of "hyper-verbalization," means, in plain language, that Emily talks without thinking. She seems oblivious to the meaning of what she is saying, as well as the impact she is having on the listener. If you spend any length of time with Emily, you realize that you are just a glorified supporting actor, albeit more than an extra, in the play of daily life that she scripts for herself. She may ask you the same question five or six times within the same five-minute period. She has little interest in your responses and will ignore or even become irritated with you if they deviate in any manner from the answers she is anticipating.

Sit down to play any game or try to collaborate on any task and you will find, as I did, that Emily will amaze you with how rapidly she tries and often succeeds in taking complete control. She acts as if it is quite normal for seven-year-olds to dictate the rules of games they know nothing about. Her matter-of-fact voice informs me that, "Chess is the same as checkers," a game she knows well, "only the pieces look different. We will jump each other's pieces and eliminate them from the board." I tell Emily I may not play with those rules and grudgingly she tries to add small modifications, making minor concessions so as not to lose my presence. She is a perfectionist when engaged in a task. She quickly determines what standards her performance should attain and from then on is not satisfied with any other outcome.

If interrupted prior to achieving her goal, or if the task proves so difficult that her standards cannot be attained, Emily is likely to become dejected and proclaim herself a failure. Such self-imposed tyranny has resulted in her completely avoiding any performance-based activity requiring visual-motor coordination, as this is clearly her greatest weakness.

Emily's parents are young and healthy, but they are worn out. They tell me, with an ironic smile, how the doctors have told them that Emily has "mild" autism and is a "very high functioning" child with the disorder. She attends typical classes in her public school and her achievement test scores indicate that she is on grade level. The impact of her autism may not show up on achievement tests until Emily is much older when the tests begin to measure real understanding and not just memorization.

VIVIAN

Vivian is a product of over eight years of intensive speech therapy, social skills training and behavior modification. I'm told she now has a vocabulary of well over 500 words. This tall, motorically coordinated young teenager, who attends special education classes at her public school, shows little inclination to initiate any communication with me. As soon as I enter the room where she is inevitably reading a book, Vivian gazes towards me with more than a little apprehension. I do not immediately interrupt her and gradually move to her side, never making a sound or requiring any face-to-face performance. I make it to the couch without creating any disturbance and seat myself at the opposite side from her. After about 30 seconds, she briefly glances over to me, smiles in what I interpret as a welcoming manner and returns to her book. When the page ends, Vivian passively accepts her mother's request to close the book and apparently directs her attention to staring at the wall across from her. I move a bit closer to her and she seems quite comfortable with our increased proximity.

We sit quietly side-by-side on the sofa, staring at nothing in particular. She makes no move to control me, or leave my presence, as long as I do not try to get anything from her. She frequently glances over and smiles. I bounce a bit on one of the sofa cushions. She glances over, smiles and bounces a bit herself. Later I bounce harder and pretend to accidentally fall off. Vivian gazes over, laughs and holds out her hand to help me up. Then she returns to staring at the wall.

Ed

Ed, age six, appears completely unlike Emily and Vivian. He is yet a third vector of this disorder. He does not possess even a single word. His movements can be characterized as a ball of constant disorganized motion. Ed's movement seems guided by a type of mental slot machine. His eyes flow from object to object in a rapid cascade and then, for no apparent reason, they seem to pause for several seconds to attend to something at random. Most of the time Ed's focus is not combined with productive action. He typically does not study interesting, familiar objects, nor does he purposefully orient to obtain desired results—although at times his actions can be surprisingly goal-focused, if it is about one of the very few things he really desires. Unlike Emily, who seems to value my companionship as long as it coordinates with her over-active experience-scripting and Vivian, who, if we limit the language, appears quite comfortable to hang out with me, Ed doesn't stop to acknowledge my presence. Even when I slowly move towards him, he reveals no reaction. He seems unaware of me until I am physically just inches from his turned-away face.

For no apparent reason, Ed suddenly makes a high-pitched noise, runs to his mother and buries himself in her arms. Just as suddenly, he breaks from her grasp and resumes his random expedition to nowhere. His face shows little diversity of emotion—no signs of enjoyment, curiosity, apprehension or excitement. His only expressions appear to be occasional moments of distress, which may or may not be fleeting.

UNITY WITHIN DIVERSITY

These three children represent a small sample of the incredible diversity found among the ASD population. ASD individuals may or may not suffer from an extremely wide range of neural, medical and psychological disorders. Many of these conditions present significant obstacles to development and must be treated in their own right, involving the efforts of a trained, coordinated inter-disciplinary team. Their stories and those of millions of individuals like them pose an excellent beginning to the question driving my life's work: How does one go about providing individuals with Autism Spectrum Disorder (ASD) the tools to have a quality of life?

When we set about developing Relationship Development Intervention (RDI), we perceived that intervention efforts in the autism community were already well focused on recognizing and treating co-occurring conditions. There were many interventions to help people with ASD. In contrast, we found that clinical methods and programs were not evolving to address deficit areas that compose the heart of ASD. Since Dr. Leo Kanner wrote his seminal paper in 1943,[3] ASD has been considered a single syndrome, rather than a collection of individuals with a wide range of different symptoms and deficits. To use an analogy, it was as if treatment of AIDS addressed the respiratory difficulties and skin infections with medication and provided counseling for depression and other reactive psychiatric conditions but made no attempt to impact or target the AIDS itself.

We have learned to address many areas related to ASD, but the ASD itself has been like the 800 lb. gorilla in the room. We find that no matter what else we treat, these core deficits prevent people with ASD from having a quality of life.

Unlike AIDS, one might argue that by treating the symptoms and co-occurring disorders surrounding the disorder, we could provide a quality of life for ASD individuals. We would then have no need to treat the disorder itself. Perhaps by provid-

---

3   It is interesting to note the Dr. Kanner wrote his paper, the foundation of over 60 years of autism research, based upon study of just 11 children of Johns Hopkins Medical School faculty members.

ing speech to individuals who were "non-verbal," increasing behavioral compliance, reducing odd mannerisms and rituals, teaching appropriate social and self-help skills, treating allergies and nutritional intolerances, increasing sensory-motor integration and providing academic knowledge, we would enable ASD individuals to attain a quality of life. This has been an implicit assumption guiding most interventions in the autism community. Many of these efforts, when appropriately administered, are highly productive and provide significant benefit for addressing co-occurring issues.

The problem with this argument is that it is not supported by research. After 30 years of study, we have no reason to expect that these services by themselves have led to more ASD persons attaining a quality of life, regardless of the intensity with which they have been offered. Despite dramatically increasing resources for ASD intervention, we have no evidence that we are making any impact helping people with ASD to form reciprocal friendships and mature emotional relationships, conduct successful collaborations, engage in flexible, adaptive thought, or master the problem-solving abilities necessary for job attainment and success in our 21st century world.[4] The few studies that track the natural history of ASD individuals lead to similar conclusions. Researchers who attempt to differentiate and track those individuals with relatively fewer obstacles—for example, those ASD adults with at least normal IQ and language functioning—find that the prognosis for a normal life is discouraging. In the largest study to date, conducted by the National Autistic Society of Great Britain, only 12% of these "highest functioning" individuals were able to attain any kind of even menial employment, with only 3% able to live independently.

It is logical to conclude that if we are preparing ASD children for a chance at success in the real world, we must distinguish between treating the many possible co-occurring problems that people with ASD may have and remediating the chronic, core deficits of ASD itself. Both are necessary and neither is sufficient by itself. A quality of life is dependent upon it.

---

4 These abilities are collectively known as employability and have been studied extensively.

Of course, this is easier said than done. ASD has often presented itself like a Russian doll, where uncovering one layer reveals another and another and another just below the surface. It is apparent that many ASD individuals suffer from a diversity of problems and disorders. If one did not have the means to examine the condition on a deeper level, one would question why these individuals should be placed into a single syndrome. The same can be said for the strengths and skills of ASD individuals. Contained within the ASD family are individuals who do not develop speech and others who talk incessantly with highly developed vocabularies. ASD encompasses persons with a tested IQ in the genius level and others classified with significant intellectual impairment. It includes teenagers who can sink a three-point basket and others who cannot seem to lift and hold onto a basketball. Some ASD persons have allergies so severe that even a slight amount of a specific food will render them unavailable, while others can eat anything without the slightest effect. Some are easygoing and even-tempered, while others are defiant and quick to anger or cry. Some are highly disorganized to the point of appearing to wander in a random, aimless fashion, while others are highly rigid and controlling, demanding that everything occur in a scripted sameness. Some spend hours engaging in self-stimulating hand movements while others would find that boring.

Thankfully, we initiated our work in a time when many of the mysteries of ASD had begun to be revealed. Kanner himself offered some important clues in his 25-year follow-up observations of the children he originally studied in 1943. A small group of dedicated researchers, scientists like Peter Mundy, Marion Sigman, Ami Klin, Geraldine Dawson, Sally Rogers, Eric Courchesne, Margaret Bauman, Marcel Just and Nancy Minshew in the United States and Peter and Jessica Hobson, Patricia Howlin, Colwyn Trevarthen, Tony Charman and Simon Baron-Cohen in the UK, have been intent on getting past the diverse periphery to the universal core of ASD, a deep well of knowledge on which we have drawn. As I will discuss in future chapters, scientists have learned that persons with ASD are united by specific, lifelong, highly debilitating, neurologically-based information processing difficulties— severe learning disabilities— that, even in the absence of other problems and symptoms, prevent them from attaining a quality of life. Careful neurological research is revealing a unique "under connectivity" that appears to underlie these learning problems.

Relationship Development Intervention (RDI) has been developed to remediate information-processing deficits that are universal but by no means unique to persons on the autism spectrum. We use the term dynamic intelligence to represent this collection of specific cognitive, self, interpersonal and communication abilities universally deficient in persons with ASD. This is in contrast to the abilities we refer to as static intelligence—skills measured by standard I.Q. tests, which are not necessarily impacted by ASD.

In the past 20 years, Developmental Psychology has undergone an explosion of interest in better understanding children's dynamic development. Researchers have found that the sophisticated skills we take for granted as adults originate in the first years of life. These include our abilities for group collaboration, flexible problem solving, meaningful reflection, future planning and preparation. Although there are more gaps than filled-in areas, systematically cataloguing the progressive development of mental processes has provided a starting point. This is a mammoth project consuming years of time and energy and continues to this day. Nevertheless, it has reaped very useful results, as you will learn in later sections.

One scientist whose work has been seminal to this understanding is Peter Hobson, a Psychiatrist and Psychologist, who has for years been on the forefront of our understanding of ASD. He infers that in autism something interferes with the specific early parent-child learning experiences required for developing dynamic neural networks, while generally leaving the static brain pathways intact. We know that dynamic and static processing do not develop in the same manner. Static networks develop through what we commonly refer to as instruction, simple associations of neurons and external stimuli that are reinforced through repetitive pairings. Thus, if I wish to develop a static neural network, I can repetitively associate a specific stimulus, say a written math computation problem like "2 X 2 = " with a specific response, in this case "4". If I am successful, I will have created a neural pathway such that, each time the stimulus is presented, a specific, simple brain network is activated. The neural pathway would serve to visually decode the problem and then supply the correct, already associated response.

But how does the brain develop the capacity for dynamic growth? Respected scientists like Jerome Bruner, Barbara Rogoff, Alan Fogel and Alan Sroufe, believe that the neural and cognitive foundations for dynamic intelligence are typically constructed through thousands of special types of experiences choreographed through the guidance of parents and close family members. This special type of learning relationship is referred to as guided participation.

The Guided Participation Relationship (GPR)[5] is the cornerstone of parent-child functioning in every society on earth. In this special type of collaboration, an experienced guide carefully prepares situations in which a less experienced apprentice can productively struggle with uncertainty and challenge. Guides carefully balance establishing a safe environment, in which the apprentice can feel competent, with cognitive challenges that are just a bit ahead of the current level of the apprentice's understanding and stretch the apprentice's mental functioning. This creates the impetus for the formation of more complex and more highly integrated neural networks.

By the beginning of the second year of life, typically developing children have become active participants in the learning process, no longer focusing solely on behavior, but searching for meaning. They can now appraise their guide's intentions, desires and preferences and the mental aspects of their actions. They are motivated to journey with their guides into moments of uncertainty, where the more experienced guide becomes the apprentice's primary reference point and the apprentice actively seeks to appropriate the guide's thinking, appraisal and prior experience.

After learning about guided participation, I began to analyze videotapes of parents interacting with their ASD children to see if I could determine whether this process was indeed disrupted. In every single case, the GPR was either missing or severely impaired. These observations were confirmed by several hundred RDI Consultants who routinely assess the state of the parent-child GPR as part of their

---

5   Henceforth, I will use the abbreviation 'GPR' synonymously with the 'Guided Participation Relationship'.

initial assessment.[6] Equally significant, we found that in families with a typically developing sibling, the Guided Participation Relationship between parents and their typically developing child proceeded in a perfectly normal manner.

These observations provided an important clue in our quest to determine the focal point for intervention. Relationship Development Intervention (RDI) was the name chosen to represent this hope of a second chance for families with an ASD child to successfully engage in this universal developmental relationship that, through no fault of their own, had not been successful on the first go around. The mission became to restore parents to their natural roles as the primary guides of their child.

In designing RDI, we never believed that we could make up for all of the lost developmental time in a day, week, month or even a year. We hoped that by restoring a pathway to mental development, we would see the types of small moments of day-to-day mental growth that characterize typical development. We have learned not to worry about how quickly ASD children catch up with their typical peers, as long as they are gradually returning to a normal process of development.

But, how were we to restore the GPR? While there are hundreds of books, monographs and articles describing elements of this natural, intuitive process, there is no roadmap for how to proceed if the process does not develop.

We quickly found that this was no simple task. As any parent knows, raising a child with ASD is like being a blind captain of a sailing ship with a deaf crew. No matter how good a parent you are, how educated, or motivated, you are rendered inadequate by the communication barriers and seeming indifference to your efforts that are often by-products of the condition. Unfortunately, providing the child with speech does not mitigate these barriers, as parents of verbal children suffering from this condition will attest.

We recognized that to provide families with a route to guiding their ASD children, first we had to understand why the Guided Participation Relationship was not functioning. What could disrupt the GPR? It was apparent that the problem did not

---

6   This finding is also supported by recent research conducted by Dr. Jessica Hobson at the Tavistock Institute in London, presented at the 2008 International Meeting for Autism Research (IMFAR).

lie with any parental deficiency or characteristic. The same parents, who appeared unable to guide their ASD children, typically formed excellent guiding relationships with the child's typically developing siblings.

As I learned more about guided participation, I found that, unlike static learning, where the learner can maintain a relatively passive stance, the dance of guided participation requires collaboration and ongoing feedback from both partners. In other words, no matter how proficient you are as a guide, you cannot succeed unless your apprentice is taking a share of the responsibility for maintaining the process.

Furthermore, I learned that prior to assuming the role of cognitive apprentice, typical infants first master pre-requisite abilities like identification, collaboration, joint attention and social referencing that ready them to become active participants in the learning process. Early versions of these abilities are typically mastered in the first year of life. I believe it to be no coincidence that these are the very same areas most documented in the research literature as universally impaired in children with ASD.

In his groundbreaking work published over 15 years ago, Peter Hobson took this concept a step further by hypothesizing that there is no specific vulnerability, no part of the brain, no specific chemical imbalance or gene, that in and of itself is responsible for ASD. He hypothesized that ASD can be triggered by a variety of possible pre-natal and genetic abnormalities. This has now become a scientifically accepted belief about the origin of the condition. Hobson implied that if the combination and impact of the child's impairments were sufficiently great, they would interfere with his or her ability to contribute the necessary ingredients to make the parent-child relationship work and thus prevent the emergence of dynamic pathways for neurological and mental growth.

Developing the pre-requisites for guided participation typically proceeds in a completely intuitive manner. Parental guides do not typically think of, or plan the actions they are taking to provide the infant "pre-apprentice" with the necessary abilities to function as a competent cognitive apprentice. They have no systematic guidebook of sequenced objectives to guide them.

To me, this presents the crux of the problem for remediation. If something goes dreadfully wrong, as it does in ASD, parents have no reference point, no way to troubleshoot the problem and make adjustments. As a result, the process goes spiraling out of control.

I believed that by careful observation and study of developmental research, I could systematically document and make overt the intuitive process by which the early foundations of guided participation develop between parents and children. Moreover, I could then separate it into smaller steps and customize methods to compensate for each child's unique obstacles. I could then develop methods to teach parents to function in a simpler, slower and more mindful manner than had naturally been attempted the first time around. Thus, I hoped to provide parents a second opportunity to act as their child's primary guides.

THE BEGINNING OF RDI

Slow down to speed up. Help each child start at a place from where they can build momentum. The beauty of our approach is that it is based on principles that neither I nor any other psychologist, researcher or theorist had a hand in creating. The basic methods we wish to understand and systematize are those employed by every culture since the dawn of humankind. To develop our approach we did not have to reinvent the wheel. Rather the task was to carefully observe, analyze and systematize an elegant, but intuitive process and reveal it in a mindful, deliberate, gradually unfolding manner.

We did not know when we began that there would be so many years of development ahead. In addition to systematizing both a Dynamic Intelligence Curriculum and a Parent Guiding Curriculum, we had to customize the process to meet each child's unique bio-psycho-social profile as well as parents' individual readiness and the family's real world demands. Our goal was to develop a user-friendly program that the vast majority of parents would be able to learn and carry out at their own pace.

To do this we developed a successful RDI Consultant training program, a system to ensure quality assurance, a means of generalizing RDI into school settings and an internet-based communication, progress-tracking and dynamic learning system—the RDI Learning System—to serve our worldwide community. RDI is a program in continual evolution due to the efforts of a dedicated community of thousands of parents and hundreds of trained RDI Consultants in more than 20 different countries. This evolution of the program is the central momentum of RDI, which undoubtedly will continue past my lifetime.

Trained RDI Consultants serve as 'guides to the guides', by helping parents construct a slower lifestyle that still fits within the realities of their unique culture and family circumstances. They help customize parental guiding efforts to meet the unique strengths and vulnerabilities of their ASD child. Through collaboration with their consultants, mothers and fathers gradually take more responsibility for carefully choreographing an unfolding developmental progression. They slowly but continuously raise the bar and present new challenges, while providing sufficient support for the child to safely voyage without fear into areas of greater uncertainty.

Parents learn to help the child construct memories of mastery in the face of challenge. These memories are stockpiled, as guides make sure to help the child build an experiential repository of success in gradually more complex environments.

RDI embraces the premise that all family members must be nurtured and cared for and that they all sink or swim together. Every family member is critical to success. Parents are aided to recover from the feelings of desperation and emotional damage that are inevitable by-products of the disorder. Through the RDI Program, parents renew their sense of hope, feelings of competence and mutual support. Grandparents, relatives and other caregivers are taught to provide guidance as part of the family team, providing significant contributions without usurping the primary parental role. Siblings have their own lives and their needs are not neglected or burdened with care-taking or compensating roles. Rather, as they function as competent apprentices to their parents, their relationship with their ASD sibling becomes one of mutual responsibility and respect.

Both fathers and mothers are critical participants in the learning process. Current estimates of father's participation in RDI are over 90%. However, single parents are never excluded from RDI.

Part One:
Setting the Stage for RDI

Chapter One

Dynamic Brains

The brain is also dynamic, meaning that it is forever in a state of change.
—Daniel Siegel

There is a short video clip I downloaded from You Tube, which I often use in presentations. It is of Stephen, a softly spoken young man from Great Britain, nicknamed "The Human Camera" because of his amazing savant abilities. As you probably know, savants are individuals, typically, but not always with ASD, who demonstrate amazing proclivities in a single area of perception, memory and/or replication. Stephen's ability is visual duplication. He can draw anything he sees, no matter how briefly, in unbelievable detail. In a somewhat famous video, Stephen, who had never before visited Rome, is flown by helicopter over the city. After a 45-minute journey, he is returned to a room containing an enormously wide sheet of sketch paper, probably spanning more than 30 feet. Over the next three days he replicates in pencil every feature of the city, down to the tiniest cornice and windows blocks away from his flight path. His work is almost 100% accurate. While not all ASD individuals can perform these kinds of amazing feats, what Stephen does may represent an extreme version of what scientists are beginning to believe may happen as ASD brains journey down their path of development.

Regardless of the myriad symptoms and problems we observe in particular individuals, ASD is fundamentally a neurological disorder linked to the networking of the brain. I am anything but an expert in Neurology, therefore, please forgive my desire to use the following over-simplified description of neural functioning. In my account, I will distinguish two different ways in which our brains process information. These represent two different pathways of neural functioning that I refer to as static and dynamic.

At times, our brains function as if certain things that happen in the world, specific things we see, hear, touch and smell, are hard-wired to specific neural pathways in the brain. Specific stimuli seem to evoke in us the same learned associations each time we perceive them: formulas, procedures, memorized information, habits and routines. We learn to automatically multiply numbers, brush our teeth, say, "God bless you," in response to a sneeze, greet our neighbor on the elevator, stop at stop signs and perform a host of other actions with little conscious thought or effort. We do it in the exact same manner thousands of times. When our brain is operating in this static manner, we function similarly to the digital computers that are so ubiquitous in our lives. A specific event triggers a specific program that runs until completion.

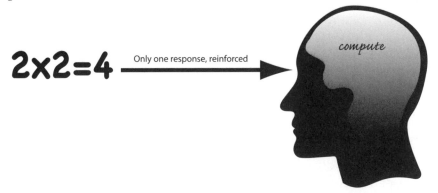

$$2 \times 2 = 4 \xrightarrow{\text{Only one response, reinforced}} \textit{compute}$$

At other times, our brains operate in a more mindful, less programmed fashion. We attend to our here-and-now experiences and integrate them with our past and potential future. We explore the nature of our minds. Problems, settings, persons and cues do not automatically trigger a specific response. We deliberate, reflect, worry, hypothesize, daydream, hang out, gossip and engage in a great deal of mental activity that cannot be predicted by the appearance of any particular stimulus. When our brains function in this manner, we operate in a uniquely human way that cannot be vaguely matched by even our most sophisticated computers.

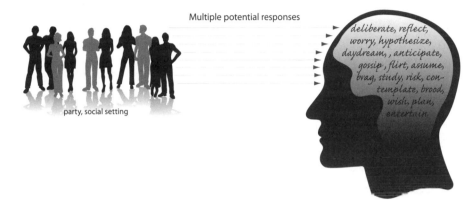

Multiple potential responses

party, social setting

deliberate, reflect, worry, hypothesize, daydream, , anticipate, gossip , flirt, assume, brag, study, risk, contemplate, brood, wish, plan, entertain

DYNAMIC NEURAL DEVELOPMENT

It is becoming increasingly clear to scientists that Autism Spectrum Disorders derive from the failure of the brain to develop normal dynamic functioning. While not present at birth, scientists observe that by the age of two, typical children have already developed sophisticated dynamic pathways, which continue to evolve as they get older.

Let me share a hypothesis I support, which is gaining increased popularity among scientists in the ASD community. What if some combination of innate vulnerabilities of the child interferes with their brain's dynamic journey at an early stage? And what if static neural growth is not impacted by these vulnerabilities and is left relatively intact? The result will be a person diagnosed at some point with an Autism Spectrum Disorder. The most recent brain imaging studies from around the world support this hypothesis. Extensive literature on the universal cognitive, social, self and emotional deficits of ASD links them to the functioning of our dynamic brain, and researchers find that the majority, but not all persons with ASD, retain intact and sometimes superior static functioning.

In making this static/dynamic distinction I refer to a certain type of brain dysfunction. I am not implying that there is a structural defect in a specific organ of the brain. CAT Scans, MRIs and other static measures of brain structure do not reveal any universal abnormalities, although this is not the case for specific ASD individuals, who may show significant structural pathology. As far as we know, after extensive study, scientists cannot find a single structural defect that is universal to individuals with ASD.

On the other hand, a consensus is emerging, pointing to deficient development of the brain's networking, as central to ASD. Networking refers to the way that various neural processing centers collaborate and form distinct, as well as integrated communication networks. Researchers are concluding that the origin of the disorder is related to, not the way that ASD individuals communicate with others, which is clearly disrupted, but how the ASD brain learns to communicate with itself.

Several research teams like those of Marcel Just, Nancy Minshew and their colleagues at Carnegie Mellon, use Functional MRI scans to observe the actual network activation of the brain during different tasks, such as sentence comprehension. They conclude that ASD brains universally suffer from network underconnectivity.[1] In an excerpt from one of their recent papers Dr. Just's team concludes that, "Individuals with ASD demonstrate significant underconnectivity in their formation of neural patterns. Specific types of problems and stimuli become rigidly linked to specific brain centers. This limits their ability to respond flexibly and in a more holistic manner to changes in their world." Drs. Minshew and Williams, also with the Carnegie Mellon group, conclude that neural connectivity deficits in ASD have been demonstrated in a robust manner. They conclude that, "Lower functional connectivity … has been found in fMRI studies involving language, working memory, problem solving and social cognition, providing evidence of a general problem with functional underconnectivity within and between neocortical systems in autism."

---

1   Underconnectivity is a rather misleading term. Scientists do not mean that there are insufficient neural connections in the brain. Rather, the term "connectivity" refers to the ability for different neural processing centers to work fluidly in an as needed, collaborative fashion. Neural Collaborativity would be a more accurate term.

According to Drs. Minshew and Williams, a not well-appreciated aspect of ASD is the second wave of deficits that emerges in the second decade of life. Frontal circuitry normally matures during this time period, and oculomotor, fMRI, and neuropsychologic studies of working memory and executive function in autism have revealed the emergence of new deficits in adolescence in autism, with the failure of frontal lobe skills to develop. Previously, it was thought that adolescents and young adults with autism fell further behind peers in adaptive function in the second decade because life became more challenging. In fact, the higher order frontal lobe skills needed to cope with these life demands may fail to develop in autism. Minshew and Williams believe that this severe frontal dysmaturity may account for the unexpectedly poor adaptive function in adult life in the majority of high-functioning ASD individuals.

TAKING IT TO THE EXTREME: THE HUMAN CAMERA

Let's return for a moment to the vignette I used to begin this chapter, that of Stephen, The Human Camera who flies for the first time over the streets of Rome and then, for three days replicates everything with which his eyes have made even the briefest contact. Most of us are awestruck by Stephen's amazing ability and cannot fathom how he can perform this feat. It is certainly a testament to the amazing processing power available to the human brain. I believe that Stephen's ability while impressive is nowhere nearly as incredible as what most of us would do if we were aloft over Rome for the same 45-minute interval. Certainly, few of us could replicate even a small fraction of what our eyes perceive. Thankfully, our brain was not designed to process in this way.

If I had the means to observe your neural functioning while for the first time carrying you aloft over Rome, I would undoubtedly see your brain virtually ablaze with communication between many different neural centers. You would be experiencing a variety of emotional states, from awe at the beauty below you, to fear at the fragility of the thin metal casing of the helicopter that alone protects you from sudden death. Though you had never been to Rome, you would be flooded with memories from years of books, photos and movies. You would be searching for familiar landmarks. You might be imagining the majesty of the Roman Empire. Your brain might be flying from perceptions, to emotions, to memories, to anticipation and plans for your walking tour the next day.

Now let us consider Stephen's neural functioning. His brain may contain as much potential raw processing power as yours or mine. However, if you were to observe his neural activity, you would find it almost all spent in the center for processing visual details. This is not some voluntary decision that Stephen makes to temporarily direct all of his brain's energy to one function. This is just what his brain does. When he journeys to a new city or for that matter, when he has any new experience, Stephen has a single way to process the information he encounters whether it is useful or not. He is trapped in a powerful but highly under-connected brain, an extreme example of what neuro-scientists are talking about.

Can you turn off your dynamic brain? *As an exercise, try to force yourself to process information like Stephen, the human camera. Don't try to replicate what he can do, but see if you can pick just a single way of processing information, like perceiving visual details, without allowing any other mode of processing to intrude. You will have to exclude all memories, future thoughts, feelings, interpretations and evaluations. It should go without saying that no creativity or imagination is allowed. How long can you remain in a one-track mind?*

DYNAMIC NEURAL FUNCTIONS

In referring to networking and terms like under-connectivity, one should not assume that scientists are referring to anything akin to an insufficient quantity of connections made between brain centers. The development of dynamic neural processing is much more complex and subtle than this type of quantitative analogy would represent. In fact, some researchers, like Dr. Eric Courchesne and his colleagues, hypothesize that a common sign of ASD vulnerability may be the presence of too many neural connections in the frontal cortex during the first year of life, resulting in a type of neural chaos that prevents meaningful neural networks from developing. On the other hand, one of the critical points of Just's group, is that neural development of individuals with ASD is too much like "hard wiring" between external stimuli and neural activation. This results in the loss of flexibility in the way that different brain centers may, or may not be called on to collaborate depending on the problem or situation being faced.

What are the consequences if your brain is becoming more static at the same time that your world requires you to function in a more dynamic manner?

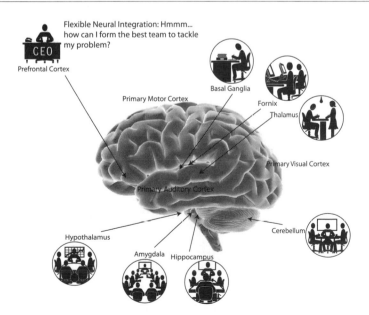

A better analogy is that our brains develop a number of increasingly sophisti-cated, specialized collaborative networks, which provide the means for integrating diverse brain processing centers into specialized think tanks. These can be called upon, as needed, by the brain's Chief Executive Officer (CEO)—the Pre-frontal Cortex—to effectively manage different aspects of our complex, constantly chang-ing world.

Dr. Daniel Siegel describes this process as neural integration, "… the capacity to link a widely distributed array of neural processes—mediated by neuronal fibers that interconnect anatomically and functionally distributed regions of the brain." According to Siegel, integration is the process that develops "coherence…the state of the system in which many layers of neural functioning become activated and cohere to each other over time."

Dr. Siegel points out that there are several different forms of neural integration including vertical and lateral processing. He provides the example of higher-lower levels of vertical integration in the collaboration between the Pre-frontal Cortex and Basal Ganglia. The Basal Ganglia mediates rule-guided behavior. The Pre-fron-tal Cortex allows for contextual evaluation and alternative action. This Basal Gan-glia-Pre-frontal Cortex network can rapidly respond when rules apply but reject irrelevant rules that do not apply to a particular context.

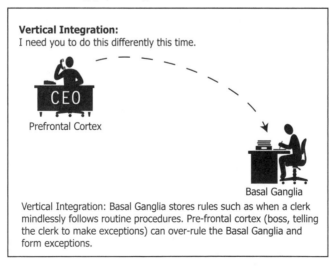

Vertical Integration:
I need you to do this differently this time.

CEO
Prefrontal Cortex

Basal Ganglia

Vertical Integration: Basal Ganglia stores rules such as when a clerk mindlessly follows routine procedures. Pre-frontal cortex (boss, telling the clerk to make exceptions) can over-rule the Basal Ganglia and form exceptions.

An example of lateral integration is found in the way we process communication. As we will discuss in greater detail later, when you engage in face-to-face communication, you are simultaneously processing facial, gestural, postural, auditory non-verbal, linguistic and contextual information. Lateral neural integration allows for these centers to collaborate, so that you perceive the communication as a single packet of information.

The development of neural integration is experience-dependent. In other words, it develops only when the brain is challenged by facing specific types of learning experiences, particularly those that provide problems which the current state of neural connectivity is insufficient to manage.

Emotions and emotional communication appear to be central to the integration process. According to the world famous neurological researcher Albert Damasio, "It would be unreasonable not to single out emotion among the critical integrative components". Emotions provide meaning to our experience; experiences with higher subjective meaning make neurons hypersensitive and thus more easily activated. This leads to greater neural plasticity and the development of increased synaptic connections.

Neural integration appears to derive from a strong innate tendency of human brains to evolve towards maximal complexity. As Dr. Siegel points out, complexity is not derived from random activation of neurons. Instead, it evolves from an ongoing balance of the continuity and flexibility of the neural system.

According to Siegel, continuity "...refers to the strength of previously achieved neural states and therefore the probability of their repetition" and is experienced as sameness, familiarity and predictability. Continuity is produced by inherent recursive tendencies, which reinforce patterns of neural responses learned from prior experiences. Flexibility, the other side of the balance, is comprised of "the system's degree of sensitivity to environmental conditions." It is promoted by the emergent properties of our brain. According to Siegel, this is a uniquely human, innate tendency to move towards greater freedom and adaptation. Flexibility comes into play under situations of novelty and uncertainty, where we are challenged to develop new adaptations to the environment.

Complexity evolves from an ongoing balance of the continuity and flexibility of the neural system.

The following charts provide a brief glimpse into several, but by no means all, integrated neural processes. The first chart provides a brief description of processes and functions, while the second contrasts dynamically integrated processes with their static equivalents:

Dynamic Neural Functions

Neural Function	Description
Pre-frontal algorithms create attention filtering mechanisms.	The Pre-frontal Cortex (PFC) prioritizes information competing for limited working memory capacity, by contextually filtering irrelevant information. Cortico-Limbic networks allow for rapid appraisal of information importance and regulating degrees of vigilance.
Pre-frontal "top-down" control inhibits impulsive responding to allow for studying novel and ambiguous stimuli.	The pre-frontally mediated Studying response allows us to manage states of uncertainty in a productive manner, effectively analyzing novel information to determine safety, personal value and meaning.
Monitoring change through vertical integration.	Vertical neural networks specializing in change analysis allow for monitoring and evaluating new information. Lower-level processors signal that changes have occurred. Higher-level neural centers create filtering algorithms to determine whether change is meaningful and should be passed on for consideration.
Engaging in intuition, integrating different perspectives and multi-channel communication, through lateral integration	Lateral neural integration allows us to engage in Intuitive thinking and integrate self-and-other perspectives, emotions and ideas. Other laterally integrated networks allow us to combine communication channels into single meaning packages
Meaning-based emotional integration through "top-down" control	We modulate arousal through selectively activating the Sympathetic, Para-Sympathetic and Orienting neural systems. We develop top-down control of immediate reactions through developing "meaning-based" emotional responses.

Comparing Dynamic and Static Neural Processes

Dynamic	Static
Contextual attention filtering & regulation.	Fixed attention.
Studying novelty & uncertainty.	Novelty & uncertainty avoidance.
Vertical Change Monitoring.	Fixed response execution 1:1 stimulus-response relationship.
Lateral Neural Integration.	Single network activation.
Meaning-based emotional regulation.	Unmodulated emotional reactions.

When the brain is severely stressed, the balance between continuity and flexibility can be lost. Either type of imbalance will interfere with dynamic development. Excessive flexibility leads to chaos, while excessive continuity creates rigidity.

BRAIN-BASED LEARNING

Human brains, including the brains of most ASD children, are born with much of the necessary hardware needed for later functioning. However, the networking and communication systems in the brain are not in place at birth and must be nurtured, especially in the first years of life. ASD represents an extreme example of the failed development of neural integration.

How does the brain's neural architecture develop? Scientists believe that neural connectivity is dynamic and experience-dependent. Our brain is plastic, meaning that it can and does transform throughout our lives. Clinical studies show that our brain can repair itself, even after serious injuries and insults, such as strokes.

Only specific types of experiences will foster neural integration. Scientists have concluded that the growth of productive neural integration is the result of immersing the child in a learning environment that optimally balances cognitive challenge and safety—the environmental equivalents of neural flexibility and continuity.

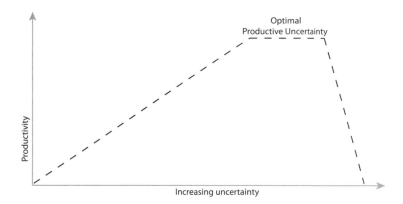

The growth of neural integration occurs only when our brain is faced with problems, discrepancies and incongruities that challenge the current adequacy of the brain's networking configuration. Optimal learning environments provide such safe challenges.

This new understanding has led to the mushrooming of educational approaches termed brain-based learning. A quotation from the influential educational group, The 21st Century Learning Alliance, summarizes what educators believe about brain-based education: "This much we now know. The brain learns best when it is trying to 'make sense'. When it is building on what it already knows. When it is working in complex, situated circumstances. When it accepts the significance of what it is doing. When it is exercising in highly challenging, but low threat environments."

What we do all day long, how we use our minds, especially how we are challenged to stretch our thinking and perceiving, determines the growth and development of our brain. The quality, not the quantity of thinking that the child engages in, determines how his or her brain will develop.

What is the consequence to a child's brain, if he is spending his day involved in learning discrete, rote and static skills? What is the consequence to a child's brain, if you create supports that substitute for his need to dynamically process?

The way that we as adults choose to interact with our children is the greatest factor impacting the development of the child's neural growth. The implications of this new understanding are profound. Parents and educators *are* the architects of the child's neural integration whether that child has ASD or not. How we conceive of our goals, how we perceive our roles with our children and the methods we choose have a profound impact far beyond what most of us recognize.

Reflection Questions

1. If you were to construct an educational program that enhanced dynamic neural integration, what would it look like?

2. What would students be doing during the course of the day?

3. What would you eliminate?

4. How would you determine if the program were effective? Review the charts above and think about how you would structure your school day to develop dynamic neural processes.

5. As a contrast, if you were to develop a program to enhance "under-connected" neural development what would you do?

6. How would you want your teachers to act?

7. How would you measure your effectiveness?

8. Review the comparison chart and think about how you would approach education differently, depending on the desired outcome.

Chapter Two

Dynamic Intelligence

Some readers may have already inferred the impossibility of separating any discussion of neural processes from the products of those processes, the workings of our mind. On an experiential level, we perceive these internal dynamic resources as consciousness and times when we employ these sophisticated neural structures as periods of thinking.[2]

Dynamic intelligence and neural integration have a circular relationship with one another. Dynamic intelligence is the product of a neurally integrated brain. Neurally integrated brains develop through exposure to dynamic problems that challenge the brain's current neural architecture.

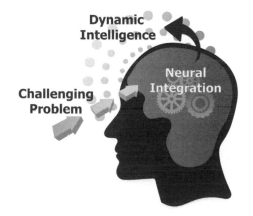

The observable product of dynamic neural development is what I refer to as dynamic intelligence. This includes abilities in the cognitive, self, communicative and relationship domains. Similarly, the external representation of static neural development is what we experience as the contents of our mind.

---

2   Alternately we might describe states such as reflecting, or intuiting, or even daydreaming. For expediency I shall refer to them all as thinking.

DYNAMIC INTELLIGENCE (MENTAL PROCESSES)

The observable product of static neural development is static intelligence. What we refer to as IQ is largely the measurement of the static functioning of our brain, a representation of what we have accumulated i.e. what we know, whereas, what are often referred to as common sense reasoning, flexible thinking, meta-cognition, executive functioning and emotional intelligence, are related to our dynamic brains i.e. what we do with what we know. As a group, people with ASD may or may not have deficits in static intelligence, yet they all have severe impairments in dynamic intelligence.

TERMS USED TO DESCRIBE DYNAMIC INTELLIGENCE

- Common Sense Reasoning
- Flexible Thinking
- Meta-Cognition
- Executive Functioning
- Emotional Intelligence

While we will spend considerable time in following sections, marveling at the achievements provided by dynamic intelligence, it is important to point out that the static brain is no slouch either. The next chart lists a small fraction of the multitude of abilities that are the product of our static intelligence. Just a casual review of these skills leads anyone to conclude that most are invaluable. A second chart contains the 20 Mental Processes that are the building blocks of my model of dynamic intelligence. You may be unfamiliar with some of these terms and they are explained in Appendix A.

Readers might find it rewarding to compare the two charts. Consider your own educational experience. What percentage of your time was spent learning static vs. dynamic abilities?

Some Important Static Abilities:	
Categorizing (provided categories)	Operating equipment and tools
Computer use (hardware/software)	Organizing (following methods)
Concept learning	Penmanship & typing
Deductive reasoning	Procedural enactment
Formula application	Reading: decode & surface meaning
Imitating	Rule-following
Instrumental referencing	Schedule following
Memorizing (facts & procedures)	Self care skills (daily habits)
Numerical computation	

Dynamic Mental Processes (Components of Dynamic Intelligence):	
Anticipating	Inferencing
Appraising	Innovating
Assimilating	Integrating
Attributing	Internalizing
Contextual Processing	Monitoring
Deconstructing	Postponing
Differentiating	Reflecting
Evaluating	Representing
Expanding	Summarizing
Fuzzy Thinking	Synthesizing

UNDERSTANDING DYNAMIC INTELLIGENCE

"In the real world, problems, persons and settings continually change. And, attempts to solve problems actually modify the problem itself. Events or activities are inherently dynamic, rather than consisting of static conditions. Change and development, rather than static characteristics, is assumed to be basic... A problem-solving approach places primary emphasis on people's attempts

to negotiate the stream of life, to work around or to transform problems that
emerge on the route to attaining the diverse goals of life."

—BARBARA ROGOFF

Dynamic intelligence is the ultimate product of our uniquely human minds. It is a gift that evolves throughout our lifetime. It allows us to adapt to an increasingly complex, continually changing world. Dynamic intelligence provides the tools to successfully solve complicated problems, prioritize multiple demands, carry on meaningful relationships and achieve long-term goals. Jobs, friendships, marriages and most aspects of daily life are primarily dynamic in nature.

Descriptions of how we employ dynamic intelligence in our daily lives are quite easy to generate. We worry about how we will have enough money for our children's college. We try to estimate the resources we will need to complete a work project to a client's satisfaction. We make multiple contingency plans, knowing that we can never really predict what will happen in the future. We evaluate whether we are making sufficient progress in our weight loss plan, or whether it is time to try something else. We struggle to prioritize among scores of demands and desires that pull on our limited time and money. We read a book containing important information and, on a sentence-by-sentence basis, determine if our level of understanding is sufficient, or whether we should stop to re-read particular passages. We find ways to collaborate with persons, even though they have significantly different areas of expertise and unique ways of thinking and perceiving the world. In doing so we enrich ourselves by gaining multiple perspectives. In a similar manner, we collaborate to enrich our joint products by integrating our contributions to create something that is more than just the sum of each of our minds.

Keep a static/dynamic diary of an average day (or even an hour!). Try to determine what percent of the time you operate in each mode. Think about what your life would be like without the dynamic component. What would you not be able to do? How would you cope?

I refer to the key elements of dynamic intelligence as mental processes. Dr. Barbara Rogoff describes mental processes in the following way:

"Instead of studying a person's possession of a capacity or an idea, the focus is on the active changes involved in an unfolding event or activity in which people participate. Events or activities are inherently dynamic, rather than consisting of static conditions... Change or development, rather than static characteristics, is assumed to be basic. Understanding processes becomes essential... Mental processes...occur in the service of accomplishing something, and cannot be dissected apart from the goal to be accomplished and the practical and interpersonal actions used. Cognitive processes serve the function of guiding intelligent, purposeful action and interaction."

An in-depth discussion of dynamic intelligence is beyond the scope of this book. However, in the following sections are several examples, which I believe will provide a glimpse into the amazing qualities of our dynamic minds.

EXPANDING YOUR MIND AT AN ART MUSEUM

The static brain seeks out a single response that matches prior associations with a specific stimulus. If the match is found, then the response is executed. In contrast, the dynamic brain is constructed to link multiple potential responses to a single problem, task or setting, rapidly shifting among multiple types and levels of analysis. In addition the dynamic brain is constructed to search out new potential responses to continually add to the repertoire of perspectives. An analogy I like to use is comparing two air traffic controllers. One controller is assigned to a rural, little used private airfield where at most he is guiding in one plane at a time to land on a single runway. The other controller works at a busy metropolitan commercial field, where continually moving planes are occupying every possible section of airspace and competing for multiple, but highly taxed approaches, departure paths and runways.

One of our most amazing, but unappreciated mental feats, is our ability to effortlessly relate to a single object, person or problem from any number of multiple, completely different perspectives in an amazingly short span of time. Dynamic intelligence frees us from the tyranny of being locked into any single stimulus-response chain. To demonstrate I'd like to ask you to participate with me in a simple exercise.[3]

To begin, try and put yourself in a relaxed, introspective state. Become aware for a moment of your breathing and use slow, deeper breaths, with particularly long exhales. When you are ready, visualize yourself standing in front of a painting, in a quiet art museum, during the time of day when there are no crowds and you are not rushed. You find yourself drawn to one particular painting, that of a woman relaxing under a shady tree alongside a flowing stream.[4] Now we will go through some mental shifts that will be quite simple for you.

First, focus on the scene itself to the point where you can briefly describe to your own satisfaction what is going on. Now think about how you would describe the painting to someone close to you when you return home. Next, shift your focus to the different elements of the painting. Focus on the tree for a while to take in its comforting shade. Then shift over to the relaxing stream and imagine it flowing on and on in its gentle manner. Now gaze more intently at the larger surroundings. Consider the grass, a nearby meadow and the unique hue of the sky. Shift your attention for a time to the woman under the tree. Think of how she is feeling. Make up a story about how she came to be there and what will happen next. Now picture yourself under a similar tree and imagine how you would feel. Find a memory from your own experience that closely matches the painting and try to trigger the experience you had.

When you are ready to move on, think about the artist. Consider for a moment what the artist was trying to achieve with the painting. Have you ever thought about being an artist? Can you picture yourself working on this painting? How would you feel if you could paint in this manner?

Now we will shift back to a more basic perceptual level. Un-focus your eyes or move far enough away so that you can no longer make out distinct figures and concentrate only on the colors. If your eyes are open, close them and visualize the

---

3   For those who would like more examples, Neuroscientist Jonah Lehrer offers a number of excellent illustrations of this dynamic ability in his book, *How we Decide*.

4   You may enhance the experience if you wish by gazing at a painting or photo in your possession, or travelling to a nearby museum or gallery.

colors in your mind. Let yourself appreciate the magnificent blends. Now move right up to the painting. Without actually touching the canvas, consider the texture of paint on canvas and experience the painting as a three-dimensional object. Study the frame and consider how it does its job of setting off the canvas from the surround. Think about how much the painting is worth. What would you pay for it? Where would you put it if you owned it?

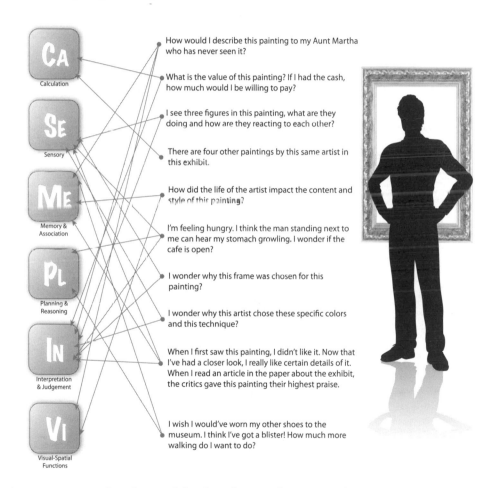

As we come to the close of this brief mental journey, focus once again on your breathing and state of comfort or tension. You can slowly return to your real world and gaze pleasantly at something completely different in your surroundings for a moment. Now you may return to your normal worries and thoughts.

If you wish, you can complete this entire mental exercise in a couple of minutes. In doing so you would have activated numerous, complex dynamic neural networks involving the integration of perception, emotion, memory, self-awareness, motor regulation, visualization, imagination and hypothetical thinking, all quite easily linked to the single stimulus of the painting. You were functioning like the master conductor of your own splendid mental symphony, with all the instruments at your disposal. You could have added many more perspectives had you wished.

In contrast, with significantly greater effort, you could have limited yourself to a single perspective and excluded all others, let's say focusing only on examining the colors, or the life of the artist.[5]

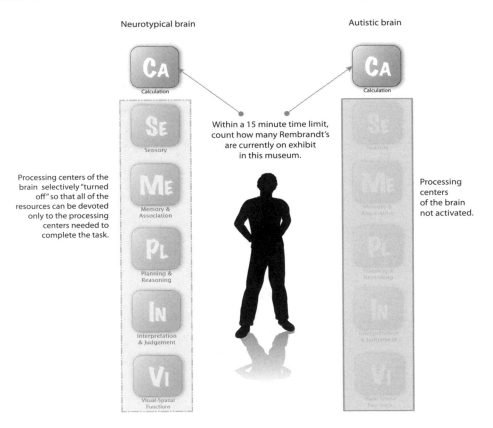

---

5   Ironically, this would be a much more difficult task for you to do.

At any moment, you could broaden or narrow your field at will depending on your needs and desires. You could add the dimension of time, considering past, present and future experiences. You could even include your assumptions about the reactions of others in contrast to your own, through the process scientists call intersubjectivity.

We conduct this amazing mental symphony throughout our waking and most probably our sleeping lives. We do it with little thought or reflection. Yet, we have not always been so proficient. Somehow we learned to function in this amazing manner. We just don't remember how we learned to do it.

As a way of understanding ASD, imagine Stephen, the Human Camera from my prior example, entering the same museum. My guess is that after a brief visit, if given enough time and paper, he could replicate every painting in the museum with amazingly accurate detail. However, I want you to consider the price Stephen pays for this talent. He has to go through life with only a single perspective, a very limited and often counterproductive way of obtaining meaning from his world.

INTEGRATING EMOTION AND COGNITION

Spock to Kirk: *Captain you seem to place a lot of trust in a feeling.*
Kirk to Spock: *Sometimes, Mr. Spock, a feeling is all we have to go on.*

As I discussed in the last chapter our human dynamic brains function more powerfully, through the integration of subjective, emotional information, along with objective factual data. As we all know, information learned in a context of greater meaning, translated as feeling something about the information, is learned in a more rapid and deeper fashion than if the data is simply inputted in a neutral manner.

Appraisal is a uniquely human mental process, in which we integrate our subjective feelings and objective data to try and pre-evaluate the meaning, value and importance of various persons and things in our world. We cannot and do not want to separate our emotions and cognitions in our appraisals. We buy expensive automobiles, select school and careers, choose our city of residence, pick our friends and determine whom we will marry through some remarkable neural integration of feeling and thought. Even though we use phrases like "it felt right" to describe how we make these decisions, in reality we are not simply relying on emotional reactions. Rather, thought and emotion are blended into a critical stew. We cannot fathom what life would be like if we were unable to imbue our decisions with these hybrid processes.

Several years ago, I was consulting with Linda, a very high IQ high school student with ASD. Despite her documented intelligence and extreme desire to achieve, Linda was having a hard time passing her history class. She was convinced that her teacher was singling her out for discrimination due to her disability. During one visit, Linda entered my office in a state of extreme agitation and proceeded to tell me that she felt cheated by her teacher and was not going to take it anymore. I inquired as to why she felt that such unfairness had been visited upon her. Linda's reply was, at the time stunning, but in retrospect perfectly understandable: "I know that if I study for four hours I will get an 'A' on my tests. I studied for four hours before every single one of his [the teacher's] tests and the best I have gotten is a 'D.' So last week I studied for eight hours and I still received a 'D.' I am going to go to his office and demand the 'A' that I deserve."

Up until this particular class, Linda's four-hour-rule had worked for her. Inevitably, she encountered a class where her lack of a deeper level of understanding, or her inability to provide what the teacher required made the rule absurd. Linda had no ability to appraise the problem. In fact, she had no idea that the rest of us would routinely do so. Therefore, she was baffled and angered when her rule-based method no longer worked. Back when you were in school preparing for a test, how did you decide when you had studied enough? I am certain you would probably answer with something like, "I studied until I felt like I knew the material. It felt right." Imagine if I were to take away the emotional feel you use to make your decisions. You would be left with no better recourse than Linda's.

Imagine how your problem solving would change if you could not integrate emotion with thought. What decisions would you have made differently in your life? Would you even be able to make decisions?

SAILING: A CONTINUOUS, REGULATORY PROCESS

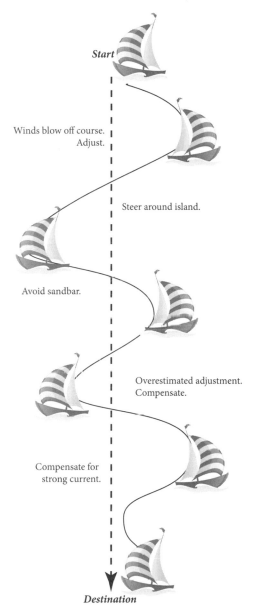

Start

Winds blow off course.
Adjust.

Steer around island.

Avoid sandbar.

Overestimated adjustment.
Compensate.

Compensate for
strong current.

Destination

When your brain is operating in a static way, once you get started, you are really at the end. Most of the work of the static brain takes place in initially matching a stimulus with the correct learned responses and then executing those responses. Once that is done you can often turn on your mental automatic pilot and stop thinking.

In contrast, when using dynamic intelligence, your initial response is just a beginning approximation—a best guess to get you started. Most of the time, you are involved in what scientists and mathematicians refer to as a continuous regulatory process. You are facing problems that require continuous monitoring and evaluation of information from many sources and frequent regulatory adjustments based on what you learn along the way.

One metaphor I like to use for the constant change and adaptation characterizing our daily lives is that of sailing. I am not a sailor myself, but when I speak with recreational sailors, what they love the most is the continual need to make course corrections. When piloting a motorboat, you can often point your craft in the direction of your destination, assuming there are no obstacles in the way and you will get there. The boat can even be placed on a type of automatic pilot.

When you are sailing, you never assume that you will reach a destination by keeping your boat pointed in the right direction. There is no such thing as automatic pilot for a sailboat (unless you cheat and install a motor). In fact, when you sail, you never really expect to be on course, if that means being headed exactly in the direction of your destination. Sailing, like most of life, involves a continual regulatory process.

When sailing, we assume that we will need to obtain feedback from the wind, currents, depth, obstacles, other boat traffic and similar nautical factors. However, another important source of feedback are your own actions. You cannot predict the effect of your actions until you actually take them and evaluate their impact. What is unique in continuous regulatory activities like sailing, or conversations, is that every action you take to be more on course will inevitably have the effect of eventually moving you off course. If the wind is blowing you off course in one direction and you tack to correct this, you will have to modify your tacking at some point or you will sail in the opposite or wrong direction.

Additionally, as you progress, you may learn new information about the problem or task: think of a surgeon doing a biopsy or a mechanic opening up the car hood to see what is going on. New information can be introduced at any moment or the wind may suddenly shift direction.

Therefore, any good sailor will anticipate that he will spend a fair amount of time monitoring and evaluating many factors, while simultaneously taking the actions of steering, adjusting the sails and carrying out the scores of other duties need to maintain sailcraft while afloat. The good sailor will frequently shift attention from whatever task is at hand, to obtain different types of information. Monitoring prepares our sailor for evaluating and decision-making.

At any one time, sailing requires evaluating a multitude of factors. There is no way to combine them into some kind of optimal formula. Therefore, good sailors must become proficient in making decisions through a process we think of as intuitive thinking. They make rapid decisions, recognizing that they do not have the time to go through some formulaic process of quantifying all the variables that are impacting them. There are many situations in life where we must make decisions in such intuitive ways. In his book, *How We Decide,* Dr. Lehrer provides many examples of this form of dynamic thinking, ranging from quarterbacks determining in a split second where to pass, to deciding where you would like to eat lunch today.

Good sailors must also engage in fuzzy thinking. They make optimal decisions, recognizing that they are rarely going to find perfect or right solutions to the continual problems they face.

If you are not a sailor, try to find continuous, regulatory experiences in your daily life. Think about tasks and problems in your daily life that meet the following criteria:

1. *You cannot plan absolute right or wrong solutions before starting.*
2. *After you start, you have to check to see where you are in relation to your goal.*
3. *Multiple factors, changed and new information, may move you closer to or farther away from your goal at any moment in time.*
4. *Any action you take, even one to get back on track, may eventually lead you farther from your goal.*

FUZZY THINKING FOR A FUZZY WORLD

Everything is vague to a degree you did not realize till you have tried to make it precise.

—BERTRAND RUSSELL

Fuzzy Wuzzy was a bear

*Fuzzy Wuzzy **had just a bit of hair***

*Fuzzy Wuzzy wasn't fuzzy, **(or was he?)***

(Poem adaptation in bold by Dr. Gutstein)

Mathematicians created the term fuzzy logic to recognize that they could not employ exact calculations to predict non-exact, imprecise phenomena. Governments and large corporations spend billions annually trying to replicate the way our dynamic brains manage complex problems with multiple variables and no single right answer. They do this because those type of problems are quite common in the real world. Consider the following assignment, taken from a high school American history test: *Write a four-page essay describing what you believe would have happened to our country if Abraham Lincoln had not been assassinated.*

The assumption here is that the teacher is interested in the student's well-organized, subjective speculation about future events, rather than a single correct response. Two students arriving at opposite conclusions could both receive an "A" on the essay if their work was well supported.

A similar type of fuzzy problem has solutions that we refer to as equivalents. Here multiple solutions are interchangeable; for example, "It's too dark in here. I don't care who replaces that burned out light bulb as long as someone does it!"

An interesting type of fuzzy logic is employed when we have to pre-determine what I refer to as good-enough performance criteria. Let's assume you are taking notes while reading this book. The act of reading with comprehension along with note-taking could be sufficient to over-stress attentional capacity. The way our dynamic brains manage this feat is to unconsciously pre-determine good-enough criteria for each of the processes we are going to engage in. For example, I would hope that while reading, in order to maximize the quality of your comprehension and reflection, you would minimize the attention paid to handwriting, grammar and spelling while note taking. In this example, good enough note taking is just above the threshold where you will later be able to decipher your notes. In such good-enough cases we are actually deciding to produce a less than perfect product, including accepting the inevitability of a certain number of mistakes. However, we gladly sacrifice perfection in pursuit of our actual goal.

Consider how your good-enough perspective would change if you were asked to take notes for a stranger. Suddenly you have to shift more resources to note-taking to ensure that your writing is more legible. Certainly, this wouldn't be at the level of a job application letter, but it would probably require significantly more attention than your personal notes.

Yet another type of fuzzy logic is required when we face problems that we cannot solve in the correct manner, no matter how much we would care to do so. We have to make do with the time, resources and information that we have and accept this as the best we can accomplish. I have provided several such problems for you to consider at the close of this chapter. As you read them, you may want to think about how representative they are of the challenges you face in your day-to-day life.

Try to remember times in your life (even in the present), when you faced problems that you knew were not going to have good solutions, but nonetheless had to be addressed. How did you cope with these situations?

WHICH BOX SHOULD I OPEN FIRST?

Let me share a vignette that illustrates how difficult life can be without fuzzy logic. Roger is a young man with ASD who, similar to Linda, I was privileged to consult with a number of years ago. Like Linda, Roger's measured IQ was close to the genius level. He received a 1560 out of a possible 1600 on his SAT college entrance exams. He played violin for his high school orchestra.

Roger was accepted to an Ivy League university. His first-year travails are the subject of another story. Roger survived his school year and, having no idea what to do over the summer, decided to remain on campus and attend the summer session, despite his lack of desire to take classes. As in most universities, summer session dormitory attendance is reduced. Most colleges consolidate their summer student inhabitants to a few selected dormitories. Such was the case with Roger's college. He was informed that he would have to move to a temporary dorm for the summer session.

I received a phone call from Roger at 11 p.m. on the night of the move, which had taken place earlier that afternoon. Roger's voice revealed a frantic state. Our conversation went something like this (his comments are in bold):

Hello.

I know it is late.

Who is this?

Dr. Gutstein, it's Roger. I followed the two-hour rule. Now it is two hours and 30 seconds. (Roger was referring to a rule we had made several months before when he had been calling me so often reporting emergencies that I had made him agree that he would not call unless the emergency lasted for at least two hours.)

Okay Roger. What's the matter?

I don't know what to do. I've been standing here paralyzed for hours. I don't feel like I can move!

Knowing that this was the day of the big move, I asked a series of question to try and narrow down the source of Roger's distress.

Is there a problem with your roommate?

Dr. Gutstein, don't you remember I got a single room, thank God!

Is there a problem with the way your room looks?

No. Why would I care how my room looks?

I forgot that such things did not concern Roger. After several more such questions I realized the folly of my process and finally, took my first reasonable action of the phone call.

Roger, what went wrong today?

It's the movers. They screwed the whole thing up! (I had forgotten that at Roger's exclusive university they actually provided moving men who would pack your belongings in boxes and move them to your new room.)

Oh, I'm sorry. Did they make a mess? Did they lose your things?

No. They did a great job packing everything up. I could never have done it myself. (Roger is not known for his neatness, or organizational ability.) **They put everything in boxes. The boxes are all here in the new room. In fact I've been staring at them for hours.**

Well Roger, why don't you just unpack and go to bed? (I knew that Roger would never consider going to bed unless everything was put away first, so I didn't even bother suggesting he leave unpacking until the morning.)

That's the problem. The movers left all the boxes stacked up in my room but they forgot to number them. How do I know which one to open first? Dr. Gutstein, I know that I am not supposed to care about things like this and I'm just supposed to

open any box in a random fashion. But I can't make myself do it. There's some-
thing in my brain that keeps telling me that I have to open the first box first and
the second box second.

Readers will want to know how I helped Roger understand that he could employ dynamic intelligence and make this problem go away. Alas, that was not how
the evening ended. Both of us were exhausted. This was clearly not the time to develop new neural pathways! Instead, I told Roger that he was right that the movers
had erred, but not in the manner he assumed, as box numberings were not necessary when being moved from one room to another. All the movers had omitted,
was to inform Roger of the ages-old "box opening" rule, which stated that, following a move, when confronted with a stack of boxes that require opening, you always
start from the box that is closest to the door and then proceed to gradually open
boxes based on their distance from the door. Roger was immediately relieved. He
pulled out his tape measure, went right to work measuring and unpacking and was
asleep within an hour.

PROBLEMS WITH NO SINGLE RIGHT ANSWERS

1. If you try biking to work, it takes almost an hour and sometimes you get
   sweaty. If you drive to work, it takes 30 minutes but you wind up spending a
   lot of money on gas.
2. You need to construct the kitchen table you bought at the IKEA store. You
   bought it on sale with a no-returns-policy. You start assembling it and realize that one of the four legs is not exactly the same size as the others. It is
   two millimeters shorter.
3. You have to finish a book report in two weeks. It will probably take a week
   to read the book and another three days to write the report. You look everywhere and cannot find the book. Finally, you find a copy on Amazon.
   com. The regular cost to ship it is $3.00 but it will take 5-7 days. You can get
   it express shipped, but it will cost $12.00. If you spend the $12.00, you won't
   have enough money for lunch two days next week.

4. You know that the best thing to do if you lose a ball that belongs to one of your friends is to buy him a new one. When you lose a friend's ball you immediately go out and buy one that looks identical. You present it to your friend and he refuses to accept it and says, "What good is that. That cannot replace the one I lost." What do you do?

5. You are a member of a project group. Your part of the project is to estimate how long it will take to complete a certain design. You come to the meeting with an estimate of four months. The other members of the group tell you that it is much too long because the customer requires the design completed in two months.

6. You begin working on your test. You have one hour to finish it. You will have to work very fast to finish the whole test. If you work fast, you will make more mistakes. If you slow down to check your mistakes you will not complete the test

PROBLEMS WITH NO ANSWERS AT ALL

Not only do we frequently encounter situations where we have to make-do and obtain the best result we can, given real-world limitations, or where there may be several equally good routes to take, but many times in life we encounter problems where there just doesn't seem to be *any* good answer. This is the ultimate test of fuzzy logic.

Read the following problem and you will see what I mean: *You wake up one morning and find yourself alone in a forest. You have no idea where you are or how you got here. You have no equipment. No compass. No GPS. The land is flat. You can see nothing but trees no matter where you look. You climb the highest tree but only see other trees. There is a small stream running nearby. There is no reason to think some-one is going to look for you because they don't know you are lost, and even if they did, they would have no idea where to look. What do you do next?*

There doesn't seem to be any good solution to this problem, but if you just do nothing and sit, chances are you will die. There are many problems like this in life. You have to do something. If you possess dynamic intelligence, you will eventually think of some solution that provides options knowing that you have left the world of right and wrong far behind.

As you reach the close of this chapter, you might wonder why our educational system largely neglects the development of dynamic intelligence. The reason may have to do with the way we measure progress in our schools. While it is not very hard to measure improvement in dynamic functioning, it is much cheaper to measure static progress, through group-administered, standardized tests of achievement. Progress in mental processes subsumed under dynamic intelligence is typically measured in a more individualized manner, where students must demonstrate that they can use their knowledge to solve real-world, fuzzier problems, requiring intuitive thinking, good-enough products, multiple perspectives, alternate solutions and effectively evaluating and integrating new information inserted mid-stream.

Reflection Questions:

1. How often in your typical day do problems arise that require intuitive, fuzzy thinking?

2. How common is it for you to feel completely certain about your decisions?

3. Are the proper tools and resources always available when you need them? How do you manage when they are not?

4. What would happen if you were unable to hypothesize and speculate?

5. When you do a Google search and hundreds of websites emerge, how do you quickly determine which sites to discard and which to focus on?

6. How many times in a day do you employ "good enough" thinking (where you determine what criteria is good enough rather than worrying about being perfect)?

7. How do you know when a change is central and must be attended to, or peripheral and can be ignored?

Chapter Three

Dynamic Communication

Human communication seems to me to provide the most poignant illustration of dynamic intelligence and therefore I have granted communication its own chapter. In truth, we develop both static and dynamic forms of communication referred to respectively as instrumental and experience sharing.

Instrumental communication, just as it sounds, implies that the other person is being used as an instrument, a means to an end, to achieve a non-interpersonal goal. Examples of instrumental communication include using polite mannerisms so that you won't stand out, requesting a desired object, questioning someone who can provide you with needed information, obtaining permission to go somewhere, or finding someone to fill the role of a second player in a board game that requires at least two participants. Once we receive the object, information or permission, once the other person has assumed the prescribed rules and has served his purpose, we have no further need to communicate. When we operate instrumentally, we seek the most efficient, predictable ways to communicate. We have no interest in the feelings, ideas, perceptions or any other aspect of the internal world of those with whom we communicate.

Instrumental communication relies almost completely on static neural processing, employing rules with scripted, predictable interchanges. We reasonably expect that when we step up to a movie theatre ticket window, the ticket seller will ask us which show we want to attend. We will respond with the name of the movie, hand over the money, the seller will provide the ticket and that will end the communication. Communication processes of this nature bypass the Pre-frontal Cortex and require little neural integration. We don't need to include any emotional processing. We can rely completely on the verbal text and ignore facial, gestural, postural and prosodic information channels. We don't have to wonder (unless suffering from paranoia) about the real meaning of the ticket seller's question. All we have to do is select the program that fits the instrumental goal we seek to achieve, run it and assume that the result will follow in due course.

THE WORK NEVER STOPS

Experience sharing communication requires a good deal of neural integration. From an information-processing standpoint, human communication is a messy business where rules are the exception. Experience sharing relies on our expectation that involved parties understand that communication is always a work in progress requiring continual effort. It is never completed and, no matter how smoothly it appears to be going in the moment, it can never be taken for granted.

There are clearly some rules that frame human experience sharing and keep it from lapsing into chaos. For instance, you can predict that during a conversation you and your partner will try to find a common language. Nevertheless, even when speaking to someone in the same language, do you remember the last time you experienced 100% comprehension during a conversation? Usually this happens only once in our lives, the first time we fall in love. We walk around for about a week, in a pleasant, somewhat delusional state, saying things like, "We understand each other perfectly" and "I don't even have to speak and he knows what I am thinking." Unfortunately, when the week is over, we return to reality and once again act as if communication requires constant vigilance.

We assume, unless conversing with a very young child, that conversational participants will be skilled and motivated enough to take approximately equal shares of responsibility to monitor the state of our process, checking the lines to ensure there is sufficient comprehension and making necessary adjustments to improve understanding.[6] We also assume that participants recognize the fragility of the temporary bridges we construct between our minds, and accept that despite our best efforts, misunderstandings are inevitable and our mental connections will break down and require repair. When George Bernard Shaw stated that, "The greatest problem of communication is the illusion that it has been accomplished," he recognized the importance of understanding the fragility of communication and the necessary work required to build and maintain these fragile mental bridges. Danger occurs, whether in our personal relationships or those between countries, not when we fail to understand, but when we falsely over-estimate our level of comprehension.

Experience-Sharing vs. Instrumental Communication

1. *Tape record yourself communicating for five minutes with an ASD child and with a typically developing child. Analyze both tapes to determine the ratio of instrumental to experience sharing communication that you wind up using. You may be shocked.*

2. *Practice having a five-minute conversation where you use nothing but instrumental conversation. Your conversational partner should converse in a normal manner (or at least try to). Now reverse roles. How does it feel to be in both of these roles? Do you feel more or less inclined to continue conversations? Now try the same thing using only experience sharing.*

COMMUNICATION BANDWIDTH

We interpret the meaning of communication in normal conversation through several different channels. These include language, facial expression, gesture, pos-

---

6   In fact we quickly tire of a conversational partner who does not hold up his or her end of the work, an experience quite commonly found when conversing with highly verbal individuals labeled with Asperger's Syndrome.

ture, physical space, context and prosody, defined as changes in tone, emphasis, inflection and pacing that lies behind our words.

A conversation is like a dance performance that has not been choreographed, but which requires the dance partners to remain coordinated. Each partner's intentions are mediated by the transmission of many different subtle cues. When the partners are in synch and somehow accurately perceive one another's cues, the dance flows beautifully. Adults are experts in the unconscious interpretation of non-verbal meta-information and depend on this expertise to ensure meaningful encounters. Strip away the meta-information and the words alone are naked, ambiguous and subject to radical misinterpretation.[7]

Processing these multiple channels seems difficult enough, but there are factors that make this exponentially more complicated. The most obvious problem is that we receive these different channels simultaneously, all at once. People don't provide their gestural, facial and intonation changes in a nice, slow sequential order, interspersed with pauses. The second is that the information embedded within each channel can vary from second to second. You would not be amiss in considering that this places near-impossible demands upon our limited simultaneous processing ability.

Luckily, our dynamic brains have evolved an innovative way to manage this massive information demand. The dynamic integration of our brains allows us to combine different channels into a single packet of multi-channel information. Therefore, we don't have to isolate the individual meaning of a particular facial expression and then determine or couple it with a specific voice tone. We perceive this elegant, complex integrated neural process in an intuitive manner. In other words, two-year-olds do not process facial information alone but derive meaning from unique face-voice-gesture-postural packets of meaning.[8]

---

7   We refer to some ASD children as "non-verbal" because they have difficulty developing speech. However, I have yet to observe a "non-verbal" ASD child who has learned to effectively communicate using other channels of communication (gesture, facial, prosodic) that typically develop prior to speech. When you focus on speech without first developing these non-verbal channels, you may be curtailing the brain's dynamic development of communication.

8   However, six-month-olds cannot yet do this.

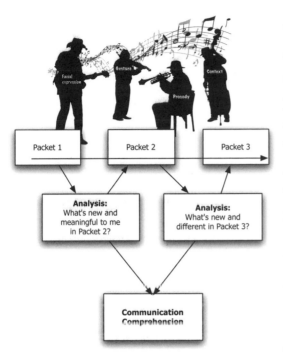

The second ingenious solution our brains have produced is a much more elegant version of what computer media engineers have learned to do when they provide a way to compress video into more manageable sizes. If you have ever tried to take video you have shot with a mini DV video-camera and transfer it to a computer, you know that in its raw form even a half hour of video can take up a huge chunk of your hard drive. That is because there is so much information that has to be translated from the analog to the digital.

Moreover, if you want to put the video on the internet and stream it for viewing on line—say on YouTube—you will run into a problem of bandwidth. Bandwidth refers to the transmission capacity of a communication pathway. You may have a high speed internet connection but I doubt it is high enough to provide the bandwidth to stream a raw video file on the internet. (Streaming means viewing the video on the internet without downloading it.) There is just too much simultaneous information that would have to be transmitted at once for your internet connection to manage.

Media engineers recognized a number of years ago that there is a great deal of redundant information in a typical 30 frame-per-second video clip. The odds of any significant changes in lighting, color, audio volume and objects within 1/30th of a second are very low. They also realized that the average internet video viewer is willing to accept as good enough, a less than cinema quality picture. Therefore they designed compression programs. These programs, which continue to evolve in sophistication, do not try to process every bit of data in every frame of an original video. Instead, through employing sophisticated algorithms, the compression programs determine how to scan each frame to extract and save new or changed information that was not present in the prior frame. In this way, someone can view your original ten-gigabyte file with a one megabyte-per-second internet connection.

Our dynamic brains learn to perform a much more sophisticated version of this, a form of super compression. Based on our unique culture and our experiential learning history, we develop subjective meaning programs. These complex algorithms designate certain changes in communicative information as meaningful and filter out others as not, so they never reach higher processing centers.

Additionally, based upon factors such as the specific setting and the nature of our relationship with communicative partners, for example, a best friend vs. an elevator acquaintance, we intuitively select from a variety of algorithms on the fly to find the best fit. We also adapt and revise our algorithms as needed.

In their first two years of life, typically developing children learn through intuitive parental guidance to employ initially simple, but increasingly sophisticated meaning programs tied to non-verbal channels, settings, specific persons, problems, goals and emotional states. For example, 18-month-olds will respond differently when a familiar adult suddenly shifts from a serious to an obviously teasing communicative stance. These algorithms are modified throughout life through contact with peers, teachers and interactions with the larger world.

SELF AWARENESS AND INTER-SUBJECTIVITY

A final complexity of human communication emerges from our desire to compare, contrast and integrate the product of our own mental processes with those of others, the essence of all human communication. This requires developing a set of sophisticated "you-me" algorithms that function to compare and contrast the degree of coordination between conversational partners on a moment to moment basis. These programs monitor changes in our state of connection on many different levels, such as emotional states, topic, motivation and comprehension. They employ fuzzy logic to determine if coordination is good enough on each level or if repair actions are needed. Still later, we learn to add another intuitive process to the mix, when we selectively combine some aspect of our mental process with some aspect of our partner's to produce a novel product that is different from what either of us could have produced alone.

On a more basic level, any kind of "you-me" transaction requires each partner to determine his own subjective reactions, thoughts and associations (the "me") so that he has something to share with others. Moreover, he must keep this "me" separate from the "you"; the unique contributions of communicative partners.[9] Additionally, one's initial mental products typically must be, to some degree, filtered from their initial raw form before being expressed. Attention directed to self awareness and self regulation must always be balanced by finding ways to bridge differences with others. The absence of this complex, dynamic dialectic of self awareness and inter-subjectivity renders communication meaningless.

TEACHING COMMUNICATION TO ASD CHILDREN

One of my concerns is the extent to which developing a large repertoire of rather mindless, scripted speech is seen as an important step in teaching ASD children to communicate. I understand the desire, when confronted with a child who is not communicating at all, to provide a means for her to express her needs and respond to others in a basic manner. Building a small repertoire of functional instrumental communication is often necessary. However, I frequently observe that what often starts out as a way of providing for a basic functional needs often evolves into a professional and parental obsession with increasing sentence length and vocabulary for its own sake, that may stretch on for years and dominate the child's understanding of communication.

Focusing on speech without first forming any of the neurally integrated processes that are in place in typically developing children may relieve desperate parents' fears that their child will never communicate and provide the child with

---

9   Many people do not fully appreciate the degree to which ASD individuals struggle to develop even the most primitive form of a "me", a meaningful mental self that can be shared with others. One ASD adult who has written extensively about this is Donna Williams.

some way to express immediate needs. From a longer-term and especially a neural level, it may produce incalculable damage. As illustrated in the prior section, typical communication relies on sophisticated lateral neural integration to develop in a multi-channel, integrated manner. Moreover, it requires top-down vertical integration through increasingly sophisticated filtering algorithms that rapidly determine contextual meaning and provide for intersubjective experience sharing. When typically developing children begin to employ language, it is but one more, albeit extremely powerful tool, superimposed on an already richly integrated neural process. In typical development, language from its origin is suffused with meaning, through integration with multiple channel meaning, as well as strong linkages between cortical language processing centers and connections to the Pre-frontal Cortex, Limbic System and Hippocampus.

When non-integrated speech becomes the sole way that communication is input to the brain we may be laying the seeds for future disaster. When year after year, without having any of the typical neural foundations in place, we deliberately reinforce such under-connected neural processing, we may be destroying the child's potential for later development of rich meaningful communication.

Communication Exercises

1. *Find a highly regarded foreign film, in a language of which you do not understand a word. Do not choose an action film, but rather a movie that is primarily about relationships. Make sure you do not read the sub-titles. Watch a few small segment of the film—maybe one minute at the most. Try to analyze the non-verbal communication that you are observing and how the characters impact one another non-verbally.*

2. *Try to have a conversation with an adult friend where you do not use any words. You can use all of the other modalities. Then try to use only limited modalities, like gesture and voice tone, or facial and voice, or facial and gesture.*

3. *Make sure to participate in communication with a typically developing infant between the age of ten and fifteen months who is not yet speaking. How rich is*

your communication? How much can be communicated without words? How is the work of maintaining coherence divided?

BUILDING FRAGILE, UNCERTAIN BRIDGES

Communication works for those who work at it. —JOHN POWELL

The beauty of human communication is that we discover one another and ourselves while we communicate. Human communication is all about emergence. It is a typical experience during a conversation to be suddenly surprised and exclaim, "Oh! I didn't realize you felt that way." If you knew beforehand what your partners were going to say and how you were going to respond, there would be no reason to communicate.

Conversations require a strong desire for experience sharing. If you do not want to know anything new about the actions, emotions, perceptions, ideas, feelings, opinions, preferences or beliefs of the person you are with, you will not have a real conversation no matter how much language you possess.

If you remove the unpredictable, unknown quality from experience sharing and emphasize predictability, it will quickly begin to feel like parody. Imagine you and a friend wrapping up a pleasant lunch in your favorite restaurant. You take note of the exceptional quality of your conversation and say, "I believe that was the best conversation we have ever had." Your friend concurs and you agree to meet at the same place and time for lunch on the following week. Now fast forward to the next lunch date. After you have both been seated comfortably, your friend says, "I have a great treat for you." At first, you gaze expectantly, wondering what gifts are in store. However, your mouth hangs agape in disbelief when your partner goes on to say, "Unbeknownst to you, I took the liberty of tape recording our entire conversation last week. As we both agreed, it was the most exceptional conversation we've had in some time. Rather than take the extreme risk of not performing at such a high level two weeks in a row, I thought that we could just replay and listen to the tape from last week."

While experience sharing requires that the involved parties work hard to maintain coherence, achieving mutual understanding is merely one of the goals. If you observe real human communication, you cannot fail to notice that each time we temporarily reach a state of seeming understanding, we seem to inject enough unpredictability into the conversation to once again disrupt our fragile unity. We then start building our communication bridges all over again.

Human communication revolves around moments when I cannot completely predict what you are going to say, how you are going to feel, or whether we will achieve mutual resolution. Rather than feeling threatened or disturbed by our lack of prescience, we remain curious and pleasantly intrigued as we wait to see what will emerge from our encounter. These moments of productive uncertainty are essential elements of our communicative encounters. They function in an endless dialectic peppered by temporary periods of unity and consensus.

The Challenges of Human Communication:

- It is breaking down all the time.
- There are guaranteed misunderstandings.
- It requires continual monitoring and adjustment.
- You have to manage different channels that keep changing from moment to moment.
- ***Nevertheless***...you realize that it is worth the effort because there is an enormous payoff.

COMMUNICATION IS ALWAYS A WORK IN PROGRESS

Human communication is powered by the desire to safely venture into the unknown space that exists between our minds. We want to be surprised, but not too much. We want to feel that our partner is genuinely interested in what we have to say. We want communicative encounters to create something new and unique. We wish to reach a consensus with a deepened emotional connection. The brilliant Developmental Psychologist Alan Fogel uses a play on the word *information* to describe the uncertain quality of human communication, by breaking it up into its two components *in* and *formation*. This reminds us that in human communication our meaning is always in the process of being co-created by the participants.

Human communication is full of misunderstandings, which we refer to as communication breakdowns. Typically developing children learn quite early to become very good at repairing those breakdowns, while ASD children usually do not even recognize them. Unfortunately, our response to their communication blindness is often to remain in an instrumental mode where the breakdowns are relatively rare. The trade off is that, while we won't have many misunderstandings, the child never learns about the real nature of communication. He misses out on experiencing the payoffs for why we work so hard at it and never becomes proficient in its management.

CHIMPS AND TRIBES

Dr. Michael Tomasello works at the Max Plank Institute in Germany, where for a number of years he has been studying comparative primate communication, especially contrasting chimpanzee and human abilities. He finds this an excellent method to determine what makes our communication uniquely human. Chimps don't have our voice box so they can't make our vocal noises, but by using signs they can develop a good vocabulary, put together useful sentences, make requests and ask and answer questions.

However, no matter how much Tomasello trains them—and these are undoubtedly the most linguistically capable chimpanzees in the world—they do not share experiences to collaborate with others as humans do. They do not seek to learn about the subjective experiences of a human or another chimp and integrate them with their own. They have adequate vocabulary and sentence structure, but they have no concept of how or why anyone would hold onto their own viewpoint, seek out their partner's viewpoint, and work so hard to blend these together.

Tomasello believes that human experience-sharing communication evolved to provide us with the means to form shared goals and collaborate, an exceptional survival skill. In order to maximize our potential, we learned to productively manage this uniquely human dialectic of uncertainty and consensus.

I have a fiction I play out in my mind to try to understand how experience sharing might have first developed. In my scenario, a tribe of prehistoric hunter-gatherers has learned to divide their role actions to try and maximize their potential to obtain critical information. In my story, the tribal chief, who must have been a genius for his time, sends three tribe members to scout surrounding areas for information about the terrain, potential hazards, food and water sources and other tribes. This incredible idea, "We don't all have to go together to see what there is. We can divide up our labor and obtain information many times quicker," while a stroke of genius, presents the tribe with enormous problems that must be solved for the plan to work.

The problem arises when inevitably these scouts return with different observations and perspectives, leading to a state of tribal uncertainty. At this point, the tribe needs to find ways to integrate these unique perspectives into a consensually approved decision that will increase the potential for tribal survival and satisfaction.

The diversity and subjectivity of this information would inevitably have led to very different interpretations of meaning and value, as well as conflicts related to tribal decisions. The meaning of information has to somehow be sorted out and a tribal consensus achieved, a compromise that doesn't ruffle too many feathers, literally, so that productive actions can be taken and tribal unity preserved.

As a hypothetical pre-historic tribal chief of an extremely hungry tribe, I have sent three members to forage for food, one into the forest, a second by the river and a third into the savannah. Upon returning, the first scout reports, "There are some unripe guavas in the forest. I know we hate guavas, especially the unripe ones, but at least they are food." The second scout reports that, "I think I found deer tracks by the river. I know we all love deer meat, but I'm just not certain if the tracks were fresh." The third reports that, "It's pretty smelly over in the direction I went, but I believe I smelled some good vegetables. On the other hand, I've had a cold recently and I'm not smelling things too well."

In the end, according to Tomasello, our tribe learned to take this diverse, subjective information and put it together in some fashion for the good of the group. As chief, with the help of other tribal wise persons, I can determine how much I trust each of the reports. I can consider my history with each of the reporters, as well as the unique ways they communicate. For example, I recall that scout two, our deerstalker, tends to underestimate his prowess in reading tracks. If he reports he is not sure the tracks are fresh, there is a good probability they are fresh. On the other hand, we must decide whether we are so hungry that the certainty of obtaining unripe guavas outweighs the enjoyment of somewhat less predictable dear meat. As chief, I may determine this for the good of the tribe, but I won't remain chief for long if my actions do not roughly correspond to the needs and desires of the tribal members. I will probably seek out the opinions of tribal influentials to make sure that my decision is sufficiently supported. This is just the tip of the iceberg of the types of collaborative communication that could take place. According to Tomasello, humans may have survived and evolved as a species because they became proficient in conducting this type of complex collaboration-communication process.

As in our prior tribal example, experience sharing communication is sometimes about integrating process and endpoint. Collaborative experience sharing has some of the same superficial characteristics as its instrumental counterpart. However, this is illusory. In reality when we collaborate, we are involved in determining a shared goal, working together in a synchronized fashion to achieve our goal, while maintaining an ongoing relationship with our collaborative partners. We have to reach a consensus about our goal. We have to negotiate our roles. We must synchronize our role actions. We have to develop and maintain trust with one another. We need enough prior experience to determine the context in which to interpret each other's communication.

If our communication appears to my collaborators as overly instrumental, that tribal members are just a means to my endpoint, or insufficiently focused on the group goals, they may choose not to communicate with me. On the other hand, in my tribal example, they might solve the problem by cooking *me* for dinner. Any time we engage in collaboration we are involved in the complex process of finding a joint endpoint, balancing our actions towards the endpoint and simultaneously managing a complex, ongoing relationship process.

Reflection Questions:

1. What is the main point of human communication?
2. What are the evolutionary advantages of human communication?
3. How does human communication differ from that of other species?
4. What is the role of the non-language channels of communication?
5. What happens to adults who have a stroke and lose their language? Can they still communicate?
6. Are "non-verbal" ASD children really only "non verbal"?
7. What happens if you remove thinking and deliberation from conversation? Can you imagine a conversation that did not include the desire to create bridges between minds? What else is there to talk about?

Chapter Four

Dynamic Departures

We live in a moment of history where change is so speeded up that we begin to see the present only when it is already disappearing.

—R.D. LANG

DO WE NEED DYNAMIC PROCESSING?

Some readers might still be wondering if we really should concern ourselves with dynamic processes. Perhaps a convincing argument could be made that we should simply maximize the static abilities of individuals with ASD, undoubtedly an easier task. This line of reasoning is predicated on the assumption that by exclusively building sufficient static ability, people with ASD can achieve a normal quality of life.[10] This idea has been commonly accepted and has influenced educators and clinicians to gear their academic teaching and clinical intervention methods to go-with-the-flow and build upon the relative strengths of ASD individuals, avoiding their areas of weakness. An added advantage for them is that static skills can be easily measured. ASD clinical research has almost universally employed static outcome measures such as IQ scores, increased speech repertoire and greater scripted social behaviors to bolster claims of success.

---

10   This line of reasoning may also be predicated on the belief that attaining a normal quality of life is too much to expect for almost all ASD individuals.

Unfortunately, while a tempting proposition, it is also a false one. Prominent Psychologists like Robert Sternberg have presented convincing evidence that static intelligence is not highly related to real world success. It accounts for no more than 50% of the variance, even in highly static classrooms and no more than 20% of the predictive ability for future employment. Studies like those conducted by the National Autistic Society in Britain show that the prospects, even for those persons with ASD who possesses at least normal levels of static intelligence, are dim to say the least.

Have you spent time with any adults on the autism spectrum? If you have a child with ASD or work in some manner with ASD children, interacting with ASD adults who can discuss their condition is an invaluable experience. In fact, it may change the way you look at the condition. Make sure to talk with more than one person, so you aren't influenced by their personal biases.

Scores, if not hundreds, of research studies have demonstrated statistically significant outcomes gained by employing discrete learning methods and programs. However, not a single study has demonstrated whether, after thousands of hours and years of this type of intervention, ASD individuals are more able to obtain and keep meaningful employment, live independently, develop authentic friendships, or solve problems in a more flexible, adaptive manner.

Many primarily static ASD intervention programs claim to be proven or evidenced-based. If you encounter one of these programs, be sure to ask the following question(s), "I am not doubting your program is proven, but please explain to me what it is proven to do". Similarly, you should ask, "I am sure that your program is evidenced-based. However, please tell me what evidence you are collecting and how it relates to changes in quality of life."

It is clear that our 21st century world is placing an immense dynamic strain on even typically developing individuals. We live with increasingly greater levels of uncertainty. We have to rapidly review, filter and assimilate tons of information. There are very few jobs, if any, that are repetitive, allowing the employee to repeatedly do the same thing. Today's marketplace requires the ability for responsive adaptation, rapid information assimilation and flexible collaboration.

Consider our daily lives. We rarely have the opportunity to manage only one thing at a time. We move through multiple roles in a seamless fashion: we may be worker, employer, supervisor and supervisee in the same day. A phone call received at the office from school makes us a parent. A moment later, another call places us in the role of adult-child as we are summoned to take care of our elderly parents. Criteria for progress and success seem to shift in an elusive manner. A deadline is altered and something that has been put off is now pressing and has become the number one priority. You painstakingly work to develop a budget for your company and your boss walks in and tells you that he thinks everyone needs new computers. You look at him with a shocked expression and he replies, "Just make it work," and walks out the door.

Reflection Questions:

1. If you have a child attending a K-12 school, or you work in a school, try to determine how much of the school day is devoted to static vs. dynamic intelligence. Why do you think this is? How is progress evaluated in your school? Are measures primarily static or dynamic? What percent of the day is spent teaching ways to appraise, evaluate, reflect and problem-solve that will be critical for attaining a future quality of life?

2. Do you know anyone who performed poorly in school, but went on to have a successful life? What were the attributes that led to their success?

3. Do you or your children have experiences in school where you learned something for a test, only to forget it within a week or two? How productive do you think that was?

4. What do you still remember from your own K-12 education? What percentage of your educational life wound up being productive and useful?

DYNAMIC AND STATIC

Unquestionably, both types of intelligence are necessary for obtaining a quality of life. In the real world, most daily problems contain static as well as dynamic elements. You need to know a host of formulas, facts and procedures to survive, not to mention all the passwords and user names. General rules of conduct, such as social manners and scripts are essential for most superficial encounters. There are times when you have to do things just the way you learned to do them. Driving a car requires having mastered certain procedures. Reading requires learning to decode and understand the meaning of written symbols and, unless you are a creative poet, spelling rules must be followed. Nevertheless, without their dynamic counterparts, these static skills function as empty shells, caricatures of what human minds are capable of achieving.

Modern educators understand that there is an important place for memorization and drills. But teaching critical discrete skills needs to coincide with the child making dynamic discoveries, so that the student learns to use these skills in a meaningful way. The key to integrating dynamic and static learning is to make sure that you do not introduce static skills until the child is ready to develop the associated dynamic processes needed for real-world competence. For example, do not introduce reading decoding until a child is also ready to understand reading comprehension.

THE PRICE OF AVOIDING DYNAMIC PROCESSING

We believe that the problems of people with ASD are compounded if the decision is made to avoid the weaker dynamic pathway and to instead solely focus education and intervention efforts on the child's stronger, intact static processing capacity. It is true that by placing an ASD child in the right artificial environments and selecting tests that measure static processing, we can make him appear to look better if one doesn't look too closely. In doing so, we pay an enormous price and we may be cutting off the child's future potential for normal neural development.[11]

---

11   When we encounter children who appear to be missing both static and dynamic neural development, an approach emphasizing both types of brain processing may be needed.

DYNAMIC PROCESSES FROM STATIC SKILLS?

You can practice and perfect static processing for years and not improve in the dynamic domain. This seems like common sense, but may not be obvious to everyone. The ASD literature is full of studies that attempted to teach complex, dynamic processes as if they were merely an accumulation of discrete skills.

Noted autism expert Ami Klin makes the following point to explain the failure of programs that try to teach dynamic processes in a static manner when he says, "The fact that the cognitive able [those with high static intelligence] individuals with autism are able to demonstrate so much social cognitive information is as interesting as the fact that they fail to make use of these skills."

ELIZA THE VIRTUAL SHRINK

In what I thought might be an amusing illustration of the failure to emulate dynamic intelligence through static means, I spent some time online with a computer program possessing the unlikely name of Eliza. This grand old lady was originally programmed in 1965 as an early experiment in the potential for artificial intelligence to emulate human thought. She enjoyed a short period of popularity as scientists briefly hoped that Eliza could function as a computer psychoanalyst, providing relief to the mental ailments of those who could not afford the real thing. Alas, the limitations of Eliza quickly became all too apparent and she was cast upon the virtual slagheap of history. Artificial intelligence really becomes artificial when it attempts to emulate dynamic functioning. Fortunately, Eliza still lives in the form of an online program available through the graces of the University of California at Fullerton. Go to her website and chat with her as she becomes very lonely when unused. She can be found here: http://psych.fullerton.edu/mbirnbaum/psych101/Eliza.htm.

Below I offer the following transcript from my brief session with Eliza to illustrate the clear limitations of static functioning. Eliza's responses are in bold:

Hello, I am Eliza.

Can you help me?

Don't you believe that I can help you?

I don't know if anyone can help me.

Do you wish to know if anyone can help you?

Yes.

Are you sure?

I really want help.

What does that suggest to you?

I want to feel better.

Suppose you got to feel better?

I would be happy.

That is quite interesting.

Why?

Have you asked anyone else?

No.

Why not?

Because I am asking you.

Did you come to me because you are asking me?

I came to you because I am depressed.

How long have you been depressed?

For about three months.

I'm not sure I understand you fully.

Since my goldfish died.

What does that suggest to you?

That I really miss my goldfish.

Can you elaborate on that?

Herbie, my goldfish, was the only creature I ever really loved.

I'm not sure I understand you fully.

Oh Herbie! Why did you have to die and leave me?

We were discussing you not me.

CONSTRUCTING DYNAMIC BRAINS

Education is the ability to perceive the hidden connections between phenomena.

—VACLAV HAVEL, 2000

Human infants are not born with either dynamic or static neural networks in place. As discussed earlier, the network architecture of the brain develops in what is referred to as an experience dependent manner. Our brains change based upon the types of learning experiences we are exposed to, how we ultimately find ways to derive meaning in our world. From a dynamic standpoint, we hope that as we get older, our brain develops increasingly sophisticated and subtle forms of neural collaboration. Of course, we also may wish to accumulate a host of new habits, facts, formulas, procedures and associations, the static equivalent of neural development. However, in the end it is clear that the critical factor in determining our eventual success is weighted heavily in favor of the dynamic aspects of our brain.

Children appear to develop these two forms of neural processing through vastly different types of learning experiences. Static development appears to depend upon exposure to discrete stimulus-response sequences, sometimes using operant reward mechanisms to increase the rate of learning. Repeated trials of exposure to the stimulus, making sure that the stimulus is clearly recognized, followed by the preferred response paired with the stimulus, leads to a desired automaticity.

In contrast, dynamic brain development is dependent upon exposure to cognitive challenges, provided in a careful manner. Adults intuitively expose the child to thousands of situations where he is faced with problems that are not quite solvable within the parameters of his current neural configuration. This provides the opportunity for the development of more sophisticated neural integration on a piece by piece basis. As we will discuss in the next chapter, we believe that a central part of the development of ASD is the failure of the child's brain to make use of learning opportunities of this nature.

When genuinely challenged, typically developing children struggle to solve authentic problems that cannot be assimilated through their prior understanding. They experience moments of uncertainty where they no longer perceive a familiar pattern, concept or solution, nor perceive a new one. If during these times they do not avoid the problem and are provided with the necessary supports and affordances to safely study and consider it, they learn to value moments of productive uncertainty and emerge as competent learners.

As we complete our overly brief tour of dynamic processing, I'd like you to think about the following questions: "How is it that most of us develop dynamic processing? Are we born with it? Who are our teachers? And how do they teach us?" In the next chapter, we will discuss how dynamic brains develop through our interaction with more experienced guides in cognitively challenging environments.

Reflection Questions:

1. Can you remember experiences in your life where you learned a new way of problem solving, or made a discovery that changed the way you thought about yourself, your associates, or your world?

2. Was there a period of productive uncertainty prior to the discovery?

3. What were the precipitants for these discoveries?

4. What do you remember about the process that led up to them?

Chapter Five

The Guided Participation Relationship

Children's cognitive development is an apprenticeship—it occurs through guided participation in social activity with companions who support and stretch children's understanding.

—BARBARA ROGOFF

We are not born with the ability to analyze and adapt to complex settings, simultaneously process communication channels, or handle fuzzy problems. None of us can recall taking any classes or courses on dynamic intelligence during our school years. However, beginning in our first months of life, children participate in an intensive, but implicit learning process, initially with parents and then with other adults, known as guided participation.

In 1991, Dr. Barbara Rogoff[12] published her influential book, *Apprenticeship in Thinking*, in which she examined the means whereby children become active thinkers and problem solvers. Her work was based upon the theories of brilliant Russian psychologist, Lev Vygotsky, posthumously recognized as the father of modern Developmental Psychology.

---

12   Dr. Rogoff is currently on the faculty of the University of California, Santa Cruz.

Vygotsky believed that the main purpose of learning was not the accumulation of information and procedures, but rather the growth of more sophisticated, complex mental processes. His primary thesis is that the human mind, our capacity to think flexibly, solve problems, imagine, anticipate and reflect, is the product of the relationship between the child and more experienced adults who stretch the child's understanding by providing problems that are just above his level of competence.[13]

Through extensive multi-cultural research, Dr. Rogoff concluded that in every society on earth, adults and children develop a special type of collaborative learning relationship she labeled guided participation. This process is carried out day after day, without much deliberation or conscious awareness. Children participate alongside family and community members in authentic activities as apprentices, actively seeking to appropriate meaning and expertise from adult guides who provide opportunities for the apprentice to safely encounter cognitive challenges.

Dr. Rogoff makes several points about guided participation that are well worth noting:

- Neither guides nor apprentices have to be aware of their roles in order for guided participation to be successful. Rather, in typical development the process is usually carried out in an implicit manner, built into the framework of family and cultural life.

- There is no age limit to apprenticeship. For example, Dr. Rogoff describes the Guided Participation Relationship (GPR)[14] with young South American children and their mothers, as well as with adult apprentice Nigerian tailors and their masters. If we are fortunate, we are provided with guided opportunities for mental growth throughout our lives.

- While the principles of guided participation are universal, each culture appears to customize the specific ways in which they carry out the process.

---

13 Vygotsky uses the term Zone of Proximal Development (ZPD) to describe the preferred area to construct children's learning—a zone that is right above the edge of their current competence, but not so challenging as to foster frustration and failure.

14 I will use the abbreviation GPR as a substitute for Guided Participation Relationship.

- No culture appears to have the edge of superiority in its adaptive version of guided participation.

Over the past two decades, developmental psychologists have reached a consensus in support of Dr. Rogoff's thesis. In fact, the 1990s ushered in a transformative era in developmental psychology. Dynamic Systems models, came into prominence, supporting the view of development as a fluid relationship in which both parents and children are active agents in co-constructing the child's mental development. Hundreds if not thousands of articles, monographs and books described how parents and infants engage in the special dance that forms the foundation for the child's dynamic mind.[15]

The GPR is not a technique, or artificial program developed by a psychologist or educator, but a universal learning process unfolding in every culture throughout recorded history. I hoped that analyzing this complex process would provide me with the first step in developing a systematic roadmap for constructing dynamic intelligence, in those situations, like ASD, where it fails to develop in its typical intuitive manner.

RDI seeks to restore the natural Guided Participation Relationship found in every culture.

The importance of Dr. Rogoff's work as an essential starting point in developing RDI cannot be overstated. However, her efforts, like those of other developmental psychologists, do not provide a methodology for breaking down the GPR into its essential elements and systematically re-constructing the relationship if it fails to naturally develop.

Guided participation has been viewed by developmental psychologists as such a natural process that the question is rarely asked, "If it didn't happen, where would you begin?" Scientists did not conceptualize that there would be a group of children

---

15   Psychologists love to make up their own idiosyncratic names for the same process. If we look behind different names, we find that the guided participation process has been accepted as universal.

who, despite the heroic efforts of their parents, did not naturally develop the ability to function as apprentices in guided participation relationships. This framed my primary task in developing RDI for individuals with ASD who, of course, represent these very exceptions.

In the following sections, I will recount the ways I have deconstructed guided participation to examine its various elements, first from the point of view of the guide and second from the perspective of the apprentice. Then, I will explore how the GPR provides us with a new understanding of Autism Spectrum Disorders, resulting from the failure, due to the child's vulnerabilities, to form this crucial relationship.

Chapter Six

Guided Participation: The Guide

There is no greater pleasure than serving as a catalyst for another person's journey towards fulfilling their true potential.

—STEVE GUTSTEIN

WHAT KIND OF GUIDE?

Imagine yourself as a wealthy young Englishman, traveling into the American wilderness in 1835. Your father wishes for you to get out into the world and obtain some seasoning before joining his tea import business. He invites you to take an all-expenses-paid trip to the American wilderness. Your eyes light up at the prospects of such an adventure, perhaps you will catch a glimpse of primitive tribesmen! You set sail for New York City. Arriving in New York you board a train and then take a steamboat to St. Louis. Once ensconced in your hotel, you hire a driver to take you to the address of the guide you have hired, a Mr. Johnston who has been highly recommended by an associate in London.

You find Johnston living in a posh house near the center of the city. He is a well turned-out fellow in a fine buckskin suit and beaver hat. He has a ready smile and quick wit. He tells you that he will take care of everything, even departing right from your hotel. True to his word, three days later, Johnston and his helpers are waiting outside the hotel lobby at the appointed time. Johnston has provided the horses, pack mules and all provisions necessary for the journey. You yourself bring little more than a change of clothes, sketchbook and pencils.

Each day you travel deeper into the wilderness, following a route that Johnston mapped out before your departure. Each evening you sit together by the fire and go over your route for the next day. You quickly learn to appreciate your guide as a non-stop, fast-talking, entertaining encyclopedia of the flora, fauna, native peoples and legends of the lands you travel. He is forever pointing out odd and novel things he believes you would find interesting. Your ears are filled from morning until night with fascinating information and anecdotes. You have a good but not perfect memory, so you frequently ask him to repeat his tales to make sure you retain all of this information so you can impress your family and friends back home in England.

You take for granted that Johnston will head off with his crew every day to bring back wild game to eat. They find wood to burn, even when you can't see a tree for miles. You are amazed by the way these wilderness men instantly spot tracks of the aboriginal inhabitants that you have not noticed. They hear a faint sound you would have taken for the wind and instantly tell you what animal is about. They smell potential trouble up ahead and know what to do to avoid it.

They gather wood and make fires, prepare your meals, pitch your tent and generally see to your safety and comfort, so that you can write or sketch when the whim strikes you. You decide you want to be one of the fellows, so you insist on doing some of the work. Over the weeks, you learn to make a fire with the wood they gather, prepare the food they hunt, set up and take down the tent they carry for you. You even learn to set an animal trap and catch a fish from the river. As arranged, on the 90th day, you arrive back in St. Louis, your thirst for adventure and travel well sated, desiring nothing more than to return to London and your comfortable life.

When you reach home, you are pleased to realize that you remember most of what Johnston shared with you during your journey. You have learned to talk a bit of the wilderness slang of Johnston and his crew. With the beaver hat and buckskin jacket you purchased in St. Louis, you can play the part of a real American Westerner. When you talk to friends and associates you amaze them with your knowledge of the wilderness and your explanations of how to trap a beaver, make a fire in the rain and find wild onions buried in the ground. You are left with countless memories, many sketches and amazing anecdotes to share. You intend to recommend Johnston to all of your acquaintances. In your opinion, he is the consummate guide for all those who wish to experience a taste of the real American West.

We now move to our second scenario. You are a different Englishman, also born and raised in London. You know nothing of country life, let alone traversing in the wilderness. You were born into wealth, but now, approaching manhood, through ill luck, your family has recently become penniless and you despair about making your way in life. As if ordained, at the nadir of your depression, just when you are about to humble yourself by taking a lowly clerk's job for a shipping company, you receive a letter from a solicitor requesting a meeting with you to discuss the last will and testament of your uncle. Your dear uncle Eldred has died and made you sole heir to his estate, as he never married and has no other nephews or nieces. Your spirits soar! You have not seen or heard from Eldred since he sailed off to America to make his fortune. Could this be your salvation—the answer to your prayers?

At the meeting with the solicitor, you are surprised to learn that Eldred invested his time and funds prospecting for silver in a place bearing the strange name of the Ozark Mountains. Eldred's will, dictated as he lay dying of the Influenza, expresses the desire that you continue in his footsteps, as he does not wish to have lived in vain. It contains specific instructions. You are to be provided a sum of money, which can be used only to transport you to the primitive cabin he has erected on the claim. The will reveals that the moderately successful claim is located in the middle of a wilderness area, over 100 miles from the nearest settlement and about 300 miles from St. Louis, Missouri.

The letter indicates that your uncle has arranged for a capable gentleman by the name of Thompson to serve as your wilderness and mining tutor. Thompson has agreed to spend an initial six months as a daily companion and then to make periodic visits over a second six-month period, with the purpose of teaching you all you need to know to survive this hostile place and continue Eldred's work. Thompson has been given sufficient funds to provide you with the provisions you will need during the time he is with you. Afterwards, you must survive on your own. The letter goes on to say that if you remain and work the claim for a period of no less than five years, as witnessed by Thompson, a sum of 5,000 pounds will be deposited in a bank account in London. You may also keep any silver you mine.

With more than a little trepidation, but with no real option, you set sail for America. After journeying by train and steamboat, you reach St. Louis. You learn that Thompson lives in a tiny settlement about 100 miles northwest of the city, so you hire a wagon and driver and finally, after four days of feeling like you've eaten half the dust in Missouri, you meet up with Mr. Thompson. He lives in a small but well-kept cabin on the outskirts of town. Thompson seems a serious but sturdy fellow. He dresses in neat, well-mended, but nondescript clothes and carries himself with an air of quiet poise and competence.

When you mentioned your upcoming journey to an acquaintance in London who had made an expedition to this very same wilderness area a year ago, he informed you that he had never heard of Thompson, but he raved about another guide, located in St. Louis, by the name of Johnston. You ask Thompson if he knows Johnston and he bursts out laughing so hard he has to sit down to keep from falling over. Finally, when he can breathe normally again he launches into the following monologue:

Sonny, Johnston and me are as far apart as the wide banks of the Missouri. Why, he takes them rich men out on them 'pleasure excursions' and brings them home safe and sound to their mommies, full of wild stories. They think they've seen danger, when he's just been traipsing them around the countryside, like they's on a picnic or some such. Sure, they can recite all this wilderness lore. Maybe they learn to light a fire, or even catch a fish if they stick their pole where Johnston tells them. But, just leave them out there on their own for a couple of days, without Johnston, his crew and all them supplies and they'd never been seen or heard from again.

Boy, I promised your uncle on his deathbed that I would do my best to prepare you for the real thing. Six months from now, I won't be around every day and you will be facing life or death. We have no time for fun and games. I don't

need you to memorize all of them pretty stories and facts that Johnston spouts
off. We've got a heap of real learning to do; hard work that will take every second
from dawn till dusk, seven days a week. We've got to re-tune all of your senses.
You've got to be able to look around you and spot things in an instant that today
you couldn't see if you had all year. You've got to taste and smell the changing
weather. You've got to talk bird talk, to seduce them to come out of their hiding
places, so you can catch them.

I don't know if the next six months is going to be enough to keep you from get-
ting yourself killed. But boy I do know this: if you went with Johnston, he'd fill you
up with fancy stories, tons of information you'd never remember and false cour-
age that would get you pretending to yourself that you were a real mountain man.
Then he'd leave you to fend for yourself, with as little common sense as the day you
arrived and you'd be dead in no time.

You have no reason to doubt Thompson's word and in any case, Uncle Eldred
has provided no options for guide selection. You steel yourself to the coming ordeal
and ask Thompson whether the two of you can set out in the morning and arrive
at the cabin in a day or two to begin mining. To your surprise, you learn that once
again he finds your words hilarious. After he recovers from a combined laughing,
coughing fit, Thompson says:

Boy, we ain't goin to be mining for a while. First, you've got to learn how to
survive them hills. You have to learn a thousand things so well you can do them
in your sleep. Why you don't even know how to make friends with a mule, so
he won't be ornery. You don't know how to read a hoof print and know if it's a
hostile or not. You don't know how to smell for the things that will eat you before
you eat them.

Thompson goes on to tell you all of the things you have to learn until your head
begins to spin. He concludes by saying that after you've learned all that, if you are
still alive and willing to go on, he will start teaching you about mining. The final
blow comes when he reminds you that you are still 400 miles from the mine. That's
fifteen days' hard journey, through a not-always hospitable country.

Exhausted, you return to your bunk in a room above a nearby barn. There are no hotels in a small place like this. As tired as you are, you cannot sleep. You realize that Thompson is right. This is no pleasure trip. You have to be able to think and perceive the world like Thompson. You have to react in an instant to a threat that you currently wouldn't be aware of until it is too late. You have to be able to see, hear, and smell things as he does. You have to know when to stop, slow down and study the world around you and when to run away as fast as you can. You have to lose your city instincts developed through years of London living and substitute them with a special kind of wilderness intuition uniquely suited for those mountains. For the first time a cold chill runs up your spine. You wonder if this is really possible. You are all too aware of the consequences if you fail.

What differences stand out when you compare the guides in the two stories? Which guide would you choose if you were the second Englishman? Why?

DIFFERENT GUIDES FOR DIFFERENT PURPOSES

Both Johnston and Thompson have serious responsibilities. However, I'm sure it's clear from the above story that the task of each is quite different. Obviously, Thompson resembles the type of guide we are interested in learning more about. He recognizes that he must somehow transfer the ways he has learned to think, perceive and feel without conscious effort, to someone from a very different culture who has none of these intuitive abilities. He will have to slow the pace for this young Englishman, become conscious of the things he does intuitively and remember back to when he was first struggling to become a mountain man.

Psychologists and educators who study the GPR are not playing semantic games. They do not use the term guide interchangeably with teacher, instructor, or tutor. Guides have a specific mission. They provide essential opportunities for the apprentice to develop the types of mental processes necessary for future success in the culture in which they live. Guides employ specific methods to carefully transfer mental processes to the mind of the apprentice in a manner that allows these mental tools to be employed in a wide variety of settings and in response to an extensive range of problems.

BALANCING STATIC AND DYNAMIC

Adults who take on guiding roles are rarely in the position of functioning purely to facilitate dynamic intelligence. For example, in teaching the young Englishman how to think like an experienced mountain man, Thompson had to instruct him in a number of static skills necessary for survival. In a like manner, parents, along with facilitating dynamic mental development, must discipline their children, keep them safe and healthy and instruct them on many life skills appropriate to their age. Certainly, teachers struggle with the conflict of limited time in which they must cover content, while hoping against hope that they can find a few moments to help their students learn to think, integrate and create.

Even in fictional allegories like the Star Wars movie saga, the various figures serving as guides to Luke Skywalker—Obi-Wan Kenobi and Yoda—have to maintain this delicate balance. The film spotlights Luke's poignant dynamic learning moments, whether visited by the ghost of Obi-Wan, or involuntarily exiled to apprentice to Yoda. Over time, Luke makes a series of mental discoveries and undergoes transformations to a new state of consciousness and control over *the Force*. However, hidden in the background of the film are the hundreds if not thousands of hours where Luke must have painstakingly learned to master the mechanics of fighting with a light saber and to operate the various spaceships and floaters he seems to fly so effortlessly.[16]

The important point for adults in the guide role is to maintain a healthy balance between the demands of today, and the foundations needed for future success. For example, the content-delivery pressures of most modern school curriculums result in school days filled with overwhelming amounts of mostly unnecessary informa-

---

16 Luke's initial strong reluctance to begin his apprenticeship with Yoda illustrates the important point that the apprentice does not necessarily have to be happy about entering the GPR, or enter on a voluntary basis.

tion. Facts are learned this week, repeated on a test and then promptly forgotten to provide room for new information. The imbalance created by this emphasis on content accumulation relegates dynamic guiding to a rare, if not non-existent, classroom occurrence.

Guides must maintain a long-term perspective, and keep focused on their primary mission, which is the apprentice's mental development. Static learning is easier, requires less planning and effort and has an immediate payoff. Thus, if we are not careful, learning in our modern, rushed society becomes dominated by the accumulation of facts, procedures, formulas and rapid answers to very specific problems. Unfortunately, these provide few foundations for mental development and growth.

The desperation and feelings of hopelessness and inadequacy experienced by parents and professionals working with ASD children often lead to a desire to obtain any kind of short-term result. Focusing solely on static skills with students whose brains are already developing in a static manner will provide an easier, quicker payoff. However, it will also curtail dynamic development, thus encroaching on or completely disregarding future mental growth.

THE GOAL BENEATH THE GOAL

Give a man a fish and you feed him for a day.
Teach a man to fish and you feed him for a lifetime.

—CHINESE PROVERB

The campus for mental development is found in the various mundane activities and settings related to our everyday existence, events such as shopping at the supermarket, or making beds. During these activities, guides consciously or unconsciously de-emphasize superficial, instrumental products, for example, getting the groceries home as quickly as possible, or making the bed in the most perfectly neat manner. They also relegate activity-related content and procedures, such as the right way to tuck in the sheets, or the specific items that must be procured at the store to the background. Instead, they use real-life activities as a vehicle for elaborating and transferring mental processes to the apprentice, while keeping the specific knowledge to a necessary minimum.

It is not that learning the specifics of tasks is unimportant. However, guides intuitively seem to know that these activities also present excellent opportunities for dynamic growth, years before the child needs to learn the specific skills required for autonomous task performance. As an example, consider three-year-olds who make amazing discoveries while accompanying their parents to the supermarket, but are clearly not ready to do the family's grocery shopping. Competent guides seem to implicitly know that they should reserve instruction for separate occasions, rather than trying to accomplish too much at one time.

---

*We refer to this process as emphasizing **the goal beneath the goal**.*

On the surface, some static skills may seem more complex than their dynamic counterparts. A dynamic process, such as monitoring potential changes in one's environment, appears simple at first glance. However, learning to actually use the process, mastering the attentional juggling to monitor the background while simultaneously engaged in a foreground task, leaves a different impression. To perfect this ability so that it can be performed almost automatically throughout the course of the day adds an entirely new level of difficulty.

While guides may sometimes temporarily deemphasize activity-related instruction, guided participation is not a theoretical exercise. *It is very real!* Guides, when they stop to reflect on their actions with apprentices, are quite aware that they are providing them with the tools they must have to thrive in their future roles.

CREATING PRODUCTIVE UNCERTAINTY

A major advantage of humans is opportunism—capitalizing on new discoveries and taking advantage of novel occurrences. The developmental value of trans-

actions with novel and unknown aspects of the environment is critical in order
to actively engage with the environment and discover new opportunities.

—Alan Sroufe

The best guides intuitively recognize that the greatest opportunities for cognitive, social and emotional growth occur during moments where the apprentice experiences heightened but safe uncertainty or ambiguity. Therefore, they strive to create lessons at the very edge of the apprentice's feelings of competence.

A state of uncertainty exists every time we encounter a new problem or new information that challenges our prior understanding. All learning in dynamic encounters occurs during states of productive uncertainty. Productive is a subjective term. If it feels productive, by definition we want more of it. Too much uncertainty results in unproductive uncertainty, better known as fear. We all have a threshold over which uncertainty feels overwhelming. Sometimes there is a very thin line between these two experiences. The optimal state is quite close to an aversive state. Think of the discovery of fire. Imagine the experience of the first human who approached a log that had been struck by lightning.

Uncertainty + Safety = Productive Uncertainty, Approach and Study.
Uncertainty + Danger = Threat, Fight or Flight.

Productive uncertainty produces a type of positive stress labeled *eustress* by Hans Selye, the founder of modern stress theory. The experience of uncertainty always produces some anticipatory anxiety. However, the over-riding emotion is curiosity—motivation to see what's going to happen next. It is exciting to be at a crossroads and not be exactly sure which road to take, as long as there is no pressure to be somewhere and no danger of making the wrong decision.

An example of productive uncertainty can be found while taking a hike in the wilderness. You have brought a map and some provisions so you won't get lost, hungry or thirsty. After hiking for a while on the main trail, you come to a crossroads where two secondary trails branch off. You check your map and see that staying on the main trail or taking either of the branches will get you where you want to go. One of the branch trails looks as if it will provide you with some mountain views. The other trail might be alongside a river. You've never taken either trail before. You stop for a few minutes, study the map and consider which trail you want to take. You flip a coin, trusting that whatever choice you make won't cause any threat or trouble. You are ready for a productive adventure. Those are the types of situations where you may learn the most about yourself and your world.

STAGING GUIDED PARTICIPATION

Staging is the larger context in which we set up a learning process. It is an over-arching concept reflecting the attitude and perceived learning position of the guide. Staging informs us about how the guide perceives his or her role as a facilitator vis-à-vis the apprentice. All learning is staged in one way or another. The ways in which we structure the learning relationship between the more experienced and less experienced person and the manner, time and effort we spend in constructing the stage for learning, largely determines what will take place.

STAYING CLOSE TO THE EDGE

I want to stay as close to the edge as I can without going over. At the edge you see all kinds of things you can't see from the center.

—KURT VONNEGUT

Human brains grow only when they are challenged. If your current level of neural integration is sufficient to successfully solve the problems you are faced with, your brain won't be pushed to develop more sophisticated, integrated neural pathways.

The challenge is to provide problems that both fit the child's current thinking process while also tempting him into trying out more powerful modes of thinking. Guides function as mediators between the apprentice and the real-world challenges that they are preparing for.

Guided participation is not about throwing apprentices into the deep end of the pool. An important function of guides is to create a background of safety and trust, so that the apprentice will approach new challenges without undue anxiety and withdrawal.

There are two elements to creating safety. The first is to clarify that the guide is the leader and authority in the collaboration. The guide must set clear limits and boundaries without stifling the apprentice's initiative and self-efficacy. The second element is maintaining a regulated level of emotional responsiveness to the apprentice. When presenting new challenges, guides must be sensitive to the apprentice's communication of distress: responding by reducing the challenge or increase their supportive efforts to keep the task proximal—slightly above the child's level of independent functioning. However, they must not be so sensitive that they become enmeshed in the apprentice's emotional state and wind up in a parallel state of distress. This is a delicate choreography.

INVESTING THE EFFORT TO CONSTRUCT CRITICAL MOMENTS

All moments of learning are not considered to be equally valuable. Most of the guide's time and energy goes into setting the stage for powerful discoveries and elaborations, moments where safely challenged learners find that they can expand their thinking, borrow another's perspective or expand prior discoveries to new settings and problems. Constructing such episodes takes preparation. Guides have to carefully select learning objectives that are just above the learner's current functioning. They have to carefully frame, scaffold and spotlight activities, terms which we will shortly discuss.

In typical development, an ongoing process emerges between parental guides and their child apprentices to prepare the learner for new challenges and then to

adding variations, employing the new tool in different settings and activities and engaging in new ways with different partners

Regulation (R¹)

new challenge

challenge

Regulation (R²)

new period of consolidation sets the stage for a future challenge

The R-C-R Cycle

provide the opportunity for the apprentice to incorporate their new discoveries into their daily lives.

Developmental Psychologist Kenneth Kaye introduced the concept of a Regulation-Challenge-Regulation (R-C-R) Cycle to describe how parents intuitively choreograph challenges with their typically developing infants. After making a new cognitive discovery, parents and infants usually go through periods where they elaborate the discovery (R1), adding variations, employing the new tool in different settings and activities and engaging in new ways with different partners. At some point in this elaboration process, a new challenge is presented and if successfully managed, it leads to a new period of consolidation (R2), which will, in turn, set the stage for a future challenge.

LEADING FROM THE SIDE

We are used to visualizing formal education as occurring from a face-to-face position. In a formal classroom, face-to-face too often describes an active instructor delivering information to a passive student receiver. It further implies that the activity used as a vehicle for learning is placed in the hands of the learner, for example, a worksheet of math computation problems that the learner will complete. The teacher would not be expected to do his or her own worksheet. Rather, the teacher's role is to provide instruction for how the learner should go about the task.

Guided participation is quite different and typically takes place in a side-by-side manner. This side-by-side position communicates that the guide and apprentice are active co-participants in the learning process with both having real responsibilities for solving problems and completing tasks.

Being side-by-side does not imply that the guide relinquishes authority to the apprentice, nor does it suggest that they have equal ability. Guides clearly communicate that the task belongs to the guide and take ownership of the activity. Guides are clear that they, not the apprentice, possess the bulk of mastery needed for success. Thus, the apprentice is a junior participant, respecting the guide's expertise and authority and assuming the roles that the guide creates for him.

The side-by-side stance also communicates that guide and apprentice, although not equals, are joined in looking out at the world together as collaborators. Their joint focus is the problem to be solved or a challenge to be surmounted. This contrasts to a typical educational setting where the student is performing to the teacher's satisfaction and providing a predetermined, desired response.

GUIDING FROM THE SIDE

- *The guide owns the task.*
- *Guide and apprentice are co-participants looking out at the task together.*
- *Each has real responsibilities designated by the guide.*

While working side-by-side, guides may not always assign themselves the more competent or complex role. Sometimes, deliberately taking a naïve position is an excellent way to stimulate the apprentice to reflect on the process to make new connections. At other times, guides deliberately define roles that may appear less powerful, but are strategically better for introducing intended challenges.

Several years ago, I received a short video clip from a family with a young teenage ASD son. The family operated a small horse farm in the southern United States. It quickly became one of my favorite examples of a guide assuming what appears to be a less powerful role for strategic reasons. In this clip, the objective chosen by the parents was for their young teenage son to learn that some interpersonal problems require grey-area thinking. Such problems cannot be solved by any right or wrong response. Another objective was to illustrate that sometimes people will act in unpredictable ways. Coping with this type of behavior, extremely characteristic of young teenage boys, requires operating outside of the box, being assertive and working out compromises with your partners.

In the clip, Jeannie and her son, Matthew, are cleaning up the tons of horse poop that naturally accumulates on their farm. The scene opens with Matthew operating a tractor that pulls the "poop cart," while Jeannie uses a pitchfork to transfer the poop into the cart. The task appears to be one of simple action coordination. Matthew drives to an area adjacent to where Jeannie is gathering poop and waits for her to pitch it into the cart. Then Jeannie goes off to the next gathering area and Matthew drives over to join her.

The coordination part of the activity is an objective Matthew had mastered some time before in his RDI Program. Jeannie treats Matthew's monitoring and regulating actions as something to be taken for granted and not something she wants to spotlight.

Two or three minutes into the video, things change dramatically. Instead of forking the poop into the cart, Jeannie raises the poop-filled pitchfork toward Matthew and, standing about two feet away, begins to smile in a teasing manner, as she gently sways her arms back and forth in his general direction. The implication of what Jeannie intends to do is clear to Matthew. Holding his hands out in a stop motion he shouts, "No!" While the idea of throwing horse poop on someone may disgust the reader, I have been told that when you grow up on a horse farm, poop takes on the same role as snow does in Maine or Vermont and Matthew smiles broadly throughout the entire clip.

Jeannie disregards his protest and flings poop toward the tractor. Matthew leaps from the tractor seat and avoids getting hit with the main barrage. However, he incurs residual damage and has to wipe the seat in order to get back on. (It is important to note that there is no directive for him to return to the tractor seat and become a victim of Jeannie's impetuousness. That would constitute learned helplessness rather than guided participation).

Intrepid soul that he is, Matthew gets right back on the tractor to resume his job. In this particular situation, non-compliance, refusing to remount the tractor until Jeannie commits to ceasing her poop attacks, would be a reasonable strategy. However, Matthew has learned to be overly compliant, in order to gain acceptance. This deeply worries his parents, since he now attends middle school.

A more assertive response does not occur immediately. It takes several minutes of threatened and actual poop tossing before Matthew finally takes a more active approach to the problem. He eventually runs to his father, Jim, who is filming the episode and tells on Jeannie by informing dad that, "Mom's getting poop on your seat". Jim, observing that Matthew is still in good spirits, introduces yet another challenge by saying, "I love it when mom gets poop on my tractor seat." Matthew reacts for about ten seconds with an amazing look of astonishment, the ultimate open mouth stare. He returns to his mother and opens negotiations: she will have to cease the poop throwing if she wants his further cooperation.

INVITING

The invitational aspect of the guide's function is best reflected in communication. Although at times guides are directive, the majority of their communication initiations are designed to invite the apprentice to share experiences. This includes times when guides may externalize their self talk process, so that the apprentice can benefit from their internal dialogue.

Guiding is not completely invitational. For example, guides may communicate in a quite powerful manner to indicate that the apprentice's attention should best be pointed in a particular direction. What guides do not try to control is whether the apprentice takes advantage of the opportunities the guide provides for cognitive growth. Guides cannot force or demand that apprentices make cognitive discoveries, but they can design experiences that offer opportunities to make new, meaningful connections about how the world works. On the other hand, because guides cannot completely predict how the apprentice will apply the opportunities they provide, unanticipated, wonderful and accidental discoveries can occur.

Invitations should not be confused with trying to entertain or make the child happy. Promoting competence, while simultaneously experiencing joy and happiness, is wonderful as an ideal, but places much too high a burden on guides.

We find that the need to entertain or keep the ASD child happy is one of the biggest obstacles to developing the GPR. We certainly can understand the motivation for this. Often your experience as a parent is that the child only attends to you when he or she wants something, or when you can be entertaining enough. When you live in fear that seemingly benign actions will provoke an outburst or tantrum, you will quickly enough develop the unconscious habit of taking actions that do not rock the boat.

We hope that the allure of new competence, coupled with the guarantee of safety, offers sufficient enticement to maintain the child's full focus on new challenges. This assumes that the guide has first successfully built a sense of trust in the relationship with the apprentice, something that typically breaks down in ASD. We will discuss this in more detail in a later chapter.

EXAMPLE OF POOR STAGING: PLAYING LITTLE LEAGUE

When I was seven, my dad got the idea into his head that I should be playing Little League Baseball. I was very uncoordinated. I'd not had the experience of hitting or catching with my father or another guide. But, my dad, in the impulsive way he often went about parenting, was determined that I play ball right then and there, despite the fact that the player selection process had already occurred, the teams had been practicing and the season was set to begin in another week. He slipped the team manager $10. This was quite a lot for a man of his modest earnings back in 1959. My dad truly loved me, misguided though he was, and purchased a baseball glove and the team uniform and, without preparing or asking me my opinion, drove me to a field and told me I was now playing on the Bears.

Not only was I horribly uncoordinated and unschooled in the mechanics of baseball, I was the youngest Bear by about a year. My coach must have sensed my problems because he assigned me right field, the place where the ball would most likely never be hit. With my undiagnosed ADD there was no way I could focus. Thus, when the occasional ball came my way I was oblivious. Looking back on this fiasco, I am surprised by my continuing love of sports but not that I never made the majors.

EXAMPLE OF POOR STAGING: PLAYING THE CELLO

In second grade, I was diagnosed with Mental Retardation. If you had observed me in my classroom back then, you might have agreed with the opinion. I was depressed as I struggled to come to grips with the cancer that would soon claim my mother's life. I was also nearsighted. Like the proverbial butcher's son who has no meat, my father the optician was not aware of the problem, spending every minute to pay the medical bills, as there was no health insurance. I had "inattentive" Attention Deficit Disorder, so I would sit in my seat, smile, and make great but vacuous eye contact. When the grim-faced Mrs. Firestone called on me, I was oblivious and typically responded with an inane answer. Even though I wasn't a behavior problem, Mrs. Firestone had little patience with me. Thus, I was seated in the back of the room, perhaps so that I wouldn't set a bad example for the other students, which was fine with me as it actually facilitated my daydreaming. Finally, even this banishment was not sufficient and she requested that I be placed in the "slow" class. The school complied without any formal evaluation.

The placement was a godsend for me. We didn't spend our time sitting at desks, nor were we passive learners. We took field trips in our neighborhood nearly every day. We tended a garden. We cut, pasted and stapled. I was the apple of my teacher's eye. Unfortunately, I brightened up and did so well, that my teacher soon realized that I did not belong in her class and lobbied successfully for my placement in the Gifted and Talented Classes. So, one day, without preparation or warning, I was escorted to yet another classroom.

In those days, the GT curriculum in New York City was experimenting with mandatory orchestral participation. Even though I had never heard an orchestra, on the day of my transfer I was led into the school auditorium, seated by myself where I listened to students play the violin, viola, cello and bass. When told to pick one, I chose the cello because it seemed to be about my size.

The cello turned out to be a bad choice for me because I had to take it home every day, ostensibly to practice, though I never did. This meant walking about a mile carrying an instrument just a bit smaller than I was and facing a fourth grade bully who considered me an excellent victim. Each day after school, he waited for me to turn a corner where he would pop out from a hiding spot and beat me up. Prior to my placement in the gifted program, I had finally learned to combine hyper-vigilance with speed. I could slide under parked cars, maneuvering to places where he couldn't reach me and wait him out (he usually got tired within a half hour and picked on someone else). Now, carrying the damn cello rendered my only coping mechanism unworkable. I could have used the violin or viola as a weapon. I could have used the bass for cover. The cello had no value—it was like throwing an anchor to a drowning man.

I "forgot" it on a regular basis. The school made heroic efforts to motivate me, even sending a cello teacher to my apartment house for extra tutoring (fighting lessons would have been more appreciated). Of course, he eventually gave up when I was not to be found at the time of the lesson. The cello was associated with trauma not competence. I was overjoyed when we abruptly moved to a new part of Brooklyn where I enrolled in a different school, finally rid of this scourge.

METHODS OF GUIDED PARTICIPATION

Guides rely on three main tools: framing, scaffolding and spotlighting. I present them in alphabetical order, because in real-life guides use these tools simultaneously (and usually unconsciously). Each tool will be briefly discussed in the next section with further elaboration in a later chapter.

FRAMING

In his groundbreaking book, *Developing through Relationships*, Alan Fogel introduces the concept of framing as, " … agreement about the scope of the discourse: its location, its setting, the acts that are taken to be significant vs. those that are irrelevant and the main focus or topic."

While scaffolding provides a roadmap for how to progressively transfer a process from a guide to an apprentice, framing, according to Fogel, is what we do in any social encounter to optimize the transfer process. It is how, on a micro level, we structure the encounter to make sure that the apprentice will focus the bulk of his attentional resources on the mental process we have chosen to transfer.

Activities of daily life constitute the background for learning in the GPR. However, proficiency in the activity itself and reaching the activity goal is typically not the main focus. The guide uses the activity as a canvas upon which he illustrates a universal dynamic process, unrelated to any specific task or problem. Guides must frame activities to make clear to the apprentice what the activity is really about. Frames help the apprentice distinguish critical from peripheral elements. They also minimize the impact of those aspects of the activity that might present obstacles to the apprentice directing her full attention to the mental process being highlighted.

Apprentices don't have to be aware of framing elements, as long as the frames are useful.

Why Do We Frame Paintings?

Dr. Fogel asks us to consider why artists frame their paintings. He makes the important point that art is no different from any other form of communication, including the GPR. Frames, while they can be ornate and lovely, primarily serve as boundaries, separating the work of art from the surround. The frame guides our focus, communicating that we should direct our attention to what is within rather than what is outside the frame. By comparison, books have chapters and covers, while symphonies have opening movements and codas. Framed activities have clear boundaries.

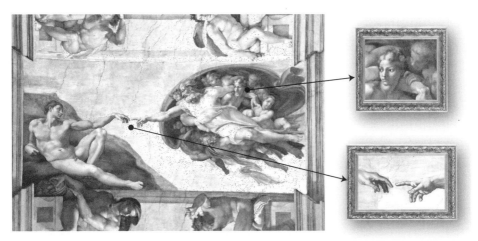

Frames create boundaries that guide our attention.

Along with creating boundaries, guides frame communication by imposing specific limits on what is to be communicated and how it is to be interpreted. Books reveal whether they are fictional, factual or something in between. Each physical volume is written in a specific language, which with rare exceptions does not change during the course of the book. Musical compositions are written with specific notation including keys, flats, sharps, tempo, intonation changes and the way that different instruments are to be integrated.

Finally, Fogel points out that all human communication differentiates figure-ground relationships. When we communicate, we intentionally or unintentionally punctuate certain information to indicate that it is more or less meaningful. For example, when writing we may **boldface** certain words and phrases, use **LARGER FONTS**, or separate key phrases from the main body by the use of extra s p a c i n g . In the same manner, framing can involve a change in pace, voice tone and space.

Competition for Attention

One important goal of framing is to minimize the impact of those aspects of the activity that might present obstacles to attending fully to the guide's main objective. It is important that peripheral elements do not wind up taking too much of the apprentice's finite processing capacity. The apprentice requires sufficient mental resources to manage the challenges being placed in the forefront.

When guides evaluate and minimize the impact of objects, sounds, tempting distractions and other "noises," they are reducing the competition for attention. This is defined as removal of any elements that are overly distracting and heightening the emphasis of critical elements, so that they are easier to perceive. Guides have to make sure to balance their removal of distracting elements with maintaining the authenticity of activities and legitimacy of roles. Whatever is removed in the short run will have to be reinstated in the long run so that real-world mastery can be established.

What constitutes competition for attention depends entirely on the apprentice's unique strengths and weaknesses. For example, the thirteen year-old in Florida who drove a tractor while his parent shoveled horse manure did not experience driving as a competition for attention. Tractor driving was something that Matthew already did on a daily basis. It was not a distraction for him. On the other hand, for an urban six year-old with visual-motor handicaps, choosing tractor driving as an authentic role would be a poor choice.

Adding or Modifying Structural Elements

An important part of framing is adding structure to an activity needed by someone who is not proficient in some aspects of their role like training wheels or written schedules. When Matt, my juggling teacher, who you will meet in the scaffolding section, was first teaching me, he had me practice throwing balls up in the air while standing in front of a wall. He knew that initially I would likely make many errant throws. If I were throwing towards an open space, I would spend the bulk of my time chasing down far-flung balls. Therefore, I would quickly become too focused on the catching. By framing the activity so that errantly thrown balls would softly bounce against a wall and come down nearby, he minimized my concern about where the balls would end up, so I could remain focused on my primary objective—learning to simultaneously keep two balls in the air.

Whether we introduce structural elements and which ones we choose to use, depends upon our objective. For example, if in the activity of riding bikes our objective is for the child to coordinate his movement with a partner and the child is not yet proficient in balancing himself, we would use training wheels so he would not have to overly attend to his balance. On the other hand, the very same training wheels would defeat the purpose if the objective is for the child to learn to make the small adjustments necessary to stay balanced. Rather we would place ourselves adjacent to the child and let go of the bicycle for a second or two at a time to provide short moments when he could safely experience balancing independently.

My next-door-neighbor and his three-year-old son collaborate to take out the trash twice each week. I love watching the slow careful pace at which they work, which is just right for the young child. My neighbor and his wife have cleverly modified the activity structure to ensure that both of the men have competent roles and also to make sure that the job gets done. Father and son each have a red wagon, in which to carry the trash bags, of a size to correspond with their height and ability. Mom has made sure to pack some of the trash in small bags that can be lifted by the son and larger bags that are clearly the purview of father. She also makes sure to place the bags in an area at the end of the driveway that is easily accessible to the wagons.

On trash days, father and son walk to their wagons parked side-by-side and roll their respective wagons to the area where the trash bags have been placed. Each lifts his respective trash bags onto his wagon and waits until his partner is finished loading. Then, side-by-side, they roll their wagons to the front curb and unload their contents. When complete, they roll their empty wagons, still side-by-side, to the back of the house and park them to be ready for the next trash day.

MEANINGFUL, AUTHENTIC ACTIVITIES AND ROLES

Apprentices learn to think, argue, act, and interact in increasingly knowledge-able ways with people who do something well, by doing it with them as legitimate peripheral participants.   —JEAN LAVE

A few years ago, my wife Rachelle and I were driving from Houston to St. Louis when we encountered a terrible thunderstorm and decided to overnight in Nacogdoches, a small, northeast Texas town. There is a lovely grand old hotel in the center of town where we spent the night in a top-floor room with great views of the rolling prairie thunder and lightning. In the morning, as we took our luggage out to the elevator, we came across a man and his son, the boy could not have been much older than four, already diligently at work, repairing the tile that had worn down around the elevator waiting area.

I gestured to Rachelle and we both slowed our pace so that we could observe this scene unfold for a few minutes without making the pair uncomfortable. Their interaction took place mostly in silence, as they went about the task of laying the tile. The son was in a peripheral role. He observed his father carefully and was quick to fetch the tools he requested. Even though the father was not teaching his son to lay tiles, this was clearly a good example of guided participation. The boy did not interrupt his father or bother him with questions. Father treated his son's role in their joint effort as authentic; he waited patiently for his son to find the correct tool and did not get it himself, even if it took his son a while. The son at one point looked up and noticed us waiting for the thankfully very slow elevator. He said nothing, but his smile told us everything of how proud he felt to be entrusted by his father as a co-worker.

Successful guides always make sure that a task has a meaningful quality that can be understood by the apprentice. Apprenticeship is not always glamorous or entertaining. For example, when I started out as a construction apprentice, my first job was pulling nails out of boards. You might think that this was just busy work but I was in a country that had a terrible shortage of lumber. They needed to re-use the boards if at all possible. My supervisor helped me understand that even though it was an entry level job, they weren't trying to torture me. My role, though minor, was actually integral to the construction process. The apprentice's role can be something that has to get done, something challenging, interesting or potentially enjoyable. But it must have some meaning, an emotional valence to it.

Similarly, in our example above, the father in his quiet way, communicated to his son that it was the son's responsibility to find the right tool and retrieve it for him. While unspoken, the father's patience, his spatial position (after asking his son for a tool he never turned around to check if the son was going to do his job), his slow pace and the calm tone of his voice, clearly framed that if the son decided not to do his job, then he was not going to do it for him. As in this example, the apprentice must know that even if a peripheral helper, the role is still essential, and if the apprentice does not perform this role, the task will not get done.

If the role is authentic, the apprentice will receive ongoing feedback from the task itself. Think about inviting an apprentice to do laundry with you. You decide to break the activity into a series of steps. The first is to carry the laundry basket into the laundry room together, face-to-face, holding up each side of the basket. (This is a good example of how the literal position of guide and apprentice may be face-to-face, while metaphorically it remains side-by-side). The objective is for the apprentice to experience himself as a true collaborator, holding up his end of the task, while moving together with you towards your goal of reaching the laundry room, with the laundry still in the basket. The apprentice must exert enough force to hold up his end of the basket, while simultaneously monitoring your pace and matching it with his own.

Now imagine holding out an empty laundry basket and asking the apprentice to help you carry it. The first problem is the apprentice will realize that the activity is meaningless: it cannot result in getting any laundry done. The second problem is that the role you are offering is not authentic. You do not really need help to carry an empty basket. Even if he does accept your invitation, the apprentice will experience no kinesthetic feedback from the task. He can use one finger and be as helpful to you as if he were using two hands. There is no way to monitor his pace to determine whether it will keep clothes from falling out. From a dynamic point of view, it is a much harder task to carry a basket with no clothes in it than one that is filled.

Neither would you invite a three-year-old apprentice to help you carry a fully laden laundry basket. This would create a task so difficult that he would most likely fail. Even if he were able to lift and carry his share of the basket, he would have no attentional resources available for the mental process of tracking whether his actions coordinated with yours, the whole point of the activity. The appropriate authentic role for him would be a basket that is sufficiently filled so that he knows the activity is for real and he can obtain the needed feedback from carrying the basket, but not so filled that just lifting it taxes all of his resources.

CHALLENGE

In guided participation, the reason we engage in an activity is to provide the apprentice with opportunities to use her mind in a new, more elaborated manner. There is no point in assigning the apprentice a role, no matter how necessary or authentic it might be, if it is not going to be mentally challenging. My rule of thumb is that any role that could be enacted by a robot is not a role worth assigning.

Let's return to our laundry example. Assume we have finally reached the washing machine with the clothes basket. Now the task is to take the laundry out of the basket and put it into the washer. We could easily set up a mindless routine where one of us grabs a piece of laundry and hands it to the other who drops it into the washer. Instrumentally, this might be quite an efficient way of reaching the goal of getting the laundry done, but is not the reason why we are spending time together. If we frame the activity in this manner, we guarantee that no dynamic learning will occur.

For the activity to be framed in a useful manner, the guide has to insert some uncertainty in the process and the apprentice's role has to be structured so that she has the major responsibility for resolving that uncertainty. One way to frame this activity is to make sure that there is a degree of unpredictability during the moments of interchange between the person taking the laundry from the basket and the person placing it in the washer. For example, assume that the apprentice is in the giver role and the guide is in the taker role. Each time the taker holds out her hand to obtain another garment, it can be in a different place, higher/lower, nearer/farther than it was the last time. This requires the giver to monitor the hand-off to make sure it is successful. Similarly, the taker might vary her readiness to receive new laundry, requiring the giver to make adjustments to his delivery.

SCAFFOLDING

If the teacher in such a system were to have a motto, it would surely be 'where before there was a spectator, let there now be a participant.' One sets the games, provides a scaffold to assure that the child's ineptitudes can be rescued or rectified, and then removes the scaffold part by part as the reciprocal structure can stand on its own.

— JEROME BRUNER

Transferring Responsibility

Scaffolding describes the manner in which guides transfer their mental processes—abilities such as analysis, appraisal, anticipation and reflection—to the apprentice in a gradual, systematic manner. Apprentices take an active role in this transfer process. There is no way that the guide can simply input his or her manner of thinking and perceiving to a passive recipient. Guides have to make sure to transfer not only ability, but responsibility as well. We already know how useless skills are when the person learning them has no concept of when they should be applied. Even more futile is teaching a skill to someone who doesn't realize he must take responsibility for actually applying that skill in his daily life.

Imagine yourself as a high wire expert in the circus who is breaking in a potential partner for a two-person balancing act. Because your apprentice has never been on the wire, the first time he goes up you will provide a strong safety net strung a few feet below the wire. You may also begin with a low wire, a few feet off the ground. In fact you may require that he purposefully fall off the wire several times to demonstrate that the net will hold him and thus he doesn't have to be afraid of getting hurt.

What you would not do is to take all the responsibility, even the very first time, to maintain your joint balance on the wire. Even though you will provide almost all of the support and balance for both of you, your partner must perceive himself as taking at least a modicum of the responsibility for maintaining his balance. If you were to begin his training by completely holding him up, he would gain nothing from the experience. What he needs is to begin to obtain feedback from his own actions, even if this means falling.

Finding simple versions

An important part of scaffolding is finding prototypes—the simplest authentic form of the process to be transferred. There are two important reasons for beginning with a basic version. The simpler version will be easier to learn and provide the earliest experience of authentic success. The second reason is that when we help the apprentice to understand a prototype, it provides an anchor for a new concept or way of thinking.

As the next examples illustrate, prototyping provides the apprentice with the experience of what a process is really about and how it differs from prior ways that he or she has thought about, or perceived the world.

Juggling two balls

Several years ago, I was conducting a workshop in Canada when, during a break, a gentleman from the audience came up to me and introduced himself. Matt told me that he was a professional juggler and that the guided participation concepts made complete sense to him. Then he asked me if I knew how to juggle. I told Matt that I had always envied people who could juggle but never seemed to get past juggling two balls. He asked if I would be willing to show him how I juggled and when I agreed, Matt produced two, soft, multi-colored juggling balls and handed them to me. I proceeded to demonstrate my juggling, which was to throw one ball in the air while transferring the second ball from one hand to the other, catching the ball that was in the air, transferring it from hand to hand, and so on.

Matt's eyes lit up as he observed me and quickly indicated that I could stop. He told me that he knew exactly what the problem was. In fact, he was so confident, he would bet me that he could teach me to juggle in five minutes if I did exactly what he told me to do. I willingly agreed to be his apprentice for five minutes, and so we began.

Matt explained that many people don't understand what juggling is about. They assume that juggling is primarily catching balls, so they develop a juggling strategy that maximizes their ability to catch. That is what I had done. But, as Matt pointed out, this is a false prototype for juggling. The real prototype has nothing to do with catching balls: it is about throwing them both up in the air at the same time and simultaneously keeping them aloft. Once you get the hang of throwing, you can then work on the catching part. Most important, one must stop worrying about whether the balls are caught or not caught. So my first exercise was to practice throwing two balls up in the air at the same time, making sure that I did not catch them.

Matt had intuitively deconstructed a complex process and had extracted the single basic prototype of throwing the balls in the air as the way to begin. The most important part of this prototype is that it is the only way that you can ever progress from two to three and more balls. Using my false method, I was forever limited to two balls.[17]

As I stated earlier, Matt also intuitively framed my participation by asking me to face a wall and stand a foot away from it while I threw the balls up. That way, when I didn't catch the balls, they hit the wall and were easily retrieved.

---

17   This is similar to ASD children who have learned static conversation skills. They are forever limited to static conversations.

I was relieved and started to look forward to the exercise. Within a very short time, I had learned to throw both balls in the air and to direct my tosses so that the balls stayed within catching distance. After I demonstrated mastery of this initial prototype, Matt told me that now I could catch the balls if I wanted to, but that it really didn't matter at this point of my learning process. True to his promise, within five minutes I was juggling the two balls in an authentic manner, catching them and ready to include a third ball.

Playing One Note

For my thirty-fifth birthday, my wife Rachelle surprised me by buying me a cello and weekly lessons with Jen Cho, a talented member of the Houston Symphony. My new teacher was a fascinating character. As a youth in South Korea, he had been torn between his two loves of classical music and Buddhism. As he approached maturity, Jen had to make the painful choice of either joining a monastery or a conservatory and had chosen the musical route. However, he never gave up his love for studying the process of being in the world.

After my childhood trauma with the cello, I was determined to rise to the challenge and master the instrument and practice an hour every day. My goal was to perfect the Bach Suites, a highly complex piece of music. In one artificial way, it was achievable, as I already knew how to read music. I began my daily practice ritual and I actually learned to play all of the right notes, although the performance was horribly screechy.

Being a master guide, Jen sat side-by-side with me during our lessons, both of us straddling our cellos. I will never know what excruciating torture my screeches caused him, as he kept an even temper and maintained a gentle smile as I demonstrated the results of my misguided efforts. After several weeks he stopped me mid-stream and said, "Steve, we are going to practice in a new way. We will play just one note today. First, let me demonstrate for you. Your task is just to listen and focus on how you feel as you hear the note. Just focus on your feelings and nothing else." Jen waited until I was ready to listen and then began to play one note, over and over in a trancelike manner on his magnificent cello. For well over five minutes he produced slowly and soulfully the same note without a word or a pause, altering the rhythm and volume as he went on. It was more beautiful than anything I had ever heard. He then asked me to join and play the one note with him. He suggested that I play softly, so that the sound of his cello would completely overwhelm mine. Gradually, he asked me to increase my volume so that the two sounds joined together. I clearly remember the moment when I realized that I had made a profound discovery. I recall saying to myself, "So that's what music is! It is this feeling I have right now, not the number of notes or the complexity of the piece."

BRIDGING

The loving mother teaches her child to walk alone. She is far enough from him so that she cannot actually support him, but she holds out her arms to him. She imitates his movements, and if he totters she swiftly bends as if to seize him, that the child might believe that he is not walking alone ...her face beckons like a reward, an encouragement. Thus, the child walks alone with his eyes fixed on his mother's face not on the difficulties in his way. He supports himself by the arms that do not hold him and constantly strives toward the refuge in his mother's embrace, little suspecting that in the very same moment that he is emphasizing his need of her, he is proving that he can do without her, because he is walking alone.

—SØREN KIERKEGAARD

As the above quotation from the Danish philosopher illustrates, guides provide just enough support to lessen the apprentice's risk of venturing into new terrain, but not so much that the apprentice loses the experience of success from her own efforts. Bridging involves dividing responsibility for the pieces of a complex process, with the guide gradually giving the apprentice more pieces as she can handle them. Guides carefully remove their support in a way which allows the apprentice the ability to perform in a manner which was previously possible only with the guide's involvement.

Alan Sroufe provides another example of scaffolding using a table tennis metaphor to illustrate this progressive process:

At first one hits the ball directly to the child's paddle. Holding the paddle rigidly, the shots fly off in every direction, always being re-centered by the teacher. In time, the teacher requires the pupil to make minimal adjustments and gradually the pupil is moved towards a more equal role. Responsibility is increased at a pace that is not disheartening. What begins with the caregiver rather completely staging the interaction and responding to the infant, leads to a more mutual interaction, where each partner initiates and each responds in turn to the other.

In their highly influential article "Cognitive Apprenticeship," Allan Collins and his co-authors illustrate bridging, using the example of reciprocal teaching, an effective, well-researched model for teaching reading comprehension. In reciprocal teaching, guides scaffold by helping students learn to generate relevant questions as they take turns in the role of teacher:

Both the teacher and students read a paragraph silently. Whoever is playing the role of teacher formulates a question based on the paragraph, constructs a summary, and makes a prediction or clarification if any come to mind. Initially, the teacher models this process and then turns the role of teacher over to the students. When students first undertake the process, the teacher coaches them extensively on how to construct good questions and summaries, offering prompts and critiquing their efforts. In this way, the teacher provides scaffolding for the students, enabling them to take on whatever portion of the task they are able to. As students become more proficient, the teacher fades, assuming the role of monitor and providing occasional hints or feedback.

Bridging Poetry

During the third week in my new second grade gifted classes, the teacher asked each student to write a rhyming poem. While I am verbally capable, my handwriting, which has always been terrible, was completely illegible in the second grade. Still, I wrote a poem that actually rhymed. But I cringed as the teacher walked from student to student reading each poem silently. When she reached my desk, her response was quite gentle. She asked me to read my poem in a soft voice so that only she and I could hear. She listened with a smile on her face and when I was done, she told me that it was excellent. She further encouraged me by asking if I would share it with the class. And I still remember that it received a decent amount of applause. As I read aloud, she re-wrote the poem in her own very legible hand. Then she told me that she loved my poem so much she wanted to place it on the wall in the area reserved for the best poetry.

My teacher intuitively understood bridging. She recognized that if she required me to formulate a poem while simultaneously improving my handwriting, the activity would only end in failure and frustration. After I read my poem to the class, she said something to me that I recall to this day. "Remember Steven, good poetry comes from here (touching her head) and here (touching your heart). This (making a writing motion) is the least important part." From that moment I believed that I was a good writer. (Later I worked quite hard to improve my handwriting so that it was legible to others).

SPOTLIGHTING

The ultimate goal of engaging in any kind of learning activity is to create, elaborate, or reinforce specific synaptic connections in the learner's brain. This can only occur through creating memories that support the types of connections we wish to make.

As you might expect, dynamic intelligence relies on a more integrated form of memory than its static equivalent, which entails discrete associative and procedural memory systems. I refer to this form of more neurally integrated memory as personal memory although in the research literature it is also referred to as episodic memory and autobiographical memory. Personal memory is at the heart of the neural integration process, and relies on the collaboration of the Pre-frontal Cortex, Limbic System and Hippocampus for its formation and preservation.

As its name indicates, personal memory has to do with remembering events along with their personal meaning. It is an appraisal-based memory, where the personal meaning of an action is more important than the details of the actions themselves. Personal meanings can be about "me" or about "us". They entail learning from our experience and are employed to anticipate, prepare and plan for future events and tasks.

SPOTLIGHTING = Amplifying moments of personal experience to create productive personal memories.

We should not assume that because guides provide the right experiences and the apprentice achieves some form of success, that the lesson will be encoded in the desired manner. In other words, just because the guide herself forms a personal memory of a certain meaningful event or new experience within an activity, it doesn't ensure the apprentice will share the same memory. To guarantee that guide and apprentice perceive and capture like meaning from activities, guides increase the odds by spotlighting.

Spotlighting consists of three main elements: creating a temporal boundary around the critical challenging moments of an activity, finding ways to contrast critical actions within these boundaries so their meaning stands out from their peripheral counterparts and integrating those actions with a representation of their personal meaning.

Spotlighting does not require that the apprentice possesses a great deal of language. In fact, too much talking about the episode will dilute its emotional impact. Guides use brief punctuations that act as a trigger for the apprentice to re-experience successful challenging episodes.

Guides employ a subtle array of non-verbal actions to do this. These include altering voice tone and volume, slowing down to emphasize critical moments and spacing by moving closer or farther away. Guides may also spotlight by minimizing, or limiting, communication. The strategic use of silence or pausing mid-sentence can be quite effective. Finally, guides often amplify the climax of a spotlighted episode, so that it is differentiated from the instrumental end product of an activity.

HOW DOES THE DANCE START?

The Guided Participation Relationship is a dance requiring two active partners. Children are not born with the capabilities to function as apprentices. The initial task for all parental guides is to first help the child develop pre-requisite abilities, responsibilities and motivation to become a cognitive apprentice. This typically occurs during the first twelve-to-fifteen months of life.

In the next chapter, I will explore how parents along with their infants, develop the tools they will need to function as apprentices. Building an apprentice requires the active participation of both guide and apprentice. For example parents rely on infants to provide them with a constant stream of emotional feedback to help them adjust their responses and maintain a good balance of challenge and safety. We will also examine how critical cognitive, emotional and social discoveries provide the infant with the sense of personal agency needed to function as an active co-participant. By the end of their first year, infants use their guides as a critical reference point to increase the degree to which objects, persons and settings are understood as meaningful. Finally, we will examine how infants become highly motivated through the safe guidance of their parents to journey to the edge of their understanding and competence.

Reflection Questions:

1.   Have you any memories of guides like Mr. Thompson? If so, think about how he or she influenced your life. What would your life be like without their guidance?

2.   Have you served as a guide to an apprentice such as our second Englishman? It need not have been a life and death situation. In what ways was the process similar or different? Contrast that with your encounters with guides like Mr. Johnston, or your own experience of being the first type of guide.

3.   See if you can recall several critical personal memories that have shaped your decisions and your perceptions of yourself. What were those critical moments that have stuck in your memory? How are those memories different from memorizing facts and details?

4.   If you remove guided participation from the job of parenting, then what is left? Is there any other parent function that cannot be replaced by someone you hire?

Chapter Seven

Guided Participation: The Apprentice

The first two years of the parent-child relationship are a critical period for thousands of productive encounters between the child and caregivers, in which children are guided to participate in solving increasingly more complex problems.

—Alan Sroufe

The first and most important job of parental guides is to prepare their child to be a competent apprentice. Guiding a young child's mental development is a continuous process, regulatory task. Success can be defined as maintaining an optimal state of the child's availability for new learning. It requires ongoing evaluation, adjustment and re-adjustment. Parents must carefully monitor and evaluate the child's emotional status and degree of capability for a task or problem at any moment in time. New information and altered contextual factors are constantly entering the picture.

As I have emphasized, the problem of ASD is not one of the guide's insufficiencies. ASD emerges from a failure of the infant to sufficiently contribute to his own mental formation. The soon-to-be ASD child does not provide parental guides with sufficient active, reliable feedback so parents can achieve success in their primary mental development role.

In the following sections I will provide a brief glimpse into the process whereby a two-month-old, with only rudimentary perceptual apparatus, transforms, through the intuitive guidance of her parents, into a sophisticated mental being and highly competent cognitive apprentice.

QUALIFICATIONS FOR APPRENTICESHIP

The apprentice role I have been referring to should not be confused with a trade union training program, or the traditional guild models dating from the Middle Ages. Infant apprentices are engaged in learning to use their minds effectively in any and all settings and tasks, not in the mastery of any specific activity or job. From a very young age, apprentices function as active junior partners in their own growth. They strive to make sense of new situations. They learn to recognize and take increased responsibility for managing the important changes in their world. They seek out challenges and make their own new discoveries and elaborations.

No infant is born an apprentice and all of the pre-requisites for being one have to be learned. According to scientists like Michael Tomasello, by fifteen months of age, typically developing infants possess these prototypic skills.

What are these rudimentary abilities? Developmental Psychologists suggest three main areas of development that we should examine. The first has to do with the infant's innate drive for greater *complexity*, a strong motivation to gain greater depth of meaning in the world. Apprentices actively strive to develop more flexible and sophisticated templates for operating in their world. This means broadening and deepening what is already known, as well as expanding their understanding into new settings and domains. By the end of their first year, infants are seen as actively seeking out greater complexity from their more experienced partners.

The second criterion, *collaboration*, requires the apprentice to function as a junior co-participant in problem solving, typically in pursuit of greater complexity. This occurs many months before the acquisition of language, through ongoing non-verbal, emotion-sharing dialogues. The apprentice learns to be a responsible co-regulator during interactions with guides, evaluating and adjusting actions to maintain a state of social and emotional coordination with partners.

The final attribute, *competence*, is the ability to manage, with the support of guides, the tension and higher levels of arousal that are inevitable consequences of striving for complexity. As discussed previously, states of uncertainty are inevitably experienced when facing challenging problems and new ways of thinking and perceiving the world. As Dr. Alan Sroufe explains, "A major adaptive advantage of humans is opportunism—capitalizing on new discoveries and taking advantages of novel occurrences...For survival and adaptation, it is of fundamental importance that the human organism have special capacities for dealing with situations of uncertain consequence."

The following chart summarizes these three attributes:

Complexity	Strong desire to initiate joint attention to obtain the guide's appraisal (subjective meaning). Functioning to expand (add, deepen, transform) personal meanings. Referencing the guide's emotional reactions towards stimuli to determine safety and value. Learning to integrate contextual factors like intentionality, qualitative "attitudes" (e.g. gentleness, carefulness) and setting, familiarity into decision-making
Collaboration	Desire to interact to meet cooperative goals (e.g. role reversal, taking intentionally helpful actions). Ongoing adjustment to maintain co-ordinated role actions. Communicating and acting to maintain and increase mutual engagement.
Competence	Generalized "studying" approach to manage uncertainty in the presence of trusted guides. Persisting in the face of initial frustration. Using re-grouping, self-regulatory and social referencing strategies for emotional management. Developing trust in one's guide and oneself. Desire to accept/pursue new challenges.

The Growth of an Apprentice

The next section briefly traces the route to apprenticeship during the first two years of life through the growth of a typically developing baby, Emma. We only touch lightly on this complex developmental journey, which according to developmental scientists takes place throughout the infant's entire waking life. However, I do feel it is important to review this process. At some point in these early months, each ASD child will hit a developmental wall from which he or she will not recover.

Ten to Sixteen Weeks: Nervous System Tuning

Emma's route to becoming an apprentice begins at a quite early but typical starting point scientists call the phase of primary intersubjectivity. This is viewed as the beginning of an organized emotional relationship between parents and infant. Starting in the third month we can see two things happening with Emma. The first is that her and her parents nervous systems are being tuned to one another. This information is transmitted by their touch, voices and faces. It is mediated by the sympathetic nervous system. The very movement of parent's face and voice seems wired into Emma's neurochemical comfort and safety system. This fuels a powerful unconscious drive to maintain the facial and vocal package, which we call emotional engagement.

Emma lies flat with her father Pete reclining slightly above her. They gaze into one another's faces. He is singing the Irish lullaby, "Tura Lura Lura," and she is vocalizing along with him. Her vocals, while not as smooth as his, are timed so that she appears to be singing along with Pete in a coordinated manner. She gazes directly at him the entire time he sings and is raptly attentive.

Emma's brain is creating a connection between her father's facial movement and vocalization and something meaningful to her. She is not yet aware of the meaning of any of his emotional expressions. It is the visual pattern of his facial activity integrated with his vocal tone and regularity that she recognizes as relating directly to her own emotional state. If Pete were to suddenly stop using his face expressively and take on a neutral expression, what psychologists refer to as the *still face phenomena*, Emma would soon become distressed.

Dr. Daniel Stern has studied similar attunement episodes in his research of vocal interchanges between three-month-olds and their mothers. He found that, "… the more common vocalizing pattern during play was not that mother and infant were taking turns, but were vocalizing in unison. They seemed to be 'moved' to make sound together." These types of attunement experiences create a neural phenomenon that Daniel Siegel refers to as resonance. At such times the sympathetic nervous system creates a neurochemistry of parent and child that is quite similar. This appears to be the first real linking between them.

Ten to Sixteen Weeks: Different-but-Same

A second result of attunement is Emma's ability to use her parents' informational packages to begin to understand the recurring patterns in the world around her. From the age of two months, infants appear to seek out perceptual continuities to make sense of their world. They are not yet interested in exact sequential repetitions. Rather at a more central level their brain appears ready to process recurring patterns of movement, timing and intensity. By three months they can understand a pattern learned in one modality even when it is transferred to another, for example changes in spatial distance as a parent looms closer and recedes farther are perceived as directly related to changes in their vocal intensity.

Pete has Emma positioned in a vertical position between his legs while he reclines on the bed. She is now able to hold her neck up. She gazes straight at his face, again raptly attentive, but not smiling or laughing. He is careful to first orient her and make sure he has her attention by saying, "Hi baby. Hi baby." He deeply breathes in, releasing a clearly audible sigh and then slowly covers his face with his hands to play peek-a-boo. Emma continues to gaze raptly at Pete. She vocalizes quietly when he reveals his face but shows no emotional reaction. Pete places his hands to the sides of his eyes to frame his actions more clearly. He is not aware, but Emma looks away when he covers his eyes and shifts her gaze to be right with him when he opens his hands and reveals his face saying, "Boo!" Pete says, "Boo!" again and then, "You couldn't care less." Despite Pete's misunderstanding, Emma is hard at work trying to perceive the basic pattern and rhythm her father is revealing to her.

Different-But-Same

The variation is critical to teach the child the central *unchanging* elements that lie underneath.

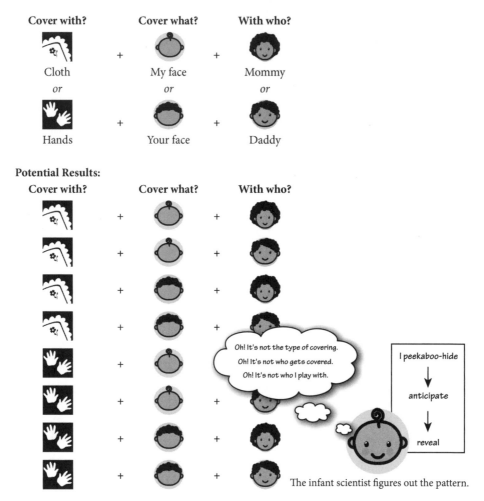

The infant scientist figures out the pattern.

The results of Emma's careful observations will soon be apparent. She is learning that the world is composed of a duality of continuity and variation. Without either realizing it, each time they play peek-a-boo, Pete alters a small feature of their game. He may delay a second, use a different tone of voice, say, "Boo!" or "peek-a-boo," cover her eyes with his hand or with a cloth. These small variations provide Emma with the information she requires to differentiate the central features from the peripheral features that are not really attached to peek-a-boo. Already she has begun to answer the question, "How do I understand the continuities in a world where things are never really the same from one time to the next?"

16 to 24 Weeks: Mutual Addiction

Our next visit to Emma and Pete occurs a couple of weeks later. Emma is now eighteen weeks of age. She is lying on her back in her crib. Pete reaches over and covers her eyes with his hands. He no longer needs to make sure he has her attention first. He perceives Emma as more resilient and is much more confident that things will work out.

Pete quickly raises his hand from Emma's face, saying, "Aah" and delivering a perfectly timed package of tactile, facial and vocal information. He covers her eyes again. She now vocalizes while her eyes are covered. He again lifts his hands and Emma greets him with a full gaze, smile and excited vocalization. This provides him with a powerful facial-vocal information package, which excites him and entices him to continue. He again quickly covers and reveals himself and this time Emma is vocalizing through most of the very rapid process. Her smile grows and this change in her face encourages her father to continue.

The most interesting parts of the story to me are the powerful neuro-chemical reactions, those incomparably rewarding opiates called endorphins, that accompany these moments between them. The key to hormonal release is not the facial expressions but the timing, the synchronization of their reactions. What captures both Emma and Pete is the impact they have on one another, the recognition that something meaningful has been revealed through this simple game. This growing synchronization and emotional coordination is pivotal to the deepening of their relationship.

16 to 24 Weeks: Non-alignments

Inevitably infant-parent interactions, like any human encounters, will break down. In this case, Pete holds his hands over Emma's face a bit too long. Emma stops vocalizing. Even though Pete's hand still covers Emma's face, she turns her head and squirms to the side as if to avoid his gaze. It takes a couple of seconds for him to recognize this cue of Emma's discomfort. When Pete lifts his hand and Emma looks up, she doesn't laugh. This is a good example of the type of non-alignment that happens all the time between typically developing infants and parents.

Psychologist Ed Tronick studied similar periods of parent-child engagement and found that typically developing infants and parents might be non-aligned up to 70% of the time. Dr. Tronick concludes that we have to alter our idealized view of infants and parents in perfect harmony:

> …*a more accurate characterization of the normal interaction, and a better basis for assessment, is that it frequently moves from affectively positive, mutually coordinated states to affectively negative, 'miscoordinated' states and back again on a frequent basis.*

Scientists believe that synchronization breakdowns are not only inevitable, but essential for infant development. Through such breakdowns, infants are introduced early on into a world where they cannot expect things to work out as desired without taking some responsibility. There are three major conclusions we hope infants draw from these imperfect encounters. The first is not to take states of emotional coordination for granted. States of connection are typically alternated with states of disconnection. Only through experiencing these brief emotional disconnections can the infant experience the importance of the connected state. Only when contrasted with the potential for disconnection do connected states become more highly valued by both infant and parent.

Experiencing disconnection is the only way that infants can learn to value moments of connection.

The second lesson is one that will take a bit more time to learn. That is to live in a dynamic world inevitably means going off-course and thus having to make temporary regulatory adjustments. Several months from now Emma will learn that she can be more active in reducing the degree of breakdowns. But even now, her gaze and postural shifting indicate she is learning to maintain her engagement by temporarily avoiding, rather than completely withdrawing. Interestingly, gaze aversion is one of the first ways that infants learn to regulate their state of arousal.[18]

Third, we hope that Emma is learning, with her guide's help, to trust herself to emotionally manage such misaligned states and continue without withdrawing. This is the onset of the process we refer to as emotional trust and resilience.

16 to 24 Weeks: Same-and-Different

Now we skip forward a few weeks. The peek-a-boo game has continued to evolve and Emma is now a peek-a-boo veteran. She fully understands the hide-reveal pattern. At twenty weeks of age, Emma already knows the critical dynamic concept of *different-but-same* that allows her brain to perceive continuities amidst ongoing variations. From a number of games like peek-a-boo she has learned that whether her father covers her eyes with a cloth or his hands, whether he covers her face or his own, whether he says "Boo!", "peek-a-boo", or nothing at all, the basic pattern does not change. Her brain can already discriminate between the peripheral and central aspects of the simple frameworks her parents create. She can distinguish beyond superficial differences. By five months the meaning of what she is seeing, hearing and doing has taken over as her primary interest.

If we judge from Pete's actions, and clearly Emma is doing a good job training him to meet her needs, what is most interesting to her now is not the pattern of hiding and revealing, but the almost frantic nature of the variations Pete introduces. Pete has a brown spotted cloth in his hand. Emma is in an infant chair, partially vertical. From the way she squirms and moves her hands and arms you can tell she yearns to be an active participant in the game, but does not quite yet have the motor control. Perhaps in a week or two she will. She gazes directly at her father for a moment and then shifts to see what her mother, who is off to the side, is doing. Her attention is no longer at the mercy of environmental stimuli. She deliberately directs and fluidly shifts her own gaze, to see what her mother is doing. She is learning to be more in control of obtaining meaning from her world.

---

18   It is ironic that ASD children are often deprived the opportunity to temporarily avoid an overwhelming situation by being forced to make eye contact. In such cases their only options are to comply or completely withdraw.

Pete doesn't attempt to elicit Emma's attention back to him. In fact, he seems to have deliberately waited until she shifted her gaze away to introduce greater surprise. He tosses the cloth onto her face without any warning. Emma uses her neck to slide the cloth off her face and then looks directly at Pete with a small smile. He gives her almost no recovery time while saying, "Where did Emma go?" and tosses the cloth back onto her face. Then he waits about two seconds and quickly removes it. He quickly replaces it again without warning. She continues to smile at him and shows no discomfort at all with his rapid unpredictably timed variations.

If you were to very carefully observe dad placing the cloth on Emma's face, you might notice that every time he places the cloth on her, he varies how long he leaves it on. Without being conscious of what he is doing, he is teaching Emma to be aware of the impact of dynamic variations. I watch four consecutive trials of peek-a-boo as he covers Emma's eyes; first for one second, then three seconds, then four and then five. It almost seems intentional. But in actuality, this wonderful scaffolding sequence is propelled along by the relationship evolving between them. He slowly prolongs his revealing as he receives feedback of her increased excitement. After this initial gradual intensity crescendo he seems to play with the variability of intensity, sometimes revealing quickly but at other times letting the anticipation build.

It is fascinating to note that the five second interval, the exact same period of delay in lifting the cloth that appeared to create her discomfort at eighteen weeks of age, has now become the highlight of Emma's excitement. Her ability to anticipate and manage arousal has grown significantly in just a few weeks. Her expectations are based on past experience and determine her emotional reactions.

Emma learns that varying the interval increases her and her partner's anticipatory excitement.

---

16 to 24 Weeks: Co-regulation

I stand adjacent and perpendicular to twenty-two weeks old Emma who is upright in a pouch in front of Pete. Pete is writing on a whiteboard with a marker and I notice that Emma is grasping her hands towards the marker. I take another marker and hand it to her. She takes it from me and drops it on the ground in what I assume is not an intentional act. She cannot yet visually track the marker as it journeys to the ground. I pick it up and as I approach her at eye level I bring the marker closer to her in a very slow, deliberate manner. She takes it from me, gazes at the marker, drops it again and then shifts her gaze to meet mine. I pick it up slowly and hand it to her again. We repeat this a third and fourth time. At some moment in this process we gaze at one another a bit differently and both realize we are involved in a joint process.

Now, instead of holding out the marker, I put it in my mouth and lean over to her. Emma takes it from my mouth. I vary the angle and elevation in which I hold the marker out to her and she takes it each time. She is visibly tracking both the marker and me as I approach her and she looks expectantly at me each time after she drops it to the floor. We engage in this process for about five minutes. I begin sharing this experience with Pete, who has been busy writing on the white board As I begin to speak to him, Emma breaks out in her first big smile of the entire episode. It is a smile that is clearly directed at me. My guess is that she remembers we engaged in this process together and were connected in a new way that is related to her growing sense of competence in the world.

Emma and I participated in what Alan Fogel refers to as a co-regulated social encounter, adjusting our actions in response to each other's prior actions. According to Fogel, this is the prototype for all future relationships. When I switched from holding the marker with my hand and held it in my mouth, Emma stopped momentarily, and adjusted her angle of reach. Neither of us had an agenda to make something happen.

While there was no specific ritual like peek-a-boo, we stayed within a framework that consisted of the following: the two of us, a marker, Emma taking and my offering and her dropping and my retrieving. We maintained these roles though Emma was certainly not aware of hers. There was continual variation, but no common goal. Her accidents, due to a five-month-old's poor motor ability, created our initial variations. After that, I deliberately varied the presentation of the marker.

Emma and I had moments of non-synchronization. However, she was never upset by them. Our engagement easily survived the times she dropped the marker and I didn't catch it and times when I held it out and Emma didn't immediately reach for it. Throughout, we managed to repair and continue. The process unfolded very slowly. Emma could not do much yet and what she could do had to be done at a very deliberate pace.

Co-regulation is often achieved with either one or both members unaware that it is happening.

---

16 to 24 Weeks: Us Memories

During this brief interval, Emma and I created an authentic type of personal memory. We formed a relationship. The next time we met, several weeks later, the bond was still there. Process moments like the one described above are very powerful learning experiences. They do not require more than one trial to be encoded in the brain and become more neurally integrated as they contain elements of our individual actions and our actions together. Emma learned to have an "us" moment with someone who is not mommy and daddy and we will continue to pick up our relationship at our future encounters.

24 to 36 Weeks: Active Roles

Now we jump ahead eight weeks, a veritable lifetime for an infant. We find Emma at thirty weeks of age, sitting upright, facing Pete who reclines on a sofa. He holds her arms to steady her. Once again Emma fluidly shifts her gaze between mother and father, choosing to do so without any cues or prompts. Again her father has no need to gain her attention before assuming his role. He places a much larger green cloth over her head and waits. This simple variation indicates that their roles have significantly evolved. Emma is now an active participant in their game and understands that their roles in joint activities must be synchronized if they are to be successful.

Pete's job has now become the simpler of the two. He only has to place the cloth on top of Emma's head while she assumes the more interesting and challenging role, that of the revealer.

Emma does not immediately pull the cloth off her face. She grasps it with one hand and pauses. Pete says, "Where's Emma, where's Emma?" in a softer voice. Emma waits. He says, "I don't see Emma," apparently a timing cue for her, since she is not yet processing the actual words, because at that moment Emma deliberately removes the cloth, looks straight at Pete and smiles. Both of their mouths are open in the exact same excited manner. Pete places the cloth back on her head and this time Emma reveals quickly and gazes at him. If you were to observe Pete's peek-a-boo timing seven weeks earlier and compare it to Emma's timing now you would be amazed. You might be even more amazed to learn that he was unaware of his timing and certainly had no intention of teaching it to Emma.

Emma has not learned about anticipation and timing in a rote fashion. She is not replicating what her father did. She has internalized the process and can use it in a flexible fashion. She has learned that the variation of timing is interesting and has apparently mastered it on her own. At seven months Emma has become a competent co-regulator. It is now Emma who is adding the ongoing variations that make the continuity of their activity worthwhile. At the same time, Emma carefully remains within her role so as not to create chaos. Amazingly, this communication is accomplished between them without a word.

24 to 36 Weeks: Intrinsic Motivation

Emma's biggest smile is reserved for moments when she takes the action of revealing herself. Her smile begins before she even notices the reactions on her parents' faces. It is not based on her their reactions, and does not result from anything they say or do. Pete's vocalizations such as "peek-a-boo" do not add any meaning, or increase her excitement, though her father still adds it at the end. His voice is not a major feature, nor is any statement of praise or reinforcement. The payoff for Emma has become intrinsic to her own actions. It revolves around her awareness of her growing capability as a collaborator. Peek-a-boo has become one of an increasing number of frameworks that provide Emma opportunities to experience her increasing competence as an active partner.

Can you see from the above illustration why providing external rewards might interfere with this critical learning process?

---

24 to 36 Weeks: Similar-but-Different

This new peek-a-boo framework continues for a while, until Maisie suggests that they take turns. Without warning, Pete modifies the framework, placing the cloth on top of his face and waits. This is the first time Pete has varied their activity in this manner. Incredibly, without instruction, Emma knows that even though the cloth is now on her father, she is still in the role of revealer. However, she also somehow realizes that this is not just another variation, or another example of different-but-same but that something fundamental has changed. I use the term *similar-but-different* to describe the infant's ability to discern when they are being presented with a cognitive challenge, where something central has changed, even though most things remain the same on the surface.

24 to 36 Weeks: Mutual Trust

Emma's parents create and Emma joins this novel, challenging situation without hesitation. This is because they have a history of mutual trust in the face of challenge and uncertainty. According to Dr. Sroufe, this is the product of many hours of parent-infant interaction in which children and parents have both learned that, "… in the presence of the caregiver, high tension need not lead to aversive experiences or behavioral disorganization, but rather can give rise to quite positive outcomes."

Dr. Sroufe explains further that in this mutual training process, parents and infants learn to maintain their organization in the face of increasingly higher levels of tension: "As caregiver and infant interact, tension is escalated and de-escalated to the edge of over-stimulation and back again. Episode by episode, day by day, the infant's capacity to modulate (and tolerate) tension is developed and a reservoir of positive feelings is created." In our example, Pete waits patiently with the cloth over his face while Emma briefly studies the situation. She is not quite sure of what to do, but she does not appear to be distressed or anxious in her current state of uncertainty.

Trust develops from hundreds of experiences of managing uncertainty productively.

---

24 to 36 Weeks: Studying

Let us observe Emma during the moment when she recognizes the challenge. Her gaze is fixed on the cloth. She does not move a muscle. She looks both alert and relaxed at the same time. We are observing Emma's newfound ability to *study* when faced with feelings of uncertainty.

The phenomenon of *studying* is characterized by distinct physiological, neurological and behavioral patterns. sensory receptors are oriented, muscles are quieted, heart rate decelerates, and blood flows to the brain. The body is providing a heightened capacity for processing environmental information without triggering a fight-flight, anxious response. On the level of brain functioning, we see an initial spurt of neural integration involving activation of areas of the Pre-frontal Cortex, the executive part of the brain and the Limbic System, the emotion-processing center.

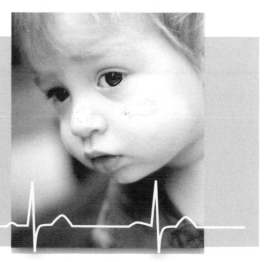

1. **Infant notices new object.**

2. **Doesn't approach.** The infant may use temporary avoidance, but does not withdraw.

3. **Studying Look:** Lowered heartrate and breathing, focus on the precipitating problem, activation of the Pre-frontal cortical (Limbic) neural pathways.

Pete decides to scaffold a bit more and provides a demonstration for Emma. With one hand he gently slides the cloth from his face. She attends intently, somehow realizing without any clear communication from her father, that this demonstration is intended for her benefit. She moves her arm in coordination with his and smiles broadly when he completes his action.

When Pete finishes his demonstration he says, "Heyyyyyy," then replaces the cloth on his head and waits. Intuitively he knows to do as little as possible, so as not to solve the problem for his daughter.

Emma, with her posture forward, alerts her body and maintains her gaze on the cloth. Now she grasps the cloth from the bottom with her two hands and looks at the cloth for a second. Suddenly she smiles, by far her brightest smile so far. At first she seems to be smiling to herself but she quickly shifts her gaze to her mother. Her smile communicates that she has solved the problem and wishes her mother to join her celebration. Emma, by figuring out what she will do, has obtained the powerful emotional payoff of her insight, even before she takes any specific action. Her gaze returns to her father and she gingerly pulls the cloth off his face, shifting her smile between parents.

Dad says, "You found me. Let's try that one more time." He covers his face again. This time Emma waits a short second and more decisively removes the cloth with a more mature expression on her face. Pete and Emma have created a powerful, shared personal memory involving challenge, uncertainty and as a climax, her discovery.

12 Months: Joint Attention

At twelve months, Emma is sitting upright on the floor across from Pete and looking at several interesting puzzle pieces. She picks up one of particular interest to her. She smiles broadly, showing that she is making her own preliminary appraisal of "this is interesting" and then fluidly shows the puzzle piece to her father. Her attention focuses on father's face as he studies the piece briefly and then smiling excitedly says, "Oh, the pointy one!" Emma puts the piece down and explores the other pieces. She picks up another that captures her interest resulting in a similar gaze shift-showing communication, followed by his response, "Oh, the big red one."

Emma is involved in a new type of communication, a qualitative milestone for the one-year-old. She is engaging in what psychologists call joint attention, an essential part of the child's drive to obtain a broader, deeper understanding of the world around her. By the close of the first year, infant-parent communication begins to revolve around a triangulating relationship—two persons and an external stimulus, such as a person, object or animal.

What is new and important is not the behavior of showing or pointing, followed by gazing at her partner's face. Those are easily acquired behaviors which Emma has already learned to do. More interesting is the reason for her actions, her desire to broaden her own subjective impressions by learning those of her partners. She is borrowing the perspective of another person's mind to enhance her own ability to obtain meaning.

1. *That's interesting to me.*

2. *What is the meaning from my guide?*
(Attention shifts from object to guide.)

3. *Point and look to see that my guide is noticing what I notice.*

4. *What is my guide's reaction?*
(Borrow guide's appraisal)

Joint Attention

This is a critical example of the type of active appropriation that characterizes the role of the apprentice in the learning process. Initiating joint attention opens the door to the understanding of the minds of others and the development of a conscious self. Thus, the young child experiences the distinction between her own unique perceptions and those of her partners.

At twelve months of age, about 60% of Emma's communication with her parents involves pointing, showing and the deliberate use of gaze and vocalization for experience sharing. The other 40% is similar but more superficial and involved with instrumental functions, for example pointing to get things she wants. As she gets older the ratio will tilt significantly more towards the experience sharing and less toward the instrumental side of the equation.

12 Months: Continuous-Process Co-Regulation

At twelve months Emma possesses what psychologists refer to as *agency*. She consciously perceives herself as an important agent in maintaining her interactions through her own regulatory actions. Emma has become a co-participant in a number of co-regulated games that require a new type of ability. In these new frameworks, both partners must maintain the coordination by making continuous adjustments. One of her favorite versions of these new games is "pull-pull." Emma and her mother each take the ends of a piece of thick string and pull it smoothly back-and-forth between them, trying not to pull so hard as to pull the string from the other's grasp. Like all of their other games, this one evolved without planning or teaching. As they pull back-and-forth, Emma jerks the string a bit too hard causing her mother to lose her grasp of it. Maisie takes no action. Without hesitation, Emma extends her hand so that her mother can take her end of the string. When they resume the game, it is clear that Emma has modulated her force and is taking care so that the episode will not be repeated. Like most early collaborative activities, pull-pull employs feedback from both tactile and visual senses. Continuous-process regulation typically begins at this tactile level, where the child can most easily feel the rhythm of co-regulation.

15 Months

As infants get older, their learning is increasingly influenced by their appraisal of an event. By fifteen months, Emma is learning even more from her joint communication experiences. Now she engages in flexible observational learning. She can deconstruct what she observes and use part of the sequence or even adapt it when needed (e.g. slowing down or speeding up). This is different from the type of automatic imitation seen in newborns and younger infants.

By the middle of the second year, infants become especially interested in the intentions of those they are observing and distinguish what is intended to be accomplished from the actual behavior. In an intriguing experiment, scientists had fifteen-month-olds watch an adult model move objects from one side of a room to the other in a deliberate manner. After an initial success, the model fell down on the second try indicating that she had hurt her leg and could not continue. The scientists then indicated that the toddlers should "go do it." Interestingly, the toddlers imitated only the successful actions, aware that the model never intended to fall.

Emma's mother is looking into a box of objects adjacent to her, but out of Emma's visual field. These are items that are unfamiliar to Emma. First, her mother lifts a rubber beetle out of the box. She gazes at it for a second, delivers a powerful facial expression and vocalization of disgust and then places the object on the floor next to her. She takes a stick, hits the beetle and tells it to, "Go away!" She reaches in the box a second time and lifts out an alien sort of doll. This time her gaze is accompanied by a very positive facial expression and vocalization. She gently strokes the doll's head and also puts it down by her side.

Several minutes later, Emma's mother removes the box but leaves the beetle, the stick and the alien doll near enough so that Emma can either engage with them or ignore them. Emma moves toward the beetle, takes the stick and whacks it three times. Then she uses the stick to turn the beetle over. While doing this, her face and voice suggest disgust, in a manner similar, but not identical to that of her mother. Next she moves to the alien doll. Her face and voice soften and she coos to the doll. She picks up the very strange looking doll, holds it in her arms and strokes it.

According to Dr. Peter Hobson, this vignette illustrates that Emma has made another major mental leap. He refers to this as *identification*. Emma can learn by observing the "softer" attitudes and emotional reactions of her mother. As Dr. Hobson states, "…infants are learning through other people and are responding to the-world-according-to-someone-else. The child starts out by reacting to the world in her own terms. She finds a toy alluring, for example. She then perceives her mother relating to that toy with disgust or fear. According to the mother's reaction, the toy is not so alluring. Its meaning has changed because of what it means to someone else."

Along with her increasingly sophisticated communication for experience sharing, Emma is also actively trying to form her own appraisals of her world. However, not all of her studies lead to engagement. A strange man and small dog approach her on the sidewalk in front of her house where she is toddling several feet from her mother. The stranger and friendly looking dog stop a few feet away to see how she will respond. Emma studies the man but particularly his dog for about a minute, sways back and forth and makes her decision. She scoots backwards, reaching for mother to pick her up. There she continues to study the dog from a safer distance.

24 Months

Emma is now a two-year-old, with a newly developed sense of self. She picks up a whoopee cushion out of a box full of interesting objects, both familiar and unfamiliar. She seems most interested in the novel, unfamiliar ones. "What's this? What's this?" she excitedly says, as she holds out the object for Ana, a family friend, to see. She gazes toward Ana who says "Yuck!" along with an expression of disgust. Emma responds "Aah!" and lifts her head in unison with Ana. Ana says "Yuck!" again and Emma says, "Go way" and throws the object. It rolls behind her. Ana gestures as if to push it away. But now, in a big change from when she was fifteen-months-old, Emma acknowledges her more experienced partner's appraisals, but does not automatically accept them. She wants to form her own opinions as well.

INTERNAL CONFLICT

After acknowledging Ana's appraisal, Emma crawls over to the whoopee cushion. She stops and looks down at it without moving, studying it for about two seconds. Her uncertainty is of a new, more complex form than it was at seven months. It emanates from the internal conflict she feels between wanting to please one of her favorite adults by accepting their appraisal, and wanting to further explore the object and form her own opinion.

FLEXIBLE STRATEGIES

Emma decides upon a proximity strategy. She picks up the object, grasps it and crawls away from Ana. She moves to the corner of the room and examines it again, believing perhaps, that she can avoid the feelings of conflict by putting enough distance between herself and Ana. Ana defeats this strategy by again grimacing and shouting, "Yuck!" to which Emma says, "Go way!" Through this action, Emma acknowledges Ana's feelings and will make the *bad* object go away. This time Emma throws the object back towards the original box and proceeds to crawl back to Ana. Interestingly, she manages to get the object close enough so that she can examine it again later.

SOCIAL REFERENCING AND COMMUNICATION RESPONSIBILITY

Emma's mother is hiding in a playroom behind one of three piles of beanbag chairs. Emma has momentarily left the playroom with Ana while her mother hides. Now Emma and Ana return. Ana looks excitedly at one of the piles and says, "There she is." Without hesitation, Emma follows Ana's gaze and moves towards the pile. There is nothing exceptional about this. Over a year ago Emma mastered this early form of social referencing and was able to use her partner's gaze as a reference point when she was uncertain.

What happens next is the interesting part. As Emma moves towards the beanbag pile her mother is hiding behind, she briefly pauses. Emma gazes back towards Ana, simultaneously pointing towards the pile where she believes mother is hiding. She is communicating for confirmation. Once she has received a nod from Ana, she pushes past the beanbags and reaches for her mother. Following this success, she runs to a different pile of beanbags to hide herself saying, "My turn."

The type of referencing, to make sure she has perceived correctly, has become automatic for Emma. It is an indication that she has become a poised, responsible communicator. She recognizes that she cannot assume she comprehends her partner's meaning on the first take and also that she must assume responsibility to make sure she clarifies what was intended.

IMPROVISATIONAL COLLABORATION

Mother and Emma are playing a game they invented with beanbag chairs. Emma lies on a tan beanbag that her mother calls bread. Then she places a red beanbag (a tomato) followed by a green beanbag (lettuce) on Emma, who watches carefully. Her mother says, "Here's a yellow like a banana," and Emma says, "Nana?" as she actively tracks the beanbag making its way toward her. Her mother suddenly changes the framework and says, "I want a turn. My turn!" With no further cues, Emma immediately gets off the beanbag and sets to work. She cannot yet lift a beanbag chair but she drags a green one over to where mother is lying. Her mother says, "Oh it's so heavy!" but allows Emma to drag it over and only helps hoist it on top of her when Emma has done all she can independently. Emma says, "It's lettuce!" and looks proudly at her handiwork. Then she rushes off to get the next beanbag chair.

She pulls a red beanbag over and quietly says, "Heavy!" Her mother echoes, "Heavy!" and Emma continues towards her. She loses her grip and takes a step forward, but recovers and continues to drag the beanbag saying, "Tomato." She cannot place the red one on top of the lettuce and her mother says, "Here, I'll help." Without further cues or instruction, Emma takes a step back and adjusts her grip at the other end of the beanbag to make room for her mother's help. They have become a team, each exerting force to get the beanbag in place. As soon as it is, Emma is off again for the next one.

PRETENSE

A couple of minutes pass. The game has changed and the role of the food has turned into pretending to be asleep. Emma is supposed to be the sleeper. Her mother says, "Close your eyes." She sees Emma's eyes peeking open and says, "Your eyes aren't closed." They both laugh and Emma begins to lift herself up.

PERSONAL CHALLENGES

Without waiting for her to get up completely, her mother suddenly says, "Let's get the pink one." This is enough communication for Emma to know that the framework has changed once again and that now they are going to be functioning as a collaborative team, building a mountain together out of the beanbag chairs, placing the pink beanbag on top of the green one upon which Emma has pretended to sleep.

Emma and her mother face each other for a split second as Emma fully stands. Then Emma's gaze shifts to the pink beanbag chair. She rushes over while saying, "OK." She knows to grasp the end of the beanbag chair that is on her side, assuming that mother will take the other end closest to her, and waits for her mother to be ready. With exaggerated groans, they begin dragging the beanbag over.

While moving toward the intended pile, Emma's gaze suddenly changes and she shifts her attention to the green beanbag they are headed towards. For a split second Emma seems entranced. Clearly this is a more sophisticated, rapidly occurring form of studying than Emma displayed at seven months, when Pete placed the cloth on his own face. It is not clear immediately why she is studying the green beanbag although the reason is quickly revealed. They are close enough for the pink beanbag to go on top of the green one. With split second timing, Emma lets go of the pink beanbag, runs to the green beanbag and falls on it in time to be covered by the pink one. (If I watch it in slow motion I am still amazed by the timing).

It took me months of analyzing this to comprehend that Emma had realized that she was facing a challenge and took responsibility for managing it. Emma had integrated their carrying collaboration with the sandwich game. Maisie did not request that her daughter fill in for the missing meat. Emma appraised the challenge all by herself and dealt with it successfully .

Emma's decision to increase complexity is really not surprising. By twenty-four months it is the challenging tasks that are most motivating for typically developing toddlers like Emma. She willingly approaches these because she has a bank of personal memories of successfully managing uncertainty. At this age, Emma's most reliable smiles come from working on difficult problems. In fact, the more difficult the problem, the more likely she is to smile.

The next chapter signals a return to focusing on Autism Spectrum Disorders. Specifically, I will try to address a very important question. What happens to children with ASD on the road to becoming mindful apprentices? Do they develop any of the necessary qualifications? What are the factors that get in the way? What are the implications for failing to become an apprentice?

Try to spend time with typically developing infants at the different age ranges described in the chapter. How are your observations similar, or different to the descriptions of Emma? How would you explain the differences?

Chapter Eight

The Breaking Point

Parents of a typically developing four-month-old assume that he is capable of supplying sufficient meaningful feedback. This communication is typically not intentional but even so, it allows parents sufficient information to make good adjustments. In my view, ASD represents a breakdown of this early process, at some point in the first fifteen months of age, due to the child's inability to provide guides with sufficient, meaningful feedback. Autism researchers have drawn several conclusions supporting this hypothesis.

Autism is not diagnosed by the presence of any specific behavioral problems. What is distinctive is not the *commission* of specific things that the child does, but rather the *omission*, what the child does not do, or is unaware of. ASD is most reliably diagnosed by the failure of the child to function in a specific social-communicative-affective domain.

Scientists believe that inborn deficits lead to the infant's failure to develop essential social-emotional readiness. This appears to be the direct result of many potential neural and physical vulnerabilities that, while present at birth, may not be expressed until sometime within the first two years of life. Autism researchers also believe that there is no single etiology or cause for ASD. Even if two infants display similar deficits and these occur at the same specific point in time, it doesn't mean that they were caused by the same originating problem. Thus, different etiologic factors can contribute to the same kind of breakdown.

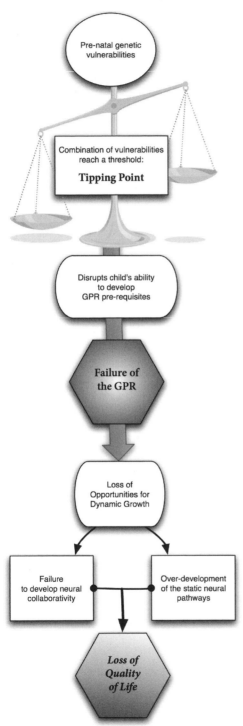

Many diseases have multiple etiologic origins resulting in common pathways of expression. For example, liver cancer can be caused by a number of different genetic and environmental factors. In fact there may be hundreds of etiologic combinations resulting in a single form of the disorder.

ASD is what we can term a threshold disorder. This refers to the fact that one can share many etiologic characteristics with individuals who go on to have ASD, but if those factors in combination are not severe enough, if they do not reach a threshold level, then the person may never suffer from a full-blown Autism Spectrum Disorder (though they may display some ASD characteristics). Another feature of a threshold disorder, is that one can have 99.9% of the factors that lead to the disorder and continue to develop normally, until an additional event occurs which tips the scale and results in the breakdown of functioning. To use the analogy of a different threshold disorder, why is it that on one day cancer cells that have been dormant for years begin to multiply, while the prior day they did not?

The developmental failure leading to ASD is not due to any environmental event. Nor is it the result of any action or deficit in parents. The competence of parents, no matter how great, cannot compensate for the vulnerabilities with which these children are born. In my experience, the vast majority of family members with an ASD child are among the most capable parents, most supportive grandparents and most caring siblings in the world. Yet, when we first meet them, their expertise is insufficient when it comes to guiding their ASD child.

FIRST BIRTHDAYS

Scientists believe that most infants who are eventually diagnosed with ASD demonstrate significantly impaired functioning by their first birthdays. In 1994 Judith Osterling and Geraldine Dawson, who had been studying the early identification variable for a number of years at the University of Washington, compared first birthday party videos of children who later went on to be diagnosed with ASD, with a matched group of infants who did not receive the diagnosis. By using an observational rating formula related to eye contact, showing, pointing and orienting to name, raters were able to identify ninety-one per cent of the cases correctly.

If you've ever experienced a child's first birthday, you know that this is far from the optimal setting to observe developing apprentices. There is typically an overwhelming amount of noise and over-stimulation. Mothers and fathers run around trying to manage the chaos and rarely have time for meaningful interactions with the child. Unfortunately, these are the types of events that parents typically videotape. They rarely video quiet moments of play and interaction which characterize the majority of their time together. Therefore, the ability to predict ASD from this limited data is amazing. I believe that if these segments could have been supplemented with video clips such as those of Emma, the prediction rate would have been even higher.

JOINT ATTENTION AS A MARKER

Dr. Dawson and her colleagues have more recently published research indicating that the strongest single predictor of future ASD is whether or not the infant communicates for joint attention, a form of communication we expect to be present in at least rudimentary form by twelve months of age.[19] Their data supports the work of a number of other researchers like Peter Mundy and Tony Charman, who over the past twenty years have published scores of papers demonstrating the predictive value of joint attention. Taken as a whole, there is a compelling case for joint attention as a critical marker for the later diagnosis of ASD. This is especially so for the type of joint attention communication whose function is to share experiences with familiar adults, to expand the child's meaning in the world.

Dr. Mundy and colleagues have published convincing research that the desire to initiate joint attention through pointing is the best single predictor of future language development for young children with ASD. Instrumental pointing does not predict future language.

Defining Joint Attention

Joint attention is a dynamic process whereby the child seeks to enhance an initial subjective appraisal of something interesting or important in their environment. By definition, therefore, it is not a discrete behavior or a static skill. Using this communication the child shifts the guide's attention to the stimulus to deepen and widen the meaning obtained from it.

Joint attention is in some ways poorly named, taken literally, one might conclude that the main goal is for both parties to gaze, listen, taste, smell or touch the same thing. If limited by definition in this way, we would measure successful joint attention each time the child and partner were observed attending to the same thing.

The real success of joint attention—what makes its omissions so powerful in infants diagnosed with ASD—is based on what the child does *after* obtaining the partner's shared focus, when communicative partners provide their subjective appraisals

---

19   Reliable pointing for joint attention is not firmly in place until about fifteen months.

of the stimulus. To manage this complex process, a child must be able to generate his own subjective meaning alongside his partner's elaborated appraisal. Interestingly, this may or may not match, or even complement the child's original perception and reaction. This requires a major, sophisticated leap of neural integration.

I believe joint attention is a "marker" representing several critical dynamic intelligence discoveries typically mastered between ten to fifteen months of age. These dynamic abilities include social referencing, flexible observational learning, fluid social coordination, identification and emotional regulation of uncertainty and ambiguity. The few studies of social referencing, identification and observational learning are consistent with joint attention findings, while social coordination and emotional regulation of uncertainty have not been adequately studied.

Each of these processes requires a relatively high degree of neural integration, not observed prior to ten months of age. These mental processes are especially dependent on the development of neural networks between areas in the "executive" Pre-frontal Cortex and the "emotional" Limbic System.

This degree of sophisticated neural processing does not spring up fully formed. The one-year-old's newly demonstrated abilities are a product of the neurological growth made during the previous months, as the brain gradually develops in this direction. This occurs as the child is presented with, and successfully utilizes, hundreds of opportunities that foster such dynamic growth.

Autism researchers recognize that, while joint attention is a useful marker, we should not assume that all infants who later receive the ASD diagnosis develop normally up until late in their first year of life. Abnormal development may be observed as early as three months of age. Likewise, a child may possess neural resources that allow parents to help him master several foundational areas, without possessing sufficient ability to attain the competence of a fifteen months old apprentice.

PHILIP

Philip and his mother Kendra are in the playroom of my clinic for their first visit together. The room is about fifteen by eighteen. There is a pile of beanbag chairs in one corner. One wall is covered in floor to ceiling curtains with a small counter along a second wall. A third wall contains a one-way mirror currently covered with blinds. There are several toys on the floor.

Kendra is sitting on her knees, adjacent to the beanbags. Philip, who is almost four-years-old, hugs his mother in a jerky but genuine fashion and quickly moves away. His actions seem chaotic and disorganized. He seems to be moving just for the sake of moving. Kendra, still on her knees, moves towards her son while saying in a frantic, anxious manner, "What do you see? Hey look at this. Look at this one!"

Philip ignores her. Kendra picks up a small Frisbee, while Philip puts his hands firmly over his ears. Philip gazes vaguely in her direction and she makes a shoo noise pointing to the Frisbee. Quietly Kendra says to him, "Go get it!" He makes no move towards it so she tries to physically direct him. "Go get it. Bring it to mommy." Instead Philip glances down and picks up two small soft balls. He places one in each hand and briefly directs his attention to moving them up and down in a somewhat hypnotic fashion. Kendra does not persist in her efforts and instead tries to join in with him by saying, "Balls?"

Philip quickly walks away from his mother, still holding the balls. When he gets to the opposite side of the room, he turns and walks back, although not particularly towards Kendra. As he approaches, she holds out her hand and rapidly says, "Can you give me the balls?" Philip does not acknowledge this. He makes a noise and takes off again in the opposite direction, this time faster and more jumpily. Once he gets to the end of the room he returns quickly. Kendra again tries to gain his attention. She makes ready to toss the Frisbee saying, "Watch this Philip. Watch." Philip looks away from her while she continues to try and engage him by saying, "Phillie. Phillie!"

Philip drops one of his balls and goes to pick it up. Kendra continues her attempt at engagement by loudly and cheerfully counting, "One, two, three," before she releases the Frisbee. He is still fetching his dropped ball but chimes in to echo "three" without glancing up or acknowledging Kendra. He pays no attention to the Frisbee and again heads toward the opposite end of the room. Kendra holds out her hands and says, "Where did it go?" Philip ignores her while jumping up and down and moving across the room.

Finally Kendra accidentally catches Philip's attention while throwing the Frisbee. Philip watches for about a second and returns to his route, holding the two balls while making a rough circuit around the room.

Kendra takes the balls from Philip's hand. He does not protest nor does he seem particularly to care what he is doing. He is very close to the Frisbee and allows his mother to direct him to it. He moves to the other side of the room and he fetches the Frisbee. As he approaches she says, "Throw it. Throw it," and mimics throwing the Frisbee. Philip walks toward her, hands it to her and turns away. Kendra tries to take Philip's hand to teach him how to throw. He tolerates this without any motivation and with no gaze toward his own arm. When Kendra releases him, he is off again on his circuit. His mother tries to start something with a new toy. Philip returns to Kendra and gives her a brief hug before plunging into the pile of beanbag chairs.

BRIAN

It is Easter Sunday. Brian, now eighteen months old, has been given a basket of Easter Eggs and candy that includes yellow rabbit-shaped Peeps. He is sitting at the front of his house along the driveway. Across from him is his sister Sarah who is three years older. Adjacent are his parents Jackie and Tom. Brian has focused his gaze on the two Easter Eggs he is holding.

Jackie says in a very engaging voice, "There he is with his Easter Eggs. It's full of candy. He doesn't know." Brian is shaking the two eggs up and down. She continues, "Brian, what do you got boo boo?" Brian is oblivious to her. He drops the eggs as Jackie goes on to say, "Oh. There they go." Sarah echoes her mother, "There they go!" Jackie says, "Sissy you're so nice to play with little man." Jackie in a more powerful voice sings out, "Brian. Oh look at you! What is all that treasure?" Once again Sarah echoes her mother, "All the treasure!" There is no response from Brian. Now Jackie tries again, "Brian" followed by clucking noises. "Brian. Look, boo boo! Brian look! Look at Mama," using a highly amplified intonation. "Brian. Look at Mama!" She attempts a series of trilling noises. Brian acknowledges neither his mother or sister in any manner.

Sarah says, "Brian look what mommy and daddy and Sarah made for you." Sarah holds out the rabbit-shaped Peeps. Brian puts down the Easter Eggs and takes the candy from his sister without glancing at her. Sarah continues on and says, "Look what the Easter bunny brought you. That cute?" Brian takes a bite and then puts the candy on the ground still ignoring his sister. Jackie chuckles and says, "He took a bite! Uhm, yum. Brian. What do you got honey? You got a little rabbit?"

Throughout this entire episode, which stretches over half an hour, Brian never once glances at his family. He never shows any emotion. He also does not initiate communication, nor does he acknowledge the communication directed toward him.

Now skip to the morning of Brian's second birthday. He lies flat on his stomach on the kitchen floor with his favorite red car. He has been rolling the car back and forth for over an hour and shows no signs of tiring. He watches it as he slowly rolls it back and forth. His mother tries to get his attention by shouting out, "Brian, happy birthday," to no avail.

The third scene is Christmas morning. Brian is now twenty-six months old. The family is sitting around the tree, opening their presents. Brian briefly examines a thin package that was placed in his hands. After staring at it for about five seconds, he gently places it on the ground, slowly turns away and heads towards his favorite toy shopping cart. He begins to slowly twirl with it around the room and makes unintelligible noises. Around and around he goes in a slow circle while vocalizing, "AAAh, boinkyboinky, uhhh."

PHILIP AND BRIAN

Philip's actions appear to rely on what psychologists call bottom-up perceptual processing. Rather than using higher level neural algorithms that search for meaning and filter out peripheral information, Philip appears driven by whatever stimuli registers most strongly on lower level neural processors. He seems unable to filter out peripheral information to focus on central patterns. Philip has limited, if any, cortical control of attention. His focus seems random, as if he has no ability to deliberately regulate it. Philip seems lacking in a drive for complexity. He further appears unable to perceive meaningful continuities in his environment. There is no evidence that he is formulating his own appraisal of what is most interesting and meaningful in his environment.

In some ways Brian may appear less impaired than Philip because of the relative organization of his actions. Brian doesn't deal with the world in such a chaotic manner. He filters out almost all socially based stimuli and also carefully examines the limited things with which he involves himself.

Brian seems to select specific things he wants to interact with and is not as reactive or enslaved as Philip by the vagaries of his impulses or the environment. At the same time, his desire for meaning appears limited to maintaining replication in the few areas where he has formed associations. Brian, like Philip, seems unable to filter peripheral from central elements in the simple patterns that he perceives. But, rather than reacting in a random, chaotic fashion, his brain forms associations that include the peripheral element he encounters. That is why certain specific objects become so important. Brian will spend hours with two objects, his toy truck and his shopping cart. He cannot separate the object from the actions he has learned to employ with the object.

Neither boy has a bad temperament. They are generally not destructive, aggressive, or oppositional but both are missing the primary intersubjectivity we observed so effortlessly with Emma at four-months of age. Both children ignore the vocal and facial information so elegantly supplied by their guides. They show no recognition of emotional engagement or disengagement. In fact, they seem oblivious to whether they are emotionally connected or disconnected and take no responsibility for making or keeping the engagement.

These boys are not learning that the world is composed of the duality of continuity and variation. They seem unable to perceive underlying patterns and filter out peripheral information. Brian appears fixated on replicating specific actions while Philip may be even too disorganized for that.

Compared to Emma at five months of age, neither Brian nor Philip takes similar responsibility to co-regulate or co-participate. Neither boy seeks out the perceptions and impressions of their parents to widen their understanding of the world through joint attention. Neither is able to use parents or other significant adults as an emotional reference point to help him manage uncertainty. Brian and Philip are unaware of these situations when they occur.

Both Philip and Brian have typically developing sisters. When I observe Kendra with her daughter I witness an amazing transformation. She is as in-synch with her daughter as Emma's or any other set of parents of a typically developing child. I could easily have substituted the videos of Philip's sister Sarah with those of Emma and substantially told the same developmental story. The same is true when I observe Jackie with her daughter.

PAULIE

Like Philip, we meet Paulie for the first time during his initial visit to our clinic. We've been told that Paulie, at age three, is a high-functioning child with autism. He can do many things for himself and has a good vocabulary. We are testing his ability to use social referencing when he is uncertain. Since we do not know Paulie's capabilities, we use the simplest version of our assessment, a version with which Emma at fifteen months would have had no problems.

We set up two piles of beanbag chairs in our small playroom. The evaluator, Nancy, is getting the beanbags ready. Paulie and his mother, Barbara, are sitting on the floor. Paulie is swinging from his mother's side while grasping her hair. Barbara tells us that Paulie, if allowed, would never let go of her curly hair. Nancy says, "What's your name?" He answers, "Paulie!" using a cheerful tone of voice. He apparently feels very safe as long as he is physically hanging on to Barbara. Barbara tries to get him to stand independently but he continues to lean against her. He gazes towards Nancy and in an emotionally engaging manner says, "What's my name?" Nancy doesn't answer. He repeats himself in a louder but still positive voice, "What's my name?" After the fourth time, Nancy does respond with, "Is it Paulie?" He says, "Yeah."

Nancy goes over to Paulie and says, "Hey Paulie. Come here." She takes his hand and he stops smiling and jumping. Allowing himself to be taken from his mother, he walks the few steps with Nancy closer to the door and turns with Nancy to face it. While he is doing this, Barbara, hides behind one of the piles of beanbag chairs. The two piles are approximately six feet from where Paulie is standing. They give Barbara about five seconds to hide while Nancy quickly counts to ten with a really amplified "Tennnn".

Nancy lets go of Paulie and gazes pointedly at the pile of beanbags behind which Barbara is hiding saying, "There she is!" Paulie does not look back at Nancy, but jerkily sets off generally in the right direction, with an excited expression on his face. He moves approximately two feet away and stops, uncertain. Paulie turns back to Nancy, who is fixing her gaze on his mother's pile of beanbags. She says in an animated fashion, "Where's mommy?" He evidently cannot use Nancy's glance as a reference point. Then Paulie answers his own question with, "Mommy's finding the doctor." This is an exact repetition of what his father had told him earlier during their time in the waiting room, when Barbara had walked down a corridor to find the examiner. Nancy continues to look right at where Barbara is hiding and says, "Where's mom?"

Within a single second, Paulie's emotional state moves abruptly from excited to distressed and he repeats, "Mommy's finding the doctor," speaking to no one in particular, in a very shaky voice. Nancy moves towards Paulie while saying, "Let's find her." Paulie is close to tears and says, "Find mommy!" Nancy first takes Paulie over to the pile where his mother is not hiding and uncovers the beanbags to show that Barbara is not there. Then she quickly shows him where Barbara is hiding. Barbara emerges. Paulie runs and grabs onto his mother and they hug.

Paulie is an engaging little boy with a sweet smile. He initiated emotionally in a positive manner. He wanted to maintain engagement with his mother. However, Paulie and his mother have not developed the hallmark of the GPR, the mutual belief that the pair can safely voyage to the emotional and cognitive edge of the apprentice's competence. He has no experience of identifying and successfully surmounting challenges.

Paulie has little if any trust in himself or the adults around him to maintain a sense of safety during challenging situations where the potential for new learning and growth is optimal. Paulie becomes highly distressed by even a minor amount of uncertainty. He moves quickly into fight-flight mode; his autonomic response is near panic.

While Paulie does look to the adult, he does not know that he can use her gaze as a reference point to determine his actions. He does not have the ability to study when he is unsure. He cannot soothe himself. His words are empty and disconnected from his feelings and from personal meaning.

Paulie recovered quickly when we led him to his mother. He wound up with a big smile on his face as he clung to her during their reunion. He was able to experience other activities in our evaluation. But what did he learn about himself from this experience? We believe that each time Paulie has an experience like this, it creates a powerful indelible memory related to his inadequacy. We fear that hundreds of similar experiences have already occurred.

THE DAMAGE

The systems that Philip, Brian and Paulie have formed with their mothers and fathers have ceased to function as they were intended. Without the necessary feedback and participation, parents have lost their intuitive sense of guiding. In many ways they wind up taking the polar opposite actions from what they would do if their typically developing child were reacting in the same way. For example, in the above vignettes, the more communication fails between them, the more Kendra speeds up the pace. When she fails to obtain Philip's attention she inadvertently adds even more complexity.

With increasing desperation, there are decreasing opportunities for making cognitive discoveries. The ASD child's belief in their capacity for managing productive uncertainty similarly decreases.

The result for the child and family is a pervasive avoidance of anything that would hint of expansion and growth. We see in Brian's actions, the visible results of the unnatural inclination to pursue continuity without change. Both child and caregivers seek sameness and accumulation rather than discovery, integration and expansion. "Don't rock the boat" becomes the pervasive motto by which families survive. Parents lose their intuitive ability and wind up becoming more ineffective. When competence is destroyed, we shrink our world into nothing. Challenges become threats and setbacks are perceived as unrecoverable catastrophes.

These parents will tell you that they recognize they didn't cause their child's ASD. However, when interviewed during their initial sessions, all will admit that they often feel like failures. Kendra tells me that she feels that nothing she does is going to be right. If she leaves Philip to his own devices he will largely ignore her and engage in almost completely random, unproductive actions. When she tries to engage him, he also ignores her. She has to work incredibly hard just to get and keep his attention for a few seconds. But what is her choice? Jackie tells me she has to be very careful about changing Brian's routine. If she tries to remove his truck or shopping cart, she is sure he would tantrum for hours.

For these children and the millions of others like them, only a single autistic pathway of development appears to remain open. That pathway includes an over-reliance on static forms of learning, such as accumulating rote information, scripts and procedures, as well as frequent obsessive involvement with the single or few areas of interest or competence that the child has found to be safe.

People with ASD develop their self-concept around the ability to function in static systems. As they get older, they want to avoid more of the dynamic elements of their world. It is no wonder then that we see young adults with ASD who have high IQs and graduate from college, yet are completely unable to function in the real world, unable to get or keep a job, live independently and who are living in complete social isolation apart from immediate family members.

A STARTING POINT

While these stories might seem discouraging, for me they represent an important starting point. To understand and share my optimism you will have to avoid the trap of predicting outcomes based on current functioning. Just because we do not see these attributes during our initial observations, does not mean that Philip, Brian or Paulie cannot develop the abilities needed for apprenticeship. On the contrary, I believe that these children like everyone else, have the potential for apprenticeship and much more as well. I begin with the assumption that their potential is masked by the extreme levels of stress and confusion that has come to characterize their daily existence.

Nothing in my experience or in the research literature provided sufficient reason to give up on trying to provide these families with the means to conduct a Guided Participation Relationship. In retrospect, I know for certain I was right. Each of these three children along with hundreds of others, has developed into magnificent apprentices and you will have a chance to follow their development in later chapters.

Do you have some early videos you can watch of your child? If you have an ASD child, how do your observations line up with those of the researchers? Do you see many instances of joint attention at twelve months of age? Make sure to compare your video to one of a typically developing child at about the same age, in a similar setting. What differences do you notice?

Part Two:
The RDI® Program

Chapter Nine

Education

Remediation implies that we are embarking on a long-term marathon, not a sprint; a systematic process of correcting deficits to the point where they no longer constitute obstacles to reaching one's potential and attaining a quality of life. Remediation provides children a second chance to master areas of developmental disability that would otherwise lead to life-long marginalization and failure. When we remediate, we purposely focus on the person's greatest areas of weakness.[20] On a neural level, remediation for ASD means deliberately developing the brain's capacity for integration and neural collaboration.

I find that in the ASD community, remediation sometimes runs counter to predominant educational and treatment models. Most approaches are based on strengthening the abilities the person already has and trying to work around, or bypass areas of weakness. I decided to begin with the assumption that remediation was possible. I based this on the knowledge that cognitive interventions have been successful in changing brain pathways of people with dyslexia, obsessive-compulsive disorder, and depression. There was no research that indicated that the brains of people with autism were less malleable than those of other groups.

---

20 For example if a child has Amblyopia, also known as a "lazy eye", doctors deliberately patch the strong eye to force the weak eye to work harder, thereby strengthening it.

WHEN IS IT TOO LATE?

Parents of older children, teens and adults are concerned that there may be a critical period for neural development and that their child may be too old for remediation. Unfortunately, this "critical period" myth is sometimes fueled by professionals. The myth itself appears to go somewhat like this: Following 60 months-of-age (sometimes I hear the age as 36 or 48 months), the brain solidifies, with no further chance to influence its development. Therefore, intervention must start as early as possible, to avoid passing over this threshold.

I think of this myth as the "hard-boiled-egg" theory of the brain. Children's brains are envisioned as eggs that start out raw at birth, became soft boiled during the first few years, but if left in the pan for too long (e.g. after four years of age), harden and become unchangeable.

Fortunately, this doesn't fit with modern neurological science. We know that people's brains change throughout their lives. The brain is a dynamic organism, always altering its pathways and connections to become more efficient or solve new problems. RDI Consultants do not impose any age limit on children.[21] They may modify specific methods, especially if an adult is motivated to pursue the program. However, the basic principles of RDI remain unchanged, regardless of the age of the child.[22]

The five-year-old critical period myth may have originated from studies of the few "feral children" who have lived without any adult guidance. It appears that if children do not receive at least minimal parenting by age five, their chances for eventually developing language are poor. As interesting as this research may be, there is absolutely no reason to compare these two very different groups, or consider a parallel trajectory of development.

---

21   In fact, several consultants specialize in working with older adolescents and adults and are reporting excellent results

22   Throughout the book I refer to the ultimate recipients of RDI as "the child" or "children." I do not mean to offend those adolescents and adults who have been such excellent participants in the program. Rather, I mean the term more as a family role position, than as a statement of immaturity. From my current developmental stage, as the father of adult children, I tend to think of most teens and young adults in this manner. Ultimately, we are all children of our parents.

QUALITY OF LIFE

The goal of remediation is to enhance the potential for quality of life of ASD individuals. Defining quality of life is simple. It means providing people with opportunities for productive employment, independent living, genuine reciprocal friendship and intimate emotional relationships. One of the stranger elements of the ASD world is the absence of knowledge about whether any commonly used treatment has a positive or negative effect on attaining a quality of life. Studies have largely used measures of static learning as outcome measures. As a result, we have no idea whether any treatments increase the odds of an ASD child having a real reciprocal friendship, thinking in more flexible, adaptive ways, getting a job, living independently, or getting married some day.

Along with the general goal of Quality of Life, I have developed specific goals representing those attributes that any society would judge as essential. The attainment of these goals requires both dynamic and static abilities. Goals are described in detail in Appendix B.

Review the goals in Appendix B. Are there any that you would add? Do any appear unnecessary? Can you imagine an educational curriculum based on these goals? What do you think it would look like?

RESTORING THE GUIDED PARTICIPATION RELATIONSHIP

A primary hypothesis of RDI is that Autism Spectrum Disorders are the consequence of the child's inborn neurological and other biomedical vulnerabilities, which in various combinations, disrupt the Guided Participation Relationship early in life. I believe that if we can provide a second chance to restore or establish the GPR in a more deliberate mindful manner, while simultaneously lessening the continuing impact of co-occurring problems, we can help the majority of ASD children and families embark on a more normal path of cognitive, emotional and social development.

All infants, including those with ASD, are born with a strong drive to learn from the more expert members of their culture. This is what it means to be human. While their capacity has been overwhelmed at some point in early development, I believe that if we carefully construct a pathway for them, most ASD children will learn to be apprentices and participate in a Guided Participation Relationship.

INVESTING IN FAMILIES FIRST

A second cardinal principle of RDI is that the family unit should be the natural recipients of the bulk of service resources. Parents have a natural place as the child's first and most important guides.[23]

In two-parent families, both parents play essential roles in the guided participation process. Even if one or both parents work in demanding occupations, we want them to use the time they have reserved for parenting in the most effective manner possible. When parents have created a firm foundation and are competent in carrying out their roles, we can expand the range of guides to include extended family and family helpers.[24]

Once nuclear and extended family members establish a solid network of guidance, we expand the guided participation network to include teachers, coaches, aides and similar non-family members. For example, if staff is properly trained and settings appropriately structured, school environments can provide valuable non-family cultures, where children can participate as respected community members, with new responsibilities and opportunities for growth.

BUILDING FROM THE GROUND UP

Effective learning carefully builds upon the learners' prior understanding and experience. New development builds upon the foundations of prior development

---

23   Though certainly not their exclusive ones.
24   When working with single-parent families, we ask the parent to find a second honorary parent to serve as their co-guide. We prefer this to be a non-paid, permanent member of their social network such as a grandparent, other relative or close friend.

as sophisticated processes are constructed from more basic versions. We cannot arbitrarily pick our objectives based upon observing a child's deficits.

Lets briefly return to Emma, whose development I chronicled during her first two years of life. Emma has become a capable apprentice, demonstrating a good deal of dynamic intelligence. However, her abilities did not emerge fully formed at birth. Emma's competence at 24 months is a result of the foundations developed from as early as three months. The emotional attunement and awareness of continuities we witnessed at three months of age, were essential pre-requisites for the co-regulation and synchronized vocal-facial communication Emma displayed at five months. These abilities in turn set the stage for the active co-participation, studying and emotional regulation of seven month-old Emma and so on.

At 24 months, Emma fluidly combined social referencing with communication monitoring. However, each of these processes had to be learned individually, prior to being integrated as a single larger process of "referencing-monitoring." Similarly, Emma's brain had to gradually develop more sophisticated levels of neural integration. The degree of integration necessary for her fluid gaze shifting at five months was a building-block for the much more complex integration needed for joint attention at one year of age. Further, the neural integration displayed by two-year-old Emma is the prototype for her future development.

REAL WORLD COMPETENCE

RDI is geared towards teaching abilities that allow you to thrive in the real, messy world. Almost from the beginning, we introduce lessons about change amidst continuity, uncertainty amidst predictability, grey-areas of thinking and multiple perspectives and solutions. Children learn that most real-world problems do not have perfect solutions. Success depends on learning to operate on a good enough basis, differentially allocating sufficient resources to meet standards based on the context in which the problem resides. They learn that expectations and predictions must be tempered by knowledge, that the unexpected can occur at any time, and that if we take the surprise out of life it becomes hardly worth living.

PROGRESSIVE GENERALIZATION

As we move to higher stages in the curriculum, we gradually add greater real-world difficulty. Children learn to solve increasingly complex problems, with many different partners in continuously changing and less predictable environments. Early on, mastery in more structured, familiar settings is sufficient. As stages progress, mastery requires competence in noisier, less familiar settings. Stimuli that once distracted the child and created too much competition for his attention are gradually re-introduced. Similarly, when objectives are mastered with adults, the next stage may introduce a familiar peer. When mastery is achieved with a peer, we may move to a small group setting and so on. Guides present frameworks where communication and coordination begin to break down despite everyone's best efforts.

LIFESTYLE CHANGES

In their first two years of life, typically developing children and their guides work incredibly hard, spending literally thousands of hours constructing the foundations for integrated neural development. There is no way to rapidly make this up. Therefore, if we are going to provide ASD children a legitimate second chance, we have to use as much of each day as possible to create opportunities for dynamic development.

There are no special RDI activities. Rather, parents learn to re-think their daily lifestyle, restructuring routine activities, to provide safe, but challenging opportunities for mental growth. They make sure that children's discoveries are preserved and not buried in the flow of daily activity, by helping the child capture and consolidate critical memories to build an experiential repository for future success.

THE RDI CONSULTANT

The single most important RDI tool is the RDI Consultant. Consultants are professionals with varied backgrounds, such as Speech Pathologists, Psychologists, teachers, Social Workers, Autism Specialists, Occupational Therapists, Physicians and veteran parents. They are trained to serve as guides to parental guides-in-training. They view their role as facilitators, customizing learning programs, based on the unique needs of each family.

Consultants carefully transfer their abilities to parents over a series of clear objectives so parents can become fully independent in applying the essential tools of guided participation. Consultants help parents modify their communication, slow their pace and focus on the underlying opportunities available in their daily routines. They teach parents to conduct observation and analysis of critical processes. They break down large, complex abilities into manageable pieces. They construct clear, systematic assignments, tailored to the daily realities of the family. They make sure that parents have appropriate understanding of how they are expected to work with their child between consultant visits.

Developing dynamic intelligence and greater neural integration cannot be conducted via a cookbook approach. RDI Consultants carefully customize what they do for each parent and child. They analyze child obstacles to make learning environments as user friendly as possible. Once obstacles have begun to clear away, consultants determine each child's zone of proximal development, or edge of competence, in order to know where developmentally to proceed.

Consultants and parents require a close, working relationship. The importance of finding a good fit cannot be over-emphasized. Consultants have to help restore parents' trust in their ability to form a new guided participation relationship with their child, even though it did not work the first time around. Consultants have to be prepared to understand the trauma parents and family members have already experienced. Each family may present their own unique obstacles in this regard, resulting from the way that they have been impacted by the crisis. Consultants must also take into account the family's unique language, culture and customs. They have to sensitively explore the effectiveness of their communication style with each family member. This may include customizing their mode and frequency of communication based on each person's needs.

One of our consultants, Amy Leventhal, summarized some of the critical aspects of the consultant-parent relationship in the following manner:

When I work with a family, we begin from a standpoint of mutual respect for each other's contributions and culture and move forward with an absence of labeling or blame. Our communication is honest and clear but tempered by empathic understanding. We mutually agree upon our goals and share in the process of planning and decision-making. Our resources are freely exchanged as we work to achieve accessibility and responsiveness.

THE RDI LEARNING SYSTEM (RDILS)

A critical piece of the RDI Program was implemented in December 2007, when we launched our on line, virtual learning community—the RDI Learning System (RDILS).[25] It is a sophisticated web-based application and community site, allowing users to do many things that were previously impossible.

There are many features available to subscribers on the RDILS website. Secure and confidential multi-media online "charts" provide easy access to objectives, assignments, communication and samples of progress for that family.

Consultants, parents and other team members effectively communicate, viewing each other's work in their respective setting, as well as receiving regular feedback from one another.

Parents upload representative samples of their interaction to their consultants for review, based on specific assignments constructed by the consultant. These work samples typically consist of parental thoughts and analysis related to the specific assignment, along with video or other media files that provide a representation of their progress. Consultants rapidly respond to parents using the online system and provide valuable feedback during intervals between live meetings.

A number of other components provide additional support. Subscribers have access to weekly educational webinars, which are archived in case the subscriber cannot attend. There are discussion forums for parents and consultants, as well as built in video and text chat programs. On line courses are available for specialized topics.

---

25   In future sections I will use the abbreviation "RDILS" to refer to the RDI Learning System—our on line system of communication, education, progress tracking and documentation.

Progress tracking reports are also available allowing consultants and parents to review their gains in different areas and chart their future goals and objectives. These reports can be exported into many formats and printed for use in school ARD meetings.

The RDILS allows professionals and families around the world to contribute to increasing mutual wisdom and effectiveness. Parents and Consultants can access resources attached to specific objectives and lessons. These are video clips and other media contributed, with the consent of parents, made available only to subscribers.

THE DYNAMIC INTELLIGENCE CURRICULUM

Over the past 10 years I have constructed a curriculum, designed to carefully develop proficiency in dynamic intelligence. This curriculum, consisting of almost 1,000 objectives, is currently available to subscribers on line as part of the RDI Learning System.

When I began this process, I found that there were no guidebooks, manuals, or timelines specifying how dynamic intelligence develops. I spent thousands of hours painstakingly deconstructing and analyzing the underlying elements of scores of complex mental processes documented in the developmental psychology research literature.

I took each process and broke it down, both vertically and horizontally. Vertically I had to trace each process back to its earliest, simplest form or prototype (even the simplest three-year-olds' rudimentary conversations are built upon many earlier dynamic foundations), and then track its developmental progression as it evolved into its more sophisticated offspring.

In a similar vein, I had to look horizontally, finding non-integrated "purer" forms of processes and then determining how they gradually come to function in an increasingly integrated and elaborated manner, so intertwined, that few of us even realize the incredible degree of neural collaboration we utilize in the course of a typical day. Curriculum development continues as new research fills in gaps and provides more accurate information.

As we move through the curriculum's stages, different dimensions of mental growth are revealed. Stage progressions reflect the manner in which real-world dynamic intelligence evolves. Abilities like communication monitoring, social coordination emotional self-regulation, problem appraisal, task evaluation, critical analysis and collaboration gradually begin to function in more fluid, sophisticated and integrated ways.

For example, as stages progress objectives represent the child's movement from relying on primarily external, relationship-bound abilities like social referencing to increasing use of internal, self-contained equivalents like personal reflection, a form of self referencing (relying when uncertain, on your own past experiences). Similarly, the progression of stages reflects the ways in which children gradually learn to independently manage more complex problems with their own minds, requiring less guidance. Finally, each stage chronicles the child's increasing ability to manage dynamic problems and encounters in more novel and complex settings, with increasingly diverse and unpredictable partners.

DISCOVERIES AND ELABORATIONS

The cornerstone of the curriculum are mental discoveries. Each represents a small incremental step in the child's journey to learn to use his mind in a more powerful, competent manner. Through the gradual unfolding of many hundreds of objectives, earlier discoveries are elaborated (akin to a branch of a tree producing shoots). Elaborations themselves set the stage for, and evolve into new discoveries.

OBJECTIVES, LESSONS AND ASSIGNMENTS

Each small developmental step, whether a discovery or elaboration, is labeled as a specific, unique objective. Objectives are further sub-divided into lessons, making them more manageable for parents to implement on a daily basis. Each lesson includes observable mastery criteria as well as linkages to important resources that aid in lesson understanding and mastery. Finally, lessons are customized by the consultant into assignments, which detail the specific work to be done in the short interval between sessions.

SESSIONS WITH THE CONSULTANT

Live sessions with the consultant are customized to include practice periods, collaborative work times, sensitive listening and support as needed by family members. A family may be ready to begin work on a new objective, which must be selected and broken down into lessons. A specific lesson may be selected, along with time spent to make sure that the lesson is understood by parents and is portable enough, so that parents can access it when looking for opportunities throughout their day. Consultants and parents collaboratively construct and rehearse assignments. Subsequent meetings may focus on adjusting assignments to better fit the family's realities. Sessions may also involve troubleshooting obstacles that have crept into the family's every day life and exploring new developments that may require modifying plans.

COMMUNICATION BETWEEN SESSIONS

Because of the RDI Learning System, we have been able to make the process between parents and their consultants more closely resemble a real-world guide-apprentice relationship. Communication in between sessions makes everyone's work more effective. Consultants may ask parents to go home from a meeting and provide the consultant with a preliminary work product within a day or two, to determine if they really understand their assignment. Parents can express confusion and request clarification, and necessary modifications can be made in between office visits. Parents submit their work products on line and receive more immediate consultant feedback. Consultation meetings become exponentially more effective, because they are reserved for troubleshooting obstacles that could not be resolved on-line and for constructing new lessons and assignments.

CONSULTATION WITH SHARON AND MARTHA

One of our consultants, Sharon, was working with a mother, Martha, on understanding the difference between instrumental and experience-sharing communication. Martha's assignment was to make four short video clips using both forms of communication with both her ASD son and her typically developing daughter.

With each clip she was asked to explain why it was a good example of the type of communication it represented.

Martha submitted video clips of herself communicating with her son and her typically developing daughter. Clips with her son were full of instrumental communication, while those with her daughter were exactly what was requested. Martha did not attach any analysis of the clips, not realizing that this was the most important part of the assignment.

Sending back an edited version of a clip submitted by the parent, is one of the RDI Learning System features Sharon frequently utilizes. This creates a spotlight around those critical moments. The following day, after viewing Martha's work product on line, Sharon chose 20 seconds of a clip Martha submitted of her interacting with her son and 20 seconds of a clip with her daughter. Martha's new assignment was to compare these two video clips and analyze their differences. When Martha was able to view just these two brief segments, she was able to respond with a very accurate analysis of each and thereafter was able to modify her communication with her son.

Chapter Ten

Readiness

The Readiness Stage provides a systematic, but customizable way to help families recover from the immense stress resulting from the breakdown of guided participation and the day-to-day difficulties of living with an ASD child.

Readiness is divided into two parts: parent and child. Essential elements for parents include making sure each family member's needs are taken into consideration, learning to set and maintain appropriate limits, relieving stress and anxiety, modifying communication, maintaining a healthy marriage and slowing down routine daily activities.

I have deliberately placed child readiness after its parent counterpart. It is important to be able to look at who the real child is—what is "behind" the child's initial presenting symptoms. ASD children may be highly reactive to their environment. Often the surface expression we first encounter, has little to do with who the child really is, and more to do with how he is reacting to daily overwhelming stresses and confusion. Very often we find that we see a very different child at the end of parent readiness than when we began. Until we can see a child functioning in a calmer, less intense, less noisy world, we cannot accurately assess his needs. Therefore, we do not work on developing a plan for the child, until parents and the child's environment are operating in a "user friendly", optimal manner.[26] Otherwise

---

26 I recommend beginning the medical parts of the inter-disciplinary evaluation of the child as early as possible.

we may just be learning what the child is like in an intensely stressful environment; basically seeing the defense mechanisms the child has developed, rather than the potential that lies underneath.

The Readiness Stage requires a good deal of care and thoughtfulness. We have to be sensitive to each family's unique emotional and pragmatic needs. You cannot give people a formula to recover from crisis and trauma. Similarly, readiness can take a varied amount of time. Some families may be nearly ready soon after we begin. Others may need months. Consultants are accustomed to recognizing that every person has their own pace and should never be rushed, or made to feel guilty if they require more time.

PARENT READINESS

I know it's not my fault. I know I didn't cause my child's autism. But to tell you the truth, it doesn't really make much difference. It doesn't reduce the pain I feel every time I try so hard to make some basic contact, to do what other parents can do so easily, and fail for the millionth time.

Often, for what seems like no reason whatsoever, he will get upset and cry. When that happens it makes me feel so helpless and incompetent. So when I see that he wants things a certain way, I think to myself, "At least that is something I can do something about." So I try to do whatever I can to keep things predictable. My whole life seems to revolve around keeping him happy by not rocking the boat."

WHAT DOES THE CRISIS LOOK LIKE?

The feelings chronicled above are not unusual. Statements like these reflect feelings of intense self-doubt and inadequacy experienced by even the most competent parents, who realize that things are not working, but do not feel that there is an alternative.

When we raise a typically developing child we take the quality and quantity of feedback we receive for granted. When the child cries we usually can guess what it is about. We don't expect to have incidents where we seem to be enjoying each other and then suddenly the child walks away as if we do not exist. We don't have to figure out what to do when the child repeats the same statement or question over and over, despite our ignoring him and making repeated pleas for him to stop.

When we are raising an ASD child, our communication can seem so ineffective and our influence so sporadic, that we wind up questioning much of what we do. The experience is somewhat like being the captain of a ship where the sailors have not mutinied, they have not abandoned ship, they are just indifferent to our orders and commands, uncaring about whether the ship flounders or continues to sail in circles.

Many parents have lost their intuitive sense of empowerment. They may question their normal parenting instincts, like how to respond to a tantrum, or whether to expect the child to do basic self care actions for himself. Not infrequently, I receive a question from a parent asking me if it is okay, when the child wants to pull away in a potentially dangerous situation, to hold onto their young child. Sometimes I respond by asking the parent what he or she would do in the case of a young non-ASD child. The same parent who was confused a moment before, will respond with certainty that, "Of course I would hold on and not let go." The problem is not one of having insufficient knowledge or skill, but rather having lost trust in oneself.

Parents may develop extreme fears about changing what they have been doing, even if it hasn't worked particularly well. They may repeat the same songs and conduct the same mindless rituals over and over, because they result in some degree of predictability, like leading to a smile or at least preventing a meltdown. They set up their lives to not rock the boat because that is the only way they can find some degree of safety and not live in fear of sudden emotional breakdowns. A father may come home from work and entertain his young ASD son by performing the same repetitive rituals, or engage in somewhat chaotic roughhousing. On some level he knows he is just acting as an entertainer. But, that is better than having no role at all.

Feelings of desperation may lead some parents on a perpetual quest for cures and new treatments that promise recovery. Enormous amounts of energy may be spent scouring the Internet. In their fragile state, parents are highly susceptible. In desperation they may hang onto anyone that seems to have more influence; anything that provides, even momentarily, a sense that they are getting through the indifference.[27]

Parents may feel worn-out and pervasively anxious. After years of enduring stress, some parents develop immune-system disorders. Others may suffer from reactive depression or post-traumatic stress disorders. We have to make sure that these problems are carefully assessed and treated by experienced professionals.

MOVING OUT OF CRISIS

When depressed, panicked, or in a desperate mode searching for rapid solutions, we are not fully available for new learning. Typically, the hardest time for us to assume a student role is when we feel discouraged and incompetent. In those states, we are more likely to want to focus on our remaining areas of competence, or at least hide under the covers. Consultants have to help parents leave this state of desperation and crisis behind. To do so, they have to understand each family's unique response to the crisis and take whatever time is needed to repair the emotional damage that has accrued.[28]

QUIETING

I use the term "quieting" to represent the lifestyle changes encompassing every part of family life as they move through the Readiness Stage. Parents learn to slow their breathing and become more aware of their physiologic responses. They become more careful about communication and learn to stop filling the air with so much noise. They slow down and take fewer actions just for the sake of doing something.

---

27 Unfortunately, there appear to be endless companies and individuals, some of them well meaning, willing to take advantage of parental desperation.

28 Throughout the Readiness Stage, consultants must carefully assess the limits of their own professional competence and the severity of parental distress. We want consultants to be quite conservative and if in any doubt, to work on emotional repair, quieting and similar objectives in tandem with trained mental health professionals.

Physical Quieting

Parents often do not realize how their bodies have become physically enmeshed with their ASD child. Often, an enormous amount of parental anxiety becomes linked to specific behaviors of the child, especially those that trigger feelings of inadequacy or helplessness in the parent.

Some parents may have become unconsciously conditioned to respond to specific behaviors of their child with extreme physiologic stress reactions. Their heart rate may soar in response to the child's protests, screams, angry words or odd actions. Self-stimulatory behaviors, especially when done in public places may trigger a parental panic reaction. Parents may feel paralyzed or take any action that comes to mind, when the ASD child, with no provocation, suddenly disconnects physically and or emotionally, from an interaction that seems to have been going well.

When the nervous system has been on edge for a long time, many different small events, which in normal circumstances might be brushed off, will trigger a physiologic and emotional overload leading to a sudden release of adrenalin.

Parents may develop a type of anticipatory panic related to even the hint of uncertainty. This can turn into a mutual negative feedback loop, where parental anxiety triggers more stress in the child, leading to child behavior which creates more parental anxiety and so on. As this snowball effect continues, parents live in continual fear that something they do is going to trigger the child and subsequently themselves.

In contrast, parents raising a typical child, develop a type of conditional sensitivity. For example, when their child cries after cutting her knee, they may offer sympathy and aid. However, they do not become panic stricken. When their child is tantruming because he isn't allowed to go somewhere, parents often respond with something akin to, "I'm not letting you go. You can tantrum forever and it won't matter."

Unless we eliminate this underlying anxiety and avoidance, it will permeate to every part of the consultant-parent relationship. As a first step, parents evaluate the degree to which they have become physiologically conditioned to over-react to specific child actions. Through careful observation parents determine their degree of enmeshment. An important discovery for parents is recognizing that their body may have been unconsciously responding in an unproductive manner for years.

Once they are aware of physiologic reactions, parents can learn to recognize the specific child behaviors that serve as precipitants for them. These may be different for each parent and include the child's distress, extreme passivity, protests, angry words, odd actions like self-stimulation, sudden emotional disconnection, gaze aversion and rejection. Consultants next help parents uncover the often-unconscious personal meanings of the particular behavior that trigger their reactions. Typically, it is the way that the parent interprets the behavior, rather than the child's action itself, that serves as the real trigger.

We try to determine parental beliefs about the consequences of the child's actions with questions such as, "If your child starts to cry and pull away and you don't let go, what do you think is going to happen?" Because they have been unconsciously conditioned, parents have never had the opportunity to employ deliberate thought to manage their stress. For example, when asked, "What are you worried will happen if you don't answer his incessant questions?" parents may respond with, "Maybe he will just stop talking." Frequently, once parents hear themselves responding in this manner, they recognize the irrationality of their statements and revise their beliefs in a more productive manner. We have found that once parents become aware of their reactions, including their personal attributions, many report they have already overcome a good part of the problem.[29]

Communication Quieting

I also employ the quieting metaphor in the service of decreasing the intensity of communication in the entire family. Parents learn to make family communication a less frantic event. They learn to use smaller amounts of simpler, language. They find they can spend longer periods of time being fully engaged with one another, relying on non-verbal communication channels, without necessarily having to talk.

---

29   But not all. Some parents may require more extensive care, including Cognitive Therapy and/or medication.

Parents learn to monitor their communication with the ASD child and contrast it with their normal communication style. Our goal is to help parents decrease the amount of instrumental communication they use with their ASD child, which typically starts out at near 100% and replace this with experience sharing communication. We would like the see the ratio change to 60/40 experience sharing/instrumental by the end of this stage. Parents learn to reduce the amount of performance language like, "Say hello", "Say goodbye", "What is this?" and increase communication that is narrative and invitational.

Over-talking

In an earlier chapter I discussed the potential danger of over-emphasizing speech development for non-communicative children. However, quite often parents with highly verbal children tell us that their child's incessant talking is their greatest stress. I like to talk to parents of "hyper-verbal" children about what I call IPod therapy. This consists of temporarily acting as if the auditory channel of communication is not available. I ask parents to pick blocks of time where they can wear large headphones, so it is clear to the child that they cannot hear. Then I ask them to listen through their headphones to their favorite music played on a portable mp3 player, while at the same time acting in a highly available, engaging and expressive manner and using other non-auditory communication channels like facial and gestural communication. In this manner, parents communicate that while one communication channel is closed, the others are available.

Parents who employ this method under a consultant's supervision, tell me that for the first time they enjoy interacting with their child. The incessant language has become as much of a physiologic irritant to the parent as chronic pain (you don't want to cut off your arm if it is continually hurting, but you certainty wish it would stop). Their initial attributions of fear that the child will be traumatized or will stop talking forever quickly turn into relief and parents make statements like, "Oh, this is what it's like to just *be* with my child. For the first time in years I can hang out with my child, without the continual irritation."

Being Powerful without Taking Over

A final communication lesson in this stage involves learning to be powerful in directing the child's attention without promoting the child's mindless compliance and thoughtless behavior. Parents learn to use what we refer to as indirect prompts. Unlike a direct prompt, such as "look at me," or "raise your hand," indirect prompts do not tell you what to do. Rather, they provide the child with information about the location of the most important information at that moment in time, without any directive about how to react or act in relation to the information, for example saying, "It's over here!"

Parents learn to employ various communicative tactics such as sudden movement changes (coming to an abrupt stop), non-verbal amplifications (suddenly pausing mid-sentence, or placing your hands over the child's eyes or ears), changes in body placement (placing yourself in front of the child's line-of-sight, with your back to the child) and elaborative, brief phrases ("Watch out!" "Oh no!"). These provide a strong signal for the child to stop and monitor their environment for something important, without instructing them what to do.

PARENTAL EMPOWERMENT

Regardless of whether they communicate their appreciation for our efforts, every child needs to know that their parents are strong enough to uphold limits and boundaries that keep the child safe and accessible for parent guidance. Children with ASD are no different. Unfortunately, parents can feel so inadequate and helpless that they lose their natural parental instincts. Over the course of several years, the consequences can be disastrous. I have seen too many ASD teens who have become tyrants in their households, having wielded too much control for too many years. It is infinitely better to withstand the tantrums of a five-year-old than the threats and violence of a narcissistically entitled fifteen-year-old.[30]

A major objective in learning to regain empowerment is feeling enough trust in yourself to set clear limits without anxiety. You cannot effectively parent any child,

---

30   When we work with a teen or young adult where limits have not been enforced we have to proceed much more carefully and consider potential risk to parents of too quickly assuming the new role of enforcer.

if you do not establish an environment where they know you will, when necessary, stick to your guns.[31]

One of the major obstacles to effective limit setting is the belief that persons with ASD are fundamentally different from everyone else. Consultants have to help parents understand that their child was born with the same innate motivation as any other infant. Children with ASD were not born wanting to disengage from their parents, control them, or preferring to stare at spinning fans. That's what they learned to do when they encountered a world they had no other way to cope with. Those actions are not beneficial to them. They are not the central parts of ASD. They are simply the child's reactions to living in a very confusing world.

Consultants help parents to persevere, when they meet with initial child resistance to any type of change. Most ASD children are going to start off resisting anything that seems new and different. Consultants help parents re-frame their understanding of the child's resistance. The reframing is that the child is doing the best he can, given his limited understanding of his options in the world. The child's behavior is a defensive reaction to his experience up to this point. He is only doing what he knows to do, given his limited experience. It is not a signal that persons with ASD are fundamentally different, or that parents should stop opening new doors for their child.

Taking your role

Parents have to be prepared to don many hats on the road to raising a child. They provide for the child's health and safety. They instruct the child in proper manners and the customs of behavior of their society. They make sure that the child learns basic self-care habits and skills. They are enjoyable playmates. They provide emotional soothing and encouragement. From time to time, they act as advocates, making sure that the child receives needed services from societal institutions such as the school.

---

31   You cannot allow a typical teenager to withdraw from you all the time. You may not want to intrude every minute. But when it's time to interact, parents cannot let even the teenage child run away from communication, even if it means creating a temporarily unpleasant situation.

All of these roles are important. However, in every culture on earth, the most important role for parents is to guide their child's mental development and prepare him or her for the complexity of modern life. We have found that parenting an ASD child disrupts this natural role. We often see parents unwittingly sacrificing their guiding role, for understandable reasons but with unfortunate consequences.

Sometimes we have to help parents shift their primary role from that of entertainer or satisfier of all of the child's desires and needs. Many parents of ASD children have only felt success as a playmate, or entertainer and sometimes this can be hard to give up.

Parental expectations may have become very low. For instance, if you come home from work, believing that the only way to have a mutually enjoyable encounter with your son is to spend 10 minutes completely emulating the last episode of WWF wrestling with him, it may be hard to give this ritual up or hope for anything more. You find yourself thinking that, "At least we have our one time together."

It is hard to argue with someone who says, "I just want my child to be happy in their life." However, parents of typically developing children are quick to tell me that they have a more important responsibility—to make sure the child can grow up to get a good job, treat other people well and be a good family member. Everyone believes that joy is a wonderful thing to have. However, gainfully working, contributing to your family and being a good citizen do not bring happiness all of the time.

Some parents become highly performance oriented, and think of their role like that of an animal trainer in the circus, getting their child to perform specific behaviors in response to cues. Similar to entertaining, obtaining behavioral performance may have been the only way parents have felt successful. The problem with this type of training is that if someone is spending the whole day responding to prompts and acting based on memorized rules and scripts, they have no reason to pro-actively monitor their environment, or plan and prepare. They will face no cognitive challenges and won't learn to think on their own.

We also see parents that have defined their primary role as procuring services for their child. They are taking their child to so many different therapies that the only time they have with the child is driving in a car from therapy to therapy. Or, the child is spending so much time with therapists that he is worn out when he comes home and unavailable for parental guidance. In ASD as in most chronic conditions, more is not better. More services may have little or nothing to do with the child making progress.

We certainly do not want parents to give up every role and solely focus on being a guide. Rather, consultants help parents evaluate the way they have apportioned their roles, and make sure there is a balance that provides a significant place for guiding.

RENEGOTIATING THE CONTRACT

At some point in the readiness process, many parents recognize that they will have to forge a new implicit contract with their child. While the contract is typically not written or even verbalized, parents will want the child to understand that something fundamental has changed in the way that their relationship will work.

One aspect of the new contract may be renegotiating the way communication is managed. Parents learn to no longer compete for the child's attention while they are trying to communicate with the child. This means that they will not attempt to communicate while the child is engaged in watching TV, or some similar distraction. Similarly, they will not continue to chase the child with their words but will first make sure that the child is available to attend to their communication.[32]

The most difficult part of clearing away competition for communication space, involves managing activities, which the child has become addicted to or obsessed with. Parents often ask me whether they should eliminate their child's access to computers, video games and television. The issue of electronics is not always black and white. Some children are addicted to electronics. They need to go through withdrawal. Others can use their play station an hour per week and not be obsessed with it.

---

32 Coupled with this, parents make sure that their communication is easier to process and has more meaning for the child. They make sure their communication is clear, brief and refers to what is immediately in their joint environment, what they are presently doing together.

One way I assess the importance of removing the addiction, is to ask parents, "If you tell your child you would really like to hang out with him, will he drop the electronics, or other potentially addictive activity to be with you?" If the answer is yes, then I'm not as worried. If the answer is no, then parents may have to at least temporarily withdraw them. Playing video games is not the most productive thing to do, but not too harmful if it is not competing with the child's relationship with parents. If it is a major competition, then parents must do something about it.

An important realization for parents, as they renegotiate their parent child contract, is understanding the limitations of their child's "zone of connection." Parents must determine how physically close they need to be, so that the child will experience the parent as connected and related to them at that moment. One of the biggest mistakes parents initially make is to assume that, because a child is talking at them, they are experiencing some emotional connection.

Eliminating Elective Withdrawal

The final and often most difficult part of the new parent-child contract, is being clear that the child no longer has the right to withdraw when parents wish to continue to engage him. There are two sides to this contract; for while the child is losing his ability to run away, parents must give up their attempts to force him to perform. If this were put into words it would go something like this, "I will not force you into anything, or make you do something, unless it is absolutely necessary. I will stop prompting you all the time and getting you to perform. On the other hand, I will not allow you to physically run away, or withdraw from me."

Parents also communicate that the child no longer has the option of leaving the field indirectly, through acting in a violent, destructive or abusive manner.[33] However, they are also clear that they will not remove the child's ability to temporarily avoid an activity by, for example, averting in order to re-group. The distinction between avoidance and withdrawal is extremely important to make. Avoidance is a temporary reaction to feeling overwhelmed. It leaves you available to re-organize

---

33   This type of behavior may require additional professional resources to manage.

and return to the task. Withdrawal means the child has taken actions to leave the field and is no longer available.[34]

When I speak about this type of empowerment, I often use the term "holding on" in a metaphoric way. You don't always have to physically hold a child.[35] However, you cannot allow the child to decide when to terminate or withdraw from an interaction with you. Therefore, when parents choose to engage with the child, only they should determine how long that engagement lasts. Parents can disengage at any time, but it should be their decision.[36]

By eliminating withdrawal in the face of uncertainty, parents provide the child an opportunity to learn that this type of escape is no longer necessary. Parents can demonstrate that they are able to provide the emotional support the child needs to feel safe. On a neuro-biological level, by cutting off withdrawal, but at the same time eliminating performance demands and presenting a quieter setting, parents are extinguishing the "fight-flight" neuro-chemical response that has cut off opportunities for new learning.

Modifying the Contract With Yourself: Expecting to Bat .300

Even the best parenting is chock full of mistakes and miscalculations. Successful parenting requires developing reasonable expectations for oneself. For example, when parents of a typically developing child encounter a social coordination breakdown with the child, they typically just stop and wait. The breakdown doesn't have any significance or personal meaning.

Many parents of ASD children assume unconsciously that if their child did not have ASD they would have 100% success. Especially, if this is their only child, they have no norms. If every time something goes wrong you are reminded of how you have failed with your child, then you are in big emotional trouble. You may start to

---

34   As I mentioned in a prior chapter, the first way that young infants learn to regulate their emotional states without having to "leave the field" is through gaze aversion. I hope that makes you think twice the next time you demand that a child look at you, when he or she is feeling stressed.
35   However, with younger children who are determining themselves when to ignore you, walk away or "leave the field," holding on may become quite literal.
36   Parents should be pragmatic. It makes no sense to force engagement with a child who is clearly worn out or overwhelmed.

believe that every disturbing action the child takes, from tantrums to withdrawal, must be because you have not performed as you should have.[37] Without having reasonable parenting expectations, parents unwittingly set themselves up for failure. When their ASD child refuses to interact or suddenly withdraws with no warning, parents may become frantic. The withdrawal may be perceived as another example of personal failure. In desperation, they may wind up adding more stimulation, noise and intensity, which further disrupts the process.

To help parents understand this, I often use the baseball analogy of batting .300. If you play baseball in the U.S. major leagues and are successful three times out of ten in hitting the ball where you are supposed to, you can be paid ten million dollars per year. You are considered a star, even though you fail seven times out of ten. There is a good reason for this. In baseball, even the best hitter recognizes that he is operating in a fluid, dynamic situation where absolute prediction and control is impossible. The hitter may try to guess, but can never know for sure if the pitcher is going to throw high, or low, inside or away, a curve, fastball or change-up. These are dynamic variables. Even if you knew what the pitchers' intentions were, you would not know where the ball was actually going to wind up, as the pitcher does not have perfect control. Both hitter and pitcher are re-evaluating and making continual adjustments during each at-bat. In this sense, baseball is an excellent metaphor for parenting.

Noted marital researcher John Gottman cites the same statistic about successfully married people. When he asked them what percent of their conflicts were successfully resolved, they reported only about thirty percent. Gottman found that the difference between being happy and unhappy in your marriage is not the percent of conflicts that the couple resolves. Rather, it is the expectations couples have about their conflicts and what happens when they have these disconnections. The unhappy people tend to react to them in a more extreme

---

37   An equally destructive corollary is to blame every errant behavior on the ASD. This leads to a pervasive sense of helplessness which, in its extreme form sounds like, "What can I do? It's the autism that does this, not my child."

manner, doing things that make the situation worse and creating either esca-
lating situations, or feelings of paralysis which Gottman terms "gridlock."

LEARNING TO HANG OUT TOGETHER AND APART

Some parents of ASD children become trapped in a vicious cycle, believing they are not doing a good job unless they are getting the child to do something every minute of every day. This leads to mutual exhaustion and burnout. One of the most important things for parents to learn is that it is helpful for parent and child to sometimes just hang out together. I want parents and children to experience calm, structured times together, where no one is trying to teach something, get something to happen, or control the other person (though parents still set clear limits). I want parents to experience the relief of being together in a physiologically calm, resonating manner. Such periods are critical, as they are the only way that the couple can develop attunement and emotional trust. Sit on the old porch swing. Hang out on the sofa together, listen to music. Take a walk with no destination. Learning to hang out is not the same as giving in or doing what the child wants you to do. Rather, parent and child interact under parental guidance, but with no goal except to share the moment.

If a family is used to engaging in performance-based activities all day long, hanging out may initially create anxiety for both parent and child. The trick is finding ways to spend sufficient time hanging out, despite the initial anxiety, to desensitize your fears.[38]

In a similar manner, parents must learn to feel comfortable during times when they are apart from their child, while they are at home together (assuming that the child is ready to be alone safely). Parents may initially report that they feel guilty if they are not constantly interacting with the child because the child will not be

---

38 This rarely takes more than several hours.

engaged in anything productive, "If I'm not getting him to do something he will just twirl around. So I feel I have to be with him every second." Parents must be able to take breaks from their child. If they keep trying to make something happen every minute, they will never leave the state of crisis. Also, without some time apart, it may be difficult for the child to perceive opportunities to be together as valuable.

QUIETING THE ENVIRONMENT

While it would be ideal to require each parent to commit 30 or 40 hours a week of their time to guided participation, the realities of our world do not often present such opportunities. Moreover, consultants do not find it productive to demand that parents spend a certain number of hours per week in guided participation. The Guided Participation Relationship is something that cannot be forced, or performed in a begrudging manner. Rather, parents are asked to think of guided participation as the most valuable use of their time. Unlike times when they are chauffeuring, instructing, or cleaning up after the child, the time spent in guided participation is literally irreplaceable. Therefore, rather than asking about time for guided participation, parents are first asked to consider how much time they wish to commit to being a parent. Once this is established, consultants can help parents to prioritize their available parenting time so that it is used primarily for growth and development.

Once general time parameters are established, parents analyze their daily activities to determine which can become opportunities for mental growth. This requires that they structure the activity in a different manner, viewing it as an opportunity for thought and problem solving rather than a chore that needs to get done as quickly as possible. They plan more time for simple events like walking and routine home maintenance. They include the child in things parents have to do and things parents like to do.[39]

During the time they have reserved, parents learn to make sure they are not feeling rushed or pressured. A critical step is learning to stay "in the moment" with

---

39   Initially, when working with children who have exerted unhealthy control by typically refusing invitations to participate in activities with parents, we will select joint activities with little regard for whether the child wishes to be involved or not.

the child. There are three pieces to this. One piece is for parents to recognize that the time they have reserved to guide their child is more valuable than anything else they could be doing. The second is being able to invest all of your attention in the moment and not engage in multi-tasking. This means parents haven't scheduled twenty things that have to be done at the same time (including receiving mobile phone calls while on a walk!). The third is making sure that there is no sense of urgency to complete the tasks they choose to do with the child, like having to get the laundry done in one hour.

People always ask, how much time is enough? It is impossible to answer that question. However you can begin the process by asking yourself how many hours you wish to parent each week. Next, think about how much time you are using in other parental roles (chauffeur, homework assistant, maid, cook, funds allocator, personal shopper) and transfer a significant portion of that into guided participation, even if your other parenting jobs suffer a bit. Guiding your child is God's greatest gift to you as a parent. It is a privilege that should never be relegated to a list of 'one more thing' you have to do in your life.

Remediation, by definition requires focusing on strengthening the child's weakest areas. This means that during guided participation times, children have to be physically, emotionally and cognitively at their highest state of readiness. This can sometimes be deceptive. It is easy to delude oneself into believing that we are just going to wash the car together, or taking a walk and therefore the child doesn't have to be mentally at their best. That would be true if the activity itself were the centerpiece of the parent-child relationship. However, as I have pointed out, in guided participation activities are merely the background frame inside which the real work is done. If parents are succeeding in their guiding roles, this real work will be mentally taxing and require the child to have sufficient mental, physical and emotional resources.

To preserve the child's mental and physical resources, consultants help parents review the child's schedule and eliminate non-essential activities. They also make sure that the time being reserved for guided participation is during periods where both parent and child are physically and cognitively in a state of readiness for new challenges.

Sometimes school programs are well meaning, but do the exact opposite of what is needed. Children may be prompted all day long. The curriculum may emphasize rote learning. Adults may be shadowing the child continually. Sometimes the school can be a major source of stress. Staff may feel like they have to get the child to perform all day. The child may come home exhausted and used up, unable to participate in remediation. Parents learn to evaluate school-related stresses and develop plans to modify unnecessary, or less important school activities and demands, to preserve some of their child's resources for guided participation after school.

QUIETING FAMILY LIFE

Family members are our most valuable resource. They are the irreplaceable components and must take care of themselves. Committing to the RDI Program should not mean cutting out going to the gym. In fact, consultants encourage parents to create stress management plans, where they make sure to take care of themselves. Similarly, consultants emphasize to parents that they have to take care of their marriage. They need to go on dates. They need to have occasional weekends away from the children.

I believe that families must sink or swim together. No member of a family should feel that they are sacrificing their life for the child with ASD. Families where all members are healthy and have a good quality of life are also those that are best able to conduct guided participation.

PROVIDING OPPORTUNITIES

He who refuses to embrace a unique opportunity loses the prize as surely as if he had tried and failed.

—WILLIAM JAMES

In our modern society, we are perpetually feeling pressed for time. We rush through the supermarket, mow the lawn at record speeds while listening to our IPods and drive the car to the carwash, where we read the paper during the five minutes it takes for the car to be ready. On the other hand, traditional daily activities like doing laundry and washing cars may be delegated to someone else. In such circumstances, options for authentic parent-child collaboration may become very limited. Even if daily activities are still part of family life, the stresses of modern life typically lead to these tasks being seen as mildly aversive chores that should be done as quickly as possible.

When I'm asked about the biggest obstacle to succeeding in RDI, I sometimes respond that for many families, the biggest problem is that they no longer *have* a daily life. What I mean by "daily life" is slowing the tempo so that it does not become a daily sprint to the finish line. It means that there is time to slow down and guide the child to rake leaves beside you, or sweep the floor with you, or prepare a meal, without the rush to get it over with and move onto something else. Parents who have forgotten what normal life can be like are helped to remember that everything does not have to be a means to an end.

At the same time, we don't expect everyone to operate in a perfect world. We see many single parents and families where both parents must work hard. We have to accept that this is reality. We don't exclude anyone just because they are not in an ideal situation. Instead we try to find a workable reality for each family.

BEING CREATIVE?

Many parents initially worry that they are not creative enough to be successful guides. I used to provide anxious parents, who claimed they didn't know what to do with their child, with a big list of activities. The list contained thing like vacuuming, play catch, taking walks, playing golf, cleaning out the garage, sweeping the floor, digging a hole and filling it up, shopping, cooking, doing science experiments, estimating things and making maps of your neighborhood. I could go on forever.

The point is you do not have to be creative. When parents begin RDI they do not realize how much mileage can be obtained from a single, mundane household activity. You don't have to do any of the things on my list, but you must have a daily life where there is time to do the small routine things without rushing.

When selecting activities think of things you:

- are already doing as routines
- would like to start doing
- enjoy doing
- need to get done
- can break down into into smaller activities, with authentic pieces you can complete over time (cleaning out the garage)

PERSONAL STRENGTHS AND OBSTACLES

Before leaving the Readiness Stage, we want to make sure that our parental guides-in-training are able to use themselves as a reference point for their eventual success. Therefore, we ask parents to reflect on their personal strengths and limitations as a guide, and establish a baseline from which to track their future progress.

Although we all want to grow and become more competent, each of us has some form of resistance to functioning as an apprentice. For one thing, assuming the apprentice position requires experiencing a temporary sense of being a novice. For some of us this can be quite uncomfortable. We may have had a negative experience when placing ourselves in a similar position in the past. A potential fear related to taking on the apprenticeship role is recognizing that you are working towards giving up your dependence on an expert and assuming responsibility yourself. This can be frightening for someone whose prior experience of parenting has felt less than successful.

MISSION PREVIEWS

When they first begin RDI, many parents are overwhelmed by day-to-day pressure and haven't felt empowered or entitled enough to develop their own vision for themselves, their family and the ASD child. Parents have informed me that they have been told to, "Live one day at a time with your child." One day at a time is a very good strategy for alcoholics. But, it is a terrible one for parents. How can you be a good parent and only live one day at a time? You have to be able to look into the future, at least a little bit, and have a sufficient sense of what matters to you, to provide you with a reference point for progress.

Mission previews help parents develop a representation of a possible realistic future, that they can use as a personal reference point to maintain motivation and evaluate whether they are on the right track. We ask parents to write a short hypothetical narrative, no more than one or two paragraphs, about future periods. We don't want parents to use technical jargon, or to describe some idealistic and unrealistic future. Rather, we want them to construct a hopeful but mundane daily scene that could actually take place, a future personal memory. A good mission preview doesn't describe a child that is cured or perfect, but contains hints of the emergence of a noticeable change.

Mission previews serve as dynamic reference points. We want parents to regularly return to them and see how far they have come. They may realize that they have achieved their mission and have to raise the bar by writing a revised preview, or they may recognize that what they initially believed was an important indicator of change, for example an unusual behavior, is no longer as meaningfully to them as something else, such as the child's new desire to seek out her parents.

Mission Preview Examples

1. *I come home from work and I walk through the door and I notice that there are two baseball gloves and a ball by the door. And I realize that my son was hoping we could play catch together and had gotten the gloves and ball ready for us.*

2. *We are sitting at the dinner table and there are four French fries left. My son looks over to me and says "Dad you haven't had any French fries yet, would you like some?" For the first time he doesn't scarf them all up and he thinks about me.*

3. *Our teenager is lying on the couch when my wife and I return from shopping. I noticed on the way in, that he had not finished mowing the lawn as he had promised to do. I say to him, "The lawn hasn't been mowed*

and you haven't cleaned the kitchen." He replies with, "Chill out Dad. You know I have a big date tonight."

EVALUATING CHILD READINESS

Once parent readiness objectives have been mastered, we focus on clearing away those remaining obstacles that prevent us from evaluating the child's potential for apprenticeship, dynamic learning, and neural integration. Along with working towards minimizing the impact of bio-psycho-social obstacles, we make sure that the child has mastered critical, early developmental foundations. Finally, we construct a balanced, pragmatic plan that addresses "static" knowledge areas, helpful compensations and co-occurring conditions, along with remediation objectives. The plan is dynamic in nature and revised on an ongoing basis as needed. It may change as we evaluate progress, assess new demands and obstacles that may come into the picture and alter priorities.

It goes without saying that having access to an inter-disciplinary team is essential for the work of this stage. Team members may include many different professionals depending on the particular child. For example, Physicians, Speech Pathologists, Psychologists, Family Therapists, Occupational Therapists, Optometrists, Audiologists and Movement Therapists may participate in evaluation and planning.[40]

CLEARING AWAY OBSTACLES TO APPRENTICESHIP

Once RDI Consultants help parents create a quieter, more focused lifestyle, it is easier to evaluate the specific bio-psycho-social obstacles that the child brings to the equation, as well as the child's unique strengths and abilities and obtain a more genuine picture of his or her current functioning and potential. A listing of potential child obstacles is presented in Appendix C.

---

40   Physicians with pediatric, neurological and developmental specialties should always be involved in the process at an early stage.

GETTING BEYOND THE DIAGNOSTIC LABEL

People with ASD are complex, bio-psycho-social beings. I have found that we cannot generalize about intervention from the diagnosis of ASD. We see many children with the same diagnosis who may be on opposite ends of the developmental continuum in a number of areas.

The following examples illustrate these differences. Walk up the stairs with Mark, take three steps and suddenly stop and he will regulate his actions to adjust with you. Outdoors he cannot do this, because he needs the framing of the stairwell. Walking outside provides too much visual noise and he cannot take responsibility for regulating his actions. On the other hand Paul does just as well whether indoors or out. His problems emanate more from the way his mind quickly closes off alternatives when faced with any new situation. Erik talks non-stop. Frank is five and still has not uttered his first words but engages you with his face and eyes. Martin can make basket after basket without missing, while Ana cannot even hold onto a basketball without quickly dropping it. Jack is more flexible than Paul, but he seems flooded with ideas and thoughts that create an overload of internal stimulation, resulting in a flood of actions and verbalization.

Why do children with the same diagnosis have such different problems? The answer is found in the pathway model of ASD. Thinking about ASD as a pathogenetic disorder, with hundreds, if not thousands of possible etiologies, helps us understand how many different physical conditions can combine to disrupt a common pathway of development. Just because these factors contribute to the onset of ASD, by disrupting the Guided Participation Relationship, we should not assume that they fade away after the ASD has emerged. Many of the initial precipitating factors often remain to negatively impact the child's development. I think of them as co-occurring conditions. These problems can at times function as greater obstacles to development than the ASD itself.

LOOKING FURTHER

We have discussed ASD as a neurological disorder in which multiple physical factors disrupt guided participation and thus inhibit dynamic neural and cognitive development. Co-occurring conditions such as seizures, Attention Deficit Disorder, movement disorders and Visual and Auditory Processing Disorders are also neurological in nature and can present significant obstacles.

Many medical problems with non-neural origins can also interfere with the brain's development. A host of biomedical problems like severe allergies, intolerances and immune deficiencies may significantly impede the ability of a child to be available for guidance.

Living with ASD, inevitably results in secondary, reactive problems (conditions that emerge as a result of living with ASD) for both parents and children. Medical and mental health professionals may diagnose a variety of psychiatric and psycho-physiologic conditions, such as Generalized Anxiety Disorder, Obsessive Compulsive Disorder and Attachment Disorder. In addition, numerous pathological defensive reactions may result from children seeking to shut down or avoid uncertainty. It is important for trained professionals to carefully assess these secondary defense mechanisms and determine which may be obstacles to the development of apprenticeship.

Managing medical and psychiatric obstacles requires a close partnership between the RDI family consultant and a physician specializing in ASD, who takes the role of medical manager. The partnership works in several important directions. The RDI Consultant functions as a remediation specialist, guiding day-to-day work with the family, as well as providing the physician with necessary information for medical and psychiatric diagnosis and ongoing care. As medical expert, the physician can diminish the impact of medical conditions, so that the child can more readily take advantage of opportunities for remediation. This is true for parents as well. As I discussed in the last chapter, the crisis of living with an ASD child can create the environment for parental depression and anxiety disorders which may require physician treatment. In addition, a good number of parents may also suffer from symptoms that require care similar to that given to persons with Post Traumatic Stress Disorder.

DEVELOPING A BALANCED PLAN

Designing an intervention plan for an ASD child should involve carefully addressing the unique bio-psycho-social profile of each child. Unfortunately, many of our families start this process believing that the more services they get for their child the better. Sometimes they are presented with a long list of ASD services implying that each of the services on the list is important for any child with the diagnosis. This more is better approach goes against medical reasoning. For example, if you have cancer, the combination of chemotherapy, radiation and surgery is not necessarily better than just chemo alone. In fact it can easily kill you. Adding on more services can be confusing, counter-productive or even harmful. Children may become objectified, as patients requiring a standard menu of services. Parents can become primarily service procurers. Some of the most heavily serviced children we see are clearly suffering from the services themselves. The effort of obtaining, administering and receiving these services may leave families exhausted with few emotional or physical resources for remediation.

I do not want to imply that we should not undertake all necessary interventions. However, we have to make rational decisions based on each child's unique needs. I see children participating in weekly speech therapy with no speech impediments and excellent vocabulary because it is a recommended protocol based on the diagnosis, not the need. The service is prescribed because it is on a list and thus gets checked off. At the same time, I see children who do not realize yet that the sounds they make emanate from them. Clearly these children need intensive work with a Speech Pathologist who understands this type of severe auditory processing disorder.

We hope that parents also consider "staging treatments." For example, one child might have a degree of clumsiness that at some point will be enough of an obstacle to require Occupational Therapy but is not currently interfering with development. Another child might not even realize that his arms are part of his body and require O.T. immediately.

Developmental Foundations

Along with removing obstacles to apprenticeship, we want to make sure that the child has mastered early developmental foundations that are essential to make progress towards apprenticeship. At six months of age Emma was already emotionally attuned to both of her parents. Her ability for pattern recognition in the midst of variation showed that her mind was able to determine central from peripheral patterns—when information was specifically different but one underlying pattern was the same. Even at such a young age, Emma could focus and maintain attention long enough to observe and learn from her parents' actions. Emma was aware of her parents' deliberate nonverbal communication and had begun to show a very early form of self-awareness. Memories of trust were building and she was able to use her parents as her primary reference point. Some ASD children begin RDI with these early developmental foundations in place, while others do not.

Balancing Remediation and Knowledge Acquisition

As I stated earlier, success in life requires an optimal mix of dynamic abilities and static skills. We want to see that children are developing good habits—actions that should be taken on a routine basis without much thought. These are skills like toileting, dressing, brushing your teeth, getting ready for school, preparing for bed, getting from one place to another, following a schedule, respecting limits and doing prescribed chores. These skills do not have to be taught as dynamic abilities. In fact we want them to be rather automatic. In addition, there are many competencies such as reading, writing and mathematics that require a combination of automaticity, discrete knowledge and dynamic processing. The key is to teach these different components in a meaningful, integrated way. As all modern educators agree, there is a place for memorization and drills. But it needs to coincide with the child making dynamic discoveries that allow them to use these static tools in a meaningful way, in the proper context.

Balancing Remediation and Compensation

In an ideal world, children would not face challenges until they were developmentally ready to master them. However, in the real world, ASD children are often placed in school settings where they are developmentally unprepared for the demands they must face on a daily basis. For example, a child may be placed in a classroom which requires abilities for which he may be academically capable but socially and emotionally unprepared. An ASD child may have the intellectual capacity to understand information in a history book related to the Civil War. However he may be far from ready to function collaboratively with his peers, on a group project about the Civil War.

When constructing compensations, we have to be careful not to create an unhealthy degree of dependency or an artificial experience of success. Compensations should not wind up becoming the biggest obstacle to the child's learning to take greater responsibility and develop more dynamic ability. For example, if an aide is employed to assist the child, it is important that she does not wind up over-prompting the child and removing his need to monitor the environment and engage in social referencing.

Examples of Helpful Compensations
1. Teaching sign language to an older child who has not been able to use oral language, despite intensive, appropriate therapeutic efforts.
2. Interactively using a computer with a child with significant auditory processing or working memory problems, to develop the prototype for reciprocal conversation when he is cognitively ready.
3. Providing a student, not yet ready for unstructured peer encounters, with a challenging authentic job under adult guidance during recess.
4. Employing an aide to scaffold a student's gradual ability to monitor his or her classroom environment and employ social referencing when uncertain. The aide would show progress by phasing herself out.
5. Providing a distractible child with headphones or visual screening during independent work time.
6. Allowing a student, with attentional difficulties, or problems rapidly processing language, to engage in an alternative activity during circle time.

Chapter Eleven

Apprenticeship

Parents of a typically developing child never have to worry about whether she is preparing to take on her role as an apprentice. However, when you are guiding an ASD child, you must be prepared to start from the very beginning, if necessary, to evaluate and then develop the foundations for apprenticeship. Equally important is building trust in the guide-apprentice relationship. Parents must help the ASD child construct powerful personal memories of positive engagement with her parental guides. The child must intuitively know that when her world becomes confusing, she can rely on parents as her primary reference point, to provide just enough, but not too much support. Finally, parents must help the child develop memories where she experiences herself as more competent as a result of their shared experiences.

Try to remember times in your life when you functioned as a cognitive apprentice, even if the relationship wasn't a formal one. How did you learn to trust your guide(s)? What feelings did you experience when you were working alongside your guide(s)?

BUILDING A RELATIONSHIP

Guided participation is a very special type of relationship, with a shared goal of developing the mind of one of its members, the apprentice. Guided participation is not primarily about the mastery of specific skills. Successful guides are not concerned with predicting exactly what the apprentice will learn at each moment of the relationship. Rather, they expend their energy creating a productive learning *process*, where they can periodically insert challenges that are just beyond the child's current cognitive grasp and then carefully support the child while he productively struggles for resolution.

When parents learn to observe their process with the child, they focus on what is happening between them and their apprentice, not what they are trying to make happen. They concentrate not on what they are saying, but how they are impacting one another. They learn to focus on how the participants maintain their relationship as they journey within the task, not whether a task is being done correctly. Maintaining a productive process <u>is</u> the task!

GROUNDHOG DAY

When we are involved in guided participation, we don't rush through to get to a specific endpoint. Frantic actions typically spawned by anxiety lack sensitivity to the child and can interfere with the formation of trust. In the movie *Groundhog Day*, Bill Murray plays a callous weatherman trapped in a nightmare scenario where he must indefinitely relive the same day over and over. Initially, his goal is to try, day after day, to seduce a woman who despises him. Because he has all the time in the world, he carefully memorizes all of her preferences and she begins to warm to him. Upon completion of his final script, he has an almost perfect evening with her until at the last moment, things don't go as planned.

He now becomes frantic and over the next days he repeats the same words, takes her to the same places and duplicates the same actions. He loses the process of being *with* another person and allowing a relationship to emerge and thinks only of obtaining his desired endpoint. In his frantic state, he believes that the repetition of incantations he has memorized will get him what he wants. The woman rejects him.

Towards the end of the movie, he gives up his goal of seduction. He becomes a valued member of the town and in the one day, lived over and over, forms real relationships with the townspeople. He has given up his instrumental agenda. This is evident by the change on his face and the way he moves. He has slowed down. He is inviting and genuine with the townspeople. By the end of each day, he has become the most beloved member of the town and in true Hollywood fashion without trying to do so, wins over the woman of his dreams.

When parents are learning to analyze their process, their consultant will often stress that they should watch small segments of videotaped interaction. Two or three minutes of video will contain a great deal of information. This is because process contains redundancy and what happens once continues to recur over and over again. If I am monitoring the state of coordination and making adjustments, I will do this a number of times over a two-minute interval. If I am stopping to process your communication before replying, I will do this again and again.

EMERGENCE

Parents have to carefully plan the challenges they will present to their child at any given time, based upon a careful analysis of the child's zone of proximal development, as well as the child's unique learning style and needs. However, they must also learn to live with a degree of uncertainty in their guiding efforts. They should never try to predict exactly what the child will do with the opportunities they present.

Parents must become comfortable with the idea that the specific products of their relationship will emerge, as long as the process is functioning well. New discoveries will be co-created as guide and apprentice interact. Learning opportunities will become available at unpredictable moments, not necessarily where and when you planned them to occur. If you make a plan that goes something like, "I'm going to do A and then you will do B and then I will do C and then you will do D and then we will achieve E," you will have constructed a scripted, static sequence and destroy any opportunity for the type of cognitive discovery that characterizes guided participation. You will also be very frustrated when you, like the befuddled weatherman, never get to "E."

The concept of emergence is critical because it connotes that the product of the encounter does not exist until it is constructed from the joint efforts of the dyadic pair. I cannot completely predict what either you or I will do in Time 2, from what either of us did in Time 1. This is because a big part of what happens in time 2 is based on our subjective interpretation and emotional reactions to what happened in Time 1. However, we maintain a certain degree of predictability. We can construct a clear focus and a safe laboratory for the child to experiment in. This is because guides set up frameworks that inform us that neither of us will be engaging in actions that lie outside the limits and boundaries the guide has established.

To help parents become more comfortable being participants in an emerging process, I sometimes engage with them in a short experiential exercise. Without offering a word of explanation, I smile, as I place my hand in a bag and take out an unfamiliar, unusual object. Before revealing it to them, I examine it carefully myself with a curious expression on my face. I shift my gaze between parents and the object. After about 20 seconds, I reveal the object and slowly move it towards them.

I stop just short of the object being within their reach and provide us both a chance to gaze at the object again. Finally I reach out to hand it to them. When they grasp it, I do not immediately let go of the object. Rather we find ourselves jointly holding onto the object for about ten more seconds. Then I slowly let go. However, I keep my arm extended and my hand out, not in a gesture that communicates that I want the object back, for example an open palm, but rather to communicate that I am still engaged. If at any time I perceive that either parent is becoming anxious and that the uncertainty has become a bit unproductive, I might self-narrate and offer a bit more context about what I am doing. After a minute or two we discuss our reactions to this exercise.

EMMA'S EMERGENCE

In a previous chapter, I held out a marker to five-month-old Emma without knowing what she would do. I didn't tell her to take it and give it back. If I had already known what she was going to do, there would be no reason to hold it out. The marker was an invitation, something for her to consider. My part was to wait and see how she would respond to my invitation and what would emerge between us.

When I began the encounter with Emma neither of us knew what would happen. Furthermore, we had no stake in any specific outcome. My motivation was to spend time with her and remain curious about what we might do together. Like most adults I couldn't resist engaging her, because my general expectation is that interacting with a five-month-old who appears to be in a good mood is often gratifying.

When I introduced variation by switching from holding the marker in one place for her to grasp, to putting it in my mouth, Emma stopped for a moment and then adjusted her angle of reach and took the marker. From then on our encounter evolved. We created an experience that we would remember as an "us" moment. The next time we met the bond was still there. Six weeks later, I was greeted by a beaming smile of recognition. Such dynamic process moments are the ways that we form powerful personal memories.

When we are involved in any dynamic relationship, we share pieces of ourselves with one another and see what emerges. That is very different from thinking the encounter needs to go a certain way. In my prior example, if Emma hadn't smiled I wouldn't have been disappointed. However, if I had been trying to get the smile, I would have destroyed any opportunity for new discoveries to emerge.

PHILIP'S EMERGENCE

When I first met him at age five, Philip, his father and I began our relationship by engaging in a simple process. Philip exhibited almost no motor planning and hardly any communication. His I.Q. was judged to be quite low. His body was in continual chaotic motion. Philip's father Patrick and I gently put our arms around his shoulders as we all three stood side by side with Philip in the middle. We seated ourselves on the floor against the wall of the playroom. If we had been with a different child with different needs, we might have walked or engaged in some simple movements. However, initially my observation was that once Philip started in motion he became unavailable. Philip was not allowed to run off, but we also didn't try to get him to perform. In fact he chose to remain standing while his father and I sat down on the floor still holding onto Philip's hands and we communicated that this was perfectly fine with us.

I had only one goal for our meeting. I hoped that Philip and his father could experience being physiologically in resonance with one another for as long as possible; that for a brief time their heart rates, respiration and neural functioning could be somewhat attuned. This is the type of neural resonance that you would hope to see emerging with a typical four-week-old infant and parent. It is the most critical foundation for building a trusting relationship. I hoped to establish a safe, quieting baseline for the pair. Once we got there we could see what else they were capable of.

Patrick, Philip and I spent our first 30 minutes sometimes standing but mostly sitting and varying simple movements, like slowly rocking back and forth in a co-regulated, turn-taking manner where father and I would stop and await Philip's action when it was his "turn." At first Philip did not appear happy about this. However, after a few minutes, he seemed to understand that we were not requiring him to perform and he calmed and appeared more settled than anyone had ever seen him before. Simultaneously, Patrick also appeared more relaxed and peaceful. After several minutes, our breathing rates were all in synch. We experienced about 20 minutes of relaxed, regulated physiologic resonance.

What emerged after this initial half hour was miraculous, completely unexpected and unplanned. Philip took on a clear role, coordinated his actions with his father and me and demonstrated social referencing. He was increasingly excitedly engaged with us. Minute by minute, I observed the emergence of Philip's growing attunement, organization, comfort and competence. This provided me the feedback I needed to challenge him by adding small elaborations. The natural role of a guide is to say to himself, "Let's add just a bit more and see what happens," after each small success.

About 45 minutes into our session, the three of us happened to be sitting side by side in chairs with Philip in the middle. Father and I let go of Philip's hands for the first time. He got up, walked to the opposite side of the room, then turned back and very intentionally returned, visually engaging his father as he approached and proceeding to sit on Patrick's lap. I observed that Philip could carefully and deliberately walk away from us and return, with no goal other than to maintain his engagement with us; this type of unprompted deliberate action and motor planning had not been previously observed.

I created an activity to take advantage of my discovery. I extended my hand to invite Philip to walk with me. Philip glanced towards me but did not shift from his seat. I increased my scaffolding. I moved closer to Philip, got down on my knees to be at his level and this time reached over to touch his hand with mine but did not grasp his hands, exert any pressure or communicate any expectation. Philip took my hand but did not immediately get up from the chair. I waited until he used his own muscles to rise from the chair, careful to make sure I did not place any pressure on his arm to prompt him to get up. (It is very important for the child to perceive himself as volitionally taking actions.) We stood and held hands without moving for a few seconds to ensure that Philip was comfortable.

Remaining side-by-side and holding hands, I slowly led us in walking over to the side of the room opposite from Patrick. I made sure that I was never "pulling" on Philip and that we were walking together. Then we turned our backs to Patrick, I counted slowly to ten, turned back towards Patrick and reprised our journey back to him. As Philip neared Patrick, the facial expressions of joy they exchanged was thrilling. After this first walk, Philip needed no practice or help assuming his role. After the first time, I did not have to hold his hand, yet he synchronized his actions with mine and appeared delighted with himself. Each time we walked I added a small variation to our step and to the way we counted. Philip's enthusiasm continued to grow as he did so.

After we engaged in our simple parallel role enactment for a few times, I felt it was time to insert a challenge. The difference between an elaboration and a challenge, is the distinction between adding a new element that is "different-but-same," allowing the child to perceive the ongoing continuity amidst the new variation and inserting an element that alters the problem to one that is "similar-but-different," requiring the child to recognize that the variation has disrupted the continuity of the framework, despite superficial similarities. There was no way I could be certain that my challenge would be successful. However, I knew that Philip and I had successfully shared a framework we could use at any time to regroup and restore our feelings of competence.

I instructed Patrick that this time, while Philip and I turned our backs to count, he was to get up from his chair and hide behind the floor-to-ceiling curtains nearby. Philip and I completed our counting and started to head back. About five paces into our return, Philip suddenly stopped, as he realized that his father was not in the chair where we had left him. This was the moment of uncertainty that I hoped would be productive for Philip. He didn't have to figure out where his father was. He just had to trust me enough to assume I might be able to help him solve the problem. If my intuitive estimation of Philip was correct, this would create an opportunity. If I over-estimated the degree of challenge he could manage, I would start to see avoidance, or distress on Philip's face and would immediately have Patrick emerge from the curtain, so that we could re-group and lessen the degree of challenge, perhaps by having Philip observe his father's movement towards the curtain before turning away with me. And, if that wasn't sufficient, return to our simpler successful framework.

Philip rose to the challenge. As he abruptly stopped, to my delight, he studied the area where his father had been sitting. I had stopped moving and was frozen in place several paces behind him. I wanted to ensure that if Philip wanted my help he would choose to seek it out on his own. Then Philip turned around to gaze at my face, clearly communicating that he wished for me to act as a reference point and help him with his uncertainty. During such critical moments, guides must be careful to provide just enough information, without taking away the child's sense of personal discovery and accomplishment. I pointed to the curtain and said, "He's there." Philip immediately navigated himself to the curtain using excellent motor planning and, to the excitement of all three of us, pulled it back revealing Patrick. They smiled and hugged.

Patrick returned to his seat and Philip proceeded to sit on his lap, his excitement and sense of aliveness quite evident. Philip now shifted his gaze between the curtain, which was the source of his new discovery and therefore an interesting place, and myself, the facilitator of his newfound competence. When he gazed at me, he smiled broadly, demonstrating no anxiety. I held out my hand for Philip. This time he took more initiative. Philip immediately locked his attention onto me, smiled, got up, moved towards me, took my hand and waited for me to get up.

This time I instructed Patrick to hide on the other side of the curtain, far enough away so that if Philip returned to the last place he looked, he would not be able to locate his father. We walked away, did some variation of our ten count and headed back. Once again I deliberately remained several paces behind Philip. He immediately noticed that his father was not seated. However, this time he did not stop to study at the same place he had before. He had learned from the last time that Patrick might or might not be in his chair. Rather, Philip carefully maneuvered to the curtain and looked for his father at the place where he had previously found him. Only when he pulled back the curtain and found no father, did he stop to study and consider.

Once again Philip's face showed no anxiety or distress. Once again Philip studied the situation for a moment, then turned to shift his gaze to me and waited. I pointed to the other side of the curtain and said, "You can find him." Philip immediately walked to the other side, pulled aside the curtain and engaged in an excited reunion with his father.

Observing this episode without having access to my thoughts, one might assume that I had planned the entire event right from the beginning. However, I assure you that this was not so. I believe that if I had set out with this ambitious goal in mind, the entire hour would have been an anxiety-provoking failure. Instead, my initial goals were simple and largely achieved by setting up a calm organized process during the first 20 minutes we spent together. Acting as a guide, I took advantage of the emerging opportunities presented by Philip's growing competence and we achieved results that none of us, including Philip, would have imagined an hour before.

EXPERIENCE SHARING COMMUNICATION

Communication in the Readiness Stage was aimed mainly to quiet the environment and create a space for future success. In the Apprentice Stage, parents learn to communicate in a more pro-active manner to foster reciprocal experience sharing and thoughtfulness.

Now we construct prototypes for the unique process of human communication. To create these prototypes we must honor the incredible complexity of the process, but at the same time begin with simple versions and provide the child sufficient time to think in a more integrated manner.

The starting point for human communication is understanding that most of your communication has little to do with winning or losing, or getting it right or wrong. Rather, we spend the bulk of our communicative lives establishing and maintaining mental bridges, where we can share different aspects of our subjective experience. These are fragile bridges that require ongoing maintenance and frequent rebuilding. Nonetheless, they are essential, for they are the only means we have of learning about who we are and becoming more than just ourselves. In the Apprentice Stage, parent's initial communication objective is to create an environment where the process of "keeping the ball in play" is the norm for everyday life.[41]

DENNIS KEEPS THE BALL IN PLAY

Dennis is a 13-year-old boy with autism who was involved for many years in discrete, static learning programs. When he turned 13, his parents were told that there wasn't much more that could be done other than continuing attempts, meeting with little success, to teach social skills and help him develop friendships. Dennis had always been an easy child who didn't cause problems or bother anyone. He was happy to watch TV and play with his computer for hours on end.

---

41   Communication must sometimes be a means to an end. We must make sure that the child is developing instrumental communication ability alongside experience sharing. However, we have not encountered a single case, among the thousands of children we have seen, where experience sharing has developed without its instrumental counterpart, whereas the opposite is nearly always the case without RDI or a similar intervention.

Dennis' parents sent me two video clips. One clip represented Dennis prior to RDI. The second was a brief segment of Dennis with his mother several months after beginning RDI. In the first clip, Dennis is sitting in front of his computer flapping his hands. He shifts attention to see what his mother is doing. Lois, his mother, tells him she is setting up a video camera. He wonders why the camera is there. He receives an answer and resumes his computer game.

The next clip is a sad moment for me. The family is on a camping trip. Everyone, except for Dennis, has a task of preparing things like chopping wood and putting up the tent. The expectation for him is only that he will stay out of trouble. As long as Dennis appears content walking back and forth on a log, oblivious to the hard work being done by his father, mother and sister, the rest of the family is satisfied.

The video clip shifts to a restaurant where Dennis is seated next to his mother. Dennis makes a statement to Lois about going to a farm where he milked a cow. Lois responds, "Was it fun? What did the cow say?" He replies with, "Moo." Lois begins a barrage of questions starting with, "Whose farm was it?" Dennis shows no emotion but begins to twirl her hair. She continues with, "Was it a farm in your head?" Dennis has no time to think and the rapidity of expected responses is tiring him. He puts his hand over his ears, something he does when he is anxious, temporarily avoiding, but not completely withdrawing from interaction. He recovers and asks, "Where's dad?" (Dad tends to talk much less.) Lois responds with, "I don't know. Where is he?" Her attempts at communication have become so stressful for her that Lois is unaware she has answered his rational questions with an irrational additional question of her own. Communication is a source of great anxiety for both of them.

Lois reports that the final part of the first clip represents a transforming moment for her. In this scene, mother and son are in the street, both walking towards school, with Dennis walking about 30 paces ahead. Lois decides she would like Dennis to walk beside her. She says, "Hey Dennis, you want to walk with me?" Dennis takes off and starts running down the street.

The second clip begins about two months after they began RDI. Dennis and Lois have begun to explore a new type of communication. The clip starts with Lois and Dennis walking side-by-side in the street, practicing co-regulation by tossing a ball back and forth as they head towards school. Lois is using the phrase "keep the ball in play" to remind herself what the focus is on the process and not the product. Although the selection of a lesson phrase is usually a metaphor, rather than a specific description, in this case she uses the phrase literally. Tossing the ball back and forth as he walks with Lois is easy for Dennis, who has good visual-motor coordination and it does not absorb his attentional resources.

Lois varies each of their tosses. Sometimes the ball goes high in the air and sometimes it is bounced on the ground. Sometimes her throw is accurate and other times Dennis must reach to get it. There are times when each of them drops the ball. On one occasion when Dennis drops the ball, you can see that Lois is unsure whether he will take responsibility to retrieve it. But, before she can say or do anything, he is off to retrieve the ball, as if it were just the routine thing to do.

There is no talking between them. I am not surprised. Dennis has plenty of words but has, unfortunately over the years, learned to mentally link words with performance—right or wrong answers—a source of anxiety for him. However, their facial and vocal exchanges are rich in experience sharing.

The most amazing thing about the scene is the animation on both of their faces. Dennis is smiling and laughing, clearly perceiving himself as an active, competent participant. There is no evidence of the avoidance observed earlier. He is making sure to stay parallel to Lois, but not so close as to make it boring. Remembering the moment while watching the video with me, Lois tears up and says, "This is the moment that I knew I had my son back."

They reach the end of their quiet street and come to a busy intersection. Like a mother would do with a much younger boy, Lois starts to take Dennis' hand but instead stops herself and waits. Dennis moves close to her and locks his arm around hers, a more mature way of physically connecting. He turns to talk to her. I cannot hear what they are saying, but their non-verbal communication is animated and engaging.

CHECKING THE LINES OF COMMUNICATION

One of the earliest uniquely human discoveries about communication is realizing that keeping the ball in play is quite difficult because communication is fraught with misunderstanding; what we and our partners initially interpret may not accurately reflect our communicative intentions. This early discovery fosters the motivation for the child to develop a number of dynamic abilities designed to minimize misunderstanding.

A critical starting point is learning to continually monitor and reference ourselves and our partners in a manner that does not disrupt the flow of our communication. Later children must learn to process information from different non-verbal channels that provide the context for what is said, along with taking into account the history of the relationship, the current setting and the tasks they are involved with.

If communication is working because a more capable partner is compensating to make it work, the child will never learn to be competent and take his share of communicative responsibility. On the other hand, if we practice communication as if people always follow rules, then the child will never understand the true nature of social engagement—that the rules are the exceptions. Social encounters only work through our implicit agreement to allow one another to go off course and then to make adjustments to get back, only to go off course again. The most important skills of communication are the integration of monitoring our mutual comprehension, making small adjustments and repairing inevitable breakdowns.

START VISUAL

The visual channel defines communication as a monitoring and evaluating process. Vision is an active modality. Babies are experts at visual communication many months before they talk or understand what is being said. Typically developing infants learn that if they are going to be competent in a communication environment, they cannot wait for communication to come to them. Rather, they must continually visually check the field.

By six months of age, typically developing infants have learned to dynamically shift their attention and are taking responsibility for checking to see what is going on around them. By fifteen months of age, typical infants are carefully checking to see whether adults are attending to what the infant has pointed out for them. If he or she perceives a mismatch, a not-yet-talking infant will communicate with gestures and vocalizations to repair the temporary breakdown.

Auditory communication is more dangerous as a starting point for communication because the child can quickly become dependent on letting someone else do the monitoring and adjusting for him. A child with autism who has been taught sophisticated speech without learning to visually monitor the world in which he lives will continue to fail as a communicator over the course of his life. We often see ASD children who are highly verbal and also completely oblivious to the impact of their communication. Because they have no visual foundation for communication, they "throw language out" until they receive their desired response, or sufficiently irritate someone.

As I discussed in the last chapter, to help children who have learned to over-relay on speech, we temporarily reduce language-processing demands to give their brains a chance to develop visual monitoring and checking. This is hard work because it is difficult to retrain a brain that may have been taught to ignore rather than seek out this information. The resistance, however, does not last forever and the benefits are well worth the time it takes to get through it.

MULTIPLE CHANNELS

As I discussed in earlier chapters, human communication requires the synthesis of multiple channels of information through the formation of a complex, highly integrated neural pathway. In order to develop this sophisticated network, infant brains first construct the neural pathway for each channel separately and then gradually combine channels to form single, integrated informational packets. In RDI we recapitulate this natural developmental process, by making sure we focus on each communication channel, before combining channels. We also take apart the receptive and expressive parts of the communication process and then reintegrate them.

Developing new neural pathways for communication requires a good deal of time and consistency. Everyone with a significant involvement with the child should participate, so as not to undermine the process. The child must realize that these new channels of communication are valuable and a permanent part of his real world, not a gimmick or temporary technique. (They should NEVER become associated with specific activities, settings or persons.) Guides also make sure that the use of non-verbal communication is reciprocal. Therefore, during times when only certain channels are open they make sure that not only do they use only those channels, but that the child realizes that others can only receive those channels as well.

Steps in developing multi-channel communication:
- Construct simple dialogues emphasizing one channel at a time.[42]
- Use each channel for different functions (e.g. co-regulation, emotion sharing, sharing perceptions).
- Develop channels in simply, slowly-paced dialogues where both communicators can feel competent.
- Gradually integrate different channels, as you move from one modality to another (facial/prosodic, or prosodic/gestural).

LANGUAGE

Language is a critical communication channel. However, it is a channel that has to be developed carefully or else it becomes mindless speech, disconnected from careful thought, emotion and meaning. A second danger is that language can come to dominate neural communication processing and strangle the integrated development of multiple communication channels.

---

42   It is not always possible to keep all other channels completely neutral in order to use only one channel. For example, it would be quite strange to use vocal prosody without some form of facial communication. The goal in such cases is to emphasize a channel so the child perceives that it is primary.

In the Apprentice Stage, parents learn to minimize language use until they are certain that the child is actively processing and deliberately expressing himself with these other communication channels.[43] Ideally, rather than dominating neural development, language is deployed as yet another modality, alongside the rich non-verbal dialogues that have already been developed.

Guides demonstrate that each member's language is worth thinking about. Family members learn to allow one another time to process each other's language. They set clear limits in regards to disrespectful, annoying and unproductive language use. Parents learn to use language to enhance and elaborate what they are doing together. For example, language becomes a tool for subjective appraisal, to elaborate on the shared meaning of what is happening:

"Ooh shiny."

"Oh, it's pointy."

"Smells funny."

"Uhm, tastes good!"

We each look out a different window and take turns spotting vehicles of a certain kind:

"I see red trucks."

"Where?"

"There!"

"I can't see it!"

"There!"

"Okay, I see a red truck."

Questions reflect genuine curiosity, as parents are clear that they do not require any specific response. Rather, questions are opportunities for the parent to understand the child's subjective experience, whatever it may be.

"Which way should we go?"

---

43   The word deliberate provides an important distinction. ASD children can be expressive without having any command whatsoever of non verbal communication channels.

"What are you going to do next?"

Picture a parent blowing up a balloon asking, "Should I keep blowing?" This question reflects what they are doing together at the moment. Ther is no right or wrong answer.

INTERNAL AND EXTERNAL DIALOGUES

Another unique attribute of human communication is our discovery that each of us transacts an internal dialogue in parallel with external communication. In fact, even two-year-olds learn to communicate precisely because they wish to make an impact on their partner's subjective, internal world.

We are quite put off if we perceive that our partners are talking without referencing their internal dialogue. Their speech takes on an impulsive or scripted manner, or we feel they are just saying what they believe we wish to hear. We want to know that our communication triggers new associations in our partners' internal world. What feelings do you experience when I share something important with you? What memories do we recall? Did I have an unexpected impact on you?

Even in its most prototypical form, juggling our inner and outer worlds is no easy task. Here is an over-simplified analysis of what is required to engage in a very elementary dialogue: First, I have to distinguish between the subjective element of "you" that you are trying to share and the objective information that you may be providing. Then, I must shift from "you" to "me." I have to dredge down to my inner self and find out my subjective reaction to your communication. Finally, I must formulate this "me" in a manner that I hope will make sense to you and will in some manner fit with the piece of "you" that you have provided.

As a starting point, parents learn to strategically use small amounts of simple, slow, deliberate language and provide large chunks of time to think about their replies. They carefully differentiate self-talk from communicating with their partner to demonstrate that there is an internal process that precedes expressing oneself. They share pieces of their inner subjective selves, based on the child's capability of understanding and motivation to learn about their partner. They learn to dramatically slow down, to create space for the complex process that is gradually being elaborated. Similarly, they learn to gently stop the apprentice from responding too quickly and to be selectively responsive to verbalizations that have no relation to the ongoing process.

BUILDING COLLABORATION

The work of guided participation occurs as guides and their apprentices participate in numerous collaborations throughout the day. Collaborations are interactions in which the guide and apprentice strive to coordinate their actions, thoughts and ideas towards some common goal.

Genuine human collaboration requires participants to carry out several processes in rapid succession. They must maintain a joint focus with partners toward a shared goal. They must monitor the state of their coordination with partners and make sure that their roles remain synchronized. A third component is attending to self-regulation, which requires monitoring one's own actions. Finally, participants in a collaboration must value the integration of their actions, perceptions and positive emotional states as critical in goal attainment (You + Me = Us, then Us = Goal).

Even the simplest collaborations requires a level of neural integration that many ASD children do not initially possess. We often construct eventual collaborative processing ability and motivation by beginning with simple prototypes and gradually adding complexity and greater demand for integrated functioning.

CO-REGULATORY TURN-TAKING

In my previous illustration, Philip, Patrick and I spent our first 30 minutes together participating in co-regulatory turn-taking without specified roles or goals. This is the earliest prototype for future collaborations. There is no endpoint that must be achieved. There is no right or wrong performance and no risk of the wrong move. There is no need to check whether your actions are sufficiently synchronized with your partners'. Your actions remain safely within known parameters and clear limits. This is the way we initially built trust with Philip and thousands of other children.[44]

The shared goal is simply to remain engaged. The shared role is for each of us to take our turn, making sure we do not imitate the other person, or act in a destructive or abusive manner. By framing our interaction as turn-taking, we artificially slow down and make sequential a process that typically occurs in a much more integrated, fluid manner. We each take a simple, but unannounced action and then stop to see how our partner responds.[45] The frame could not be simpler. We remain connected and engaged. Each of us takes an action and then pauses in anticipation of how our partner will respond. From an evaluation standpoint, this period of anticipation is the most important part of the interaction. It signifies that the child is taking her action deliberately to see what her partner is going to do with it, how they will respond.

At the beginning, Philip did not take his actions in anticipation of how we would respond. However, after about five minutes he caught on. We were standing, side-by-side holding hands with Philip between the two adults. It was my turn. I decided to sit. Patrick sat as well. Philip remained standing. Initially, he appeared to be waiting to see if we would pull him down to be with us. When we didn't, he continued standing, but began to smile and gaze between his father and myself to see how he would react to the turn he had just taken (deliberately standing still can clearly be an example of taking a turn, if it is perceived that way by the participants).

Co-regulatory turn-taking is not like taking turns on a slide or taking your turn while playing a board game. Because it is a dynamic process, albeit a rudimentary one, it contains a very simple structure and clear limits, coupled with a bit of uncertainty and ongoing variation. Neither of us knows exactly what the other will do next. Parents clearly communicate that they do not expect any specific performance from the child. However, at the same time parents communicate that the child will

---

44   Some children do not require starting at this beginning level. For them we may initiate relationship development with more sophisticated forms of coordination or collaboration activities.

45   Guides make sure that their actions are not predictable, or controlled by the child. On the other hand, their actions should be ones that are within the child's experience. This is not the time for creativity.

not be in control of their joint actions.[46] Moreover, while they are not controlling the child's specific choice of action during their turn, they do insist that he remain within the limits the parent has established. Initially, as with Philip, who had a very limited zone of connection, parents may need to maintain physical contact, like holding hands, locking arms or putting hands around shoulders.

START WITH TACTILE/KINESTHETIC

In the earliest co-regulatory encounters, we want parent and child to experience the tactile and kinesthetic feel of moving together in a regulated way. As in the case of Philip and Patrick, our goal is to establish a state of physiologic resonance. We would like to see heart rates and breathing become more attuned. To accomplish this, we may initially deemphasize visual and auditory communication and may even purposefully avoid gaze if eye contact is distracting, or heightens the child's anxiety. Instead, we want to emphasize the feel of making physical contact and moving together. Movements needn't fit a specific sequence or pattern, but they should still feel connected, similar to the "marker" episode with Emma.

ADDITIONAL SCAFFOLDING

When parents begin co-regulatory turn-taking with their ASD child, there is a chance that the child will initially refuse to participate, or engage in some form of more indirect resistance. Some parents will require additional scaffolding from their consultant to help them calmly persist. Part of the scaffolding is to initially predict for parents that their child might resist and that this is a normal occurrence.

If the consultant believes that even more support is needed, he or she can begin by having parents practice regulated turn-taking with the consultant, with each parent taking on both guide and apprentice roles. Next parents may enact regulatory turn-taking with one another, again assuming both roles. The consultant may also request parents to practice with a typically developing child, before assuming the role of guide with their ASD child. From this example, it is possible to see how

---

46   Parts of this new relationship should already have been achieved during the Readiness Stage.

scaffolding supports parents as the process slowly unfolds for them. Following initial success, if later breakdowns occur with the ASD child, parents are less likely to personalize them and react in ways that make the breakdown worse.

Limited Response Variation

Some parents may benefit when we provide additional framing and scaffolding to their initial co-regulatory actions with their child. For those situations we teach a method we refer to as Limited Response Variation (LRV).

We provide parents with a small deck of 30 cards. There are six types of cards randomly placed in the deck, each containing a different action: I move with you, I move against you, I move sideways, I move up, I move down, I move around.

Parents can practice with one another first. The parent in the guide role picks a card, takes the action and waits. After parents have memorized the options we eliminate the cards. When parents are ready to practice with their child, they take their actions in a slow deliberate manner, including an enforced pause between turns to provide the child time to process and respond. If the child has difficulty perceiving the contingency when all six variations are employed, the number can be reduced to three and then gradually built back up to six.

When parents get a feel for co-regulation it can seem like second nature. However, because it first emerges as a conscious, mindful act, it may help to picture how it would develop. Visualize the following in slow motion, pausing between each action:

I move my arm up and raise both of our arms. You move our arms to the side. I hold our arms in place while our bodies sway, You move our arms down to our sides. I turn part-way away from you. You move closer to me. I slowly sink to the floor, leaving you standing. You remain standing. I feel tension in my arm. I rise up and take both of your hands. You twirl us slowly in a circle. As a consultant, participating in such a role-play, I can provide additional scaffolding by narrating my thought process out loud.

LEGITIMATE ROLES

Once we get past the initial fear of co-participation, parents re-introduce real world activities, where both participants are provided with simple, but clear and legitimate roles that must be synchronized. Coordination occurs first in a sequential manner (I hand a piece of laundry to you and you place it in the washer) and then later in a simultaneous manner (we are going to jump at the same time, so we have to time our movements so they occur together). The child's roles have to be legitimate, as well as requiring mindful thought.

While they master role-coordination, children learn to respect and help maintain common frameworks. They experience themselves as functioning through joint efforts with one guide at maintaining an "us" unit.

As quickly as possible we want the child to perceive himself as a contributor in enhancing variations to activity frameworks, rather than just a passive recipient. Parents teach the child to distinguish between variations that enhance the common framework and those that disrupt it. To accomplish this, we begin with frameworks that are easier than those we would choose if the child were only going to be a recipient of parental variations. We may also limit variation choices to two or three, so that the selection does not create anxiety.

Another part of role-coordination entails learning to take on both parallel and complementary roles. Parallel roles refer to activities where we remain synchronized while taking essentially the same action, like walking down the street together. Complementary roles occur during activities where we each take a distinctly different role, for example either sweeper or dustpan holder, and those different roles must be synchronized at a specific time or place.[47]

The most complex roles require simultaneous, continuous role-coordination. These are interactions where participants must focus on the fluid, ongoing synchronization of their designated roles, performed amidst ongoing variation. A common

---

47   Working with complementary roles helps prevent the child's dependence on automatic imitation and a tendency towards matching rather than thoughtfully evaluating and adjusting his actions to maintain coordination.

example is remaining side-by-side while walking together or even the simplest form of conversation.

Attention has to shift from oneself to one's partner, from self-regulation, to self-other regulation on a continuous basis. The critical moment in the process occurs during times when participants aren't quite synchronized. This is the moment that has the most potential for new learning and growth. During these moments, parents can gradually increase the child's responsibility to monitor and adjust his actions, to regain temporarily lost social coordination.

MEANINGFUL ACTIVITIES

To be useful, an activity must have some subjective meaning for both parent and apprentice. The meaning may not be the same for both. However, the child must recognize that something real has to get done and that he is a legitimate, if not central, part in getting it done. Meaning does not imply enjoyment or fun.[48] Feeling competent can create a more powerful payoff than laughter, a lesson we learned from adults with ASD. Nevertheless, even though an activity might be within the arena of work, doesn't mean that it cannot be approached in a playful manner.

For activities to be meaningful to the child, he must be provided with an authentic role. He must recognize that if he doesn't take his role seriously, nobody else will take over for him and the task will fail. I discussed the case earlier of one of our families who introduced a laundry activity to their child. Lilly, Ben's mother began by creating parallel roles. Lilly wanted her and her son to carry the basket to the laundry room together. The problem emerged when Lilly approached Ben with an empty laundry basket. He didn't budge, just lay on the bed staring directly at his mother, with a sort of confused look on his face while she repeated her request for help in carrying the laundry.

Lilly thought the problem might be caused by her being outside of Ben's zone of connection and therefore Ben might not feel connected to her at that distance.

---

48 Digging a ditch to replace a sewer line, an RDI project undertaken recently by a father and son was meaningful, but not necessarily fun.

However, even when Lilly approached closer and repeated her request within Ben's zone of connection, he remained unresponsive. Confused, Lilly sent the video clip to her consultant. She received the following reply, "How would you react if someone acted like they needed your help to carry an empty laundry basket?"

A parent may encounter a similar reaction if a child is asked to engage as an apprentice in an activity that he has already mastered and can do independently. Because the role of apprentice is not authentic, the child may become distrustful and perplexed by the loss of independence and autonomy.

Role actions should be constructed so that the child can initially manage them without fear of failure. However, there has to be sufficient difficulty so that the child can feel a sense of accomplishment in successfully carrying out his role. In a previous example, I related the story of my neighbor and his three-year-old son's regular routine of moving the garbage to the curb. Each had a wagon that was his size and each also had a correctly sized garbage bag to place in the wagon and carry to the curb. There was a real legitimate responsibility for each person, within the limits of his ability. Finally, roles must involve some degree of mindfulness. Many roles can quickly become mindless (e.g. I hand you the item of clothing and you place it into the washer), if variations and additional mental complexity are not a constant option.

Our families have constructed a multitude of simple role-coordination frameworks, with many revolving around daily chores and routines, like making beds, doing laundry, washing the car and taking out the garbage. While each activity is different, they retain common role relationships. For example, both carrying laundry baskets and garbage cans together provide the child the opportunity to discover underlying continuities amidst many different superficial differences and variations.

The following are a few of the thousands of ways our families work on role-coordination:

Piano Variations: We are sitting side-by-side at the piano. Each of us can only play on three black keys. We take turns, you play one and I play one key at a time. We can choose which of our three keys to play.

Hats on, Hats off: Provide each person with a hat. Stand side-by-side in front of a mirror. Start with "Do what I do" but do not repeat a specific sequence. The child should not be able to predict when the hat is placed on and off. There is a possibility for co-variation if a child remains within the framework.

Elaboration: Hat on my head or on your head.

Elaboration: Pick from several hats.

Doing Laundry: We are doing laundry. I take the clothes from the basket, give them to you and you place them in the washer. To keep this from becoming mindless or boring, try some of the following:

- Vary placement of your hands in relation to the child when giving him a piece of laundry.
- Reach over in slow motion, even slower, then faster etc.
- Change roles from giver –taker to taker-giver. Fluidly enact changes from complementary to parallel roles. Begin with giver-taker and change to getting laundry from the basket and placing it in the washer in a coordinated manner at the same time.
- Hand part of the clothing item to your partner, but don't let go.
- Create a human barrier your partner must navigate to get more laundry items.
- Secretly place non-laundry items in the basket.

OBSERVATION AND ANALYSIS

The final set of apprenticeship objectives train parents to be a good observers and analysts of their guided participation process.

There are a number of tools and techniques consultants use to help parents become better observers and analysts. For example, consultants provide video clips contributed by parents who have already mastered a particular objective. Additionally, consultants may provide parents with small snippets of clips the parent had uploaded, which illustrate critical moments that the consultant wants the parent to pay particular attention to. Finally, parents are encouraged to engage in regular journaling, to reflect on their own progress and obstacles.

OBSERVING TYPICAL CHILDREN

Parents whose only experience is with an ASD child have difficulty fully understanding the degree of ability and responsibility even a very young, typically developing child takes in order to maintain role-coordination and mutual communicative comprehension. We encourage parents to obtain experience with typically developing children under the age of 30 months. Most people have no trouble finding infants and toddlers to spend time with. If none of your friends have young children, we recommend that you volunteer at a local church, synagogue, temple, or mosque. Try to find time when you are just expected to hang out with the children. For example, my wife Rachelle has worked hard to get a low-level volunteer position at her church. She is the substitute assistant of her church's one-year-old Sunday school program. She vehemently fends off any opportunities for promotion.

PACING

True learning takes time: time to wonder, time to pause, time to look closely, time to share, and time to pay attention to what is most important.

—CHIP WOOD

Typically developing children learn to employ sophisticated top-down neural processing centers, like the pre-frontal cortex to appraise, evaluate, analyze and reflect. However, the high-level centers involved in top-down processing, require more time to work efficiently, compared to lower-level sensory processing centers related to discrete associational neural networks.

When I moved the marker toward five-month-old Emma, I did so in little steps. I slowly inched the marker towards her and then stopped for a brief moment before moving it another few inches closer. I did this until it was within her reach and then I stopped and waited, saying and doing nothing.

In the example above, I provided Emma with top-down processing time as well as scaffolding my actions to give her the opportunity. If I had moved at a faster pace, she still may have still been able to grasp and drop the object, but she would have been deprived the time to study, consider, or wonder about what was happening, including thinking about the consequences of her actions. If we act and communicate at a fast pace we shouldn't be surprised if a child becomes trained to provide automatic rote, scripted, or impulsive responses.

During this phase, parents learn to be deliberate and strategic in their use of space, time, speed and action. The right pace allows us both to act and feel competent. Guides and apprentices are able to stop to think and process and there is less emphasis on performance. However, we want the guide's pacing to be strategic and customized to the particular child and the circumstances. For example, if I were to approach an older, more competent child in the extremely slow way I approached Emma, it would make no sense and the child would find it boring.

CRITICAL MOMENTS

The most important moments in any activity are when the apprentice is faced with productive uncertainty and recognizes the need to stop, consider and study the situation. Parents learn that any time they select an activity and set up roles, they have to determine the points where they will introduce a challenge and hope that the child will experience the challenge productively. As a guide's thinking process might sound like this, "Where in this activity will I create a challenge, based on the specific dynamic lesson we are currently addressing? At what point will the child experience some degree of productive uncertainty? What sorts of things is the child supposed to be thinking about at this time? How will this challenge stretch her mind?"

Before parents engage in any activity, they should be able to anticipate how they will set up moments that will be challenging for the child and when those moments are most likely to occur. That is what it means to operate in the zone of proximal development.[49]

49   The prior section might seem to contradict my earlier statements about emergence. This is not the case. Guides have to live with the duality, that though they thoughtfully emplace challenges in their activities, they cannot predict or become overly invested in whether the challenge will produce the anticipated result.

INTERNAL EXPERIENCE

Emergent process is not just about what happens between people. We want to consider the process that goes on within our mind. It is important for parents to try and analyze their child's inner experience. For example, if you were the apprentice, would you feel passive and out-of-control, just holding onto someone while they did all the work, or would you feel like an active, competent, junior co-participant?

We cannot read people's minds to know what they are thinking. But we can observe where and how they focus their attention. Additionally, we can determine their level of engagement through their facial expressions and posture. An important way we determine whether a child is involved in a dynamic thinking process is by observing what we refer to as dynamic gaze. How fluid and meaningful, rather than static or random, is their attentional process? How well does their gaze fit the context, or the situational requirements? Parents are taught to observe their child's gaze, to determine how the child is expending his attentional resources.

Dynamic gaze is quite different from making eye contact. When Philip in an earlier example, alternated his gaze between the curtain, where he had made his recent discovery and me, the person who guided him to succeed, he was exhibiting a rudimentary form of dynamic gaze. Learning to make eye contact doesn't tell you when you should gaze at my face, or what to do with the information that you see, or how to integrate that information with communication from other channels. Eye contact, taught in a scripted manner, bypasses the limbic system and the frontal cortex. I can attest to this from my own personal experience. I have ADD and growing up I was one of the "dreamy" ones. However, I always received A's in conduct, because I taught myself to make eye contact with my teachers while I was spacing out. I was never "there." However, they rarely caught me.

A child trained to make eye contact has learned to be a static processor.[50] There is a learned mindlessness resulting from his training. Imagine the negative consequences of continuing to insist that a child keep his attention on your face, even though he doesn't know how to productively use the information you are sending and there is more important information in other parts of the setting.

---

50   Eye contact, taught in a scripted manner, bypasses the frontal cortex and limbic system.

Philip has Dynamic Attention

When Philip began RDI he seemed oblivious to the world around him. His most frequent activity was to aimlessly wander off, or spin around. Six months into his RDI program, things were quite different. His vocabulary was approximately ten words, but at this point the number of words he knew was irrelevant. He now communicated in a rich, animated, non-verbal manner. Additionally, he had learned about coordinating himself with others. I want to narrate an activity that the pair was doing at the time.

Philip and his mother Kendra are jumping towards each other, using lines she has taped onto the floor as markers to tell them where to jump next. Even though Kendra once believed that her son was severely distractible, she has correctly chosen to practice this task in their den, which is, like most normal family rooms, moderately chaotic, with books and other objects strewn around. The family dog is outside the glass doors leading to the backyard, barking loudly, trying in vain to get back in.

Six months earlier, Philip's attention would have been everywhere and nowhere. However, now the visual or auditory noise seems to have little if any negative impact. After each successfully timed jump, Philip immediately shifts his gaze to his own body. He makes sure he is steady when he lands and that he has placed his feet close enough to the next line marker. He even tugs up his pants legs to make sure he doesn't trip on them. As soon as this is accomplished, Philip shifts his gaze back to meet his mother's gaze. He looks for information to determine when she is ready to jump again, so he can synchronize his actions with hers. When they finally meet in the middle, Kendra tickles Philip and he laughs for a moment before escaping her grasp and returning to his starting place. Philip's most animated smile can be seen when he successfully regulates his actions. His real payoff emanates from feelings of competence, not sensory stimulation.

REGULATORY BREAKDOWNS

The only way a child ever appreciates the effort it takes to remain coordinated with another person, is to experience moments when coordination breaks down and must be carefully reconstructed. Without this experience, along with experiencing the payoffs for successful coordination, it would not be possible to develop the motivation needed to become proficient in monitoring, making adjustments and repairing the frequent inevitable breakdowns in our interaction and communication.

We want parents to provide many opportunities for the child to notice that he is off course and therefore must make an adjustment. Parents learn to communicate so that the apprentice perceives these moments as challenging opportunities and not failures. They become proficient, not only in setting up regulatory and repair moments, but in observing what happens when these off course moments occur naturally. Parents' initial response to an interactive breakdown should be to observe it and do nothing. This means waiting to see if the child will repair the interaction and return. If this does not occur, the parent can carefully institute a re-organization or re-grouping strategy that returns the child to a framework associated in the past with success and competence. Once this regrouping takes place, parents can return to more challenging areas more rife with potential for losing coordination, possibly with slightly increased framing or scaffolding.

REGULATORY SUCCESS

Parents learn to recognize success along with breakdowns. There are three important considerations related to observing a process that is working well. The first is to be aware of what success is and when it is occurring. When you are involved in an ongoing process, you do not have a specific product you can use to gauge success. Parents learn to perceive that the continuation of a productive process itself is the hallmark of success. One motto we have when a process is successfully running is, "Don't mess with success." However, we find that parent's who are not aware of their process goal, may inadvertently disrupt a successful process, by adding too much variation without monitoring the child's inability to manage it, or stopping a process just as it is about to become productive.

The second consideration is, to some degree, always in conflict with the first. It requires parents to continue to elaborate the process. Our second motto is that, "Like a shark the Guided Participation Relationship must keep moving or it will die." Novelty and variation make life worthwhile. From the very beginning, dynamic intelligence is based upon the child learning that their world is full of differences but that underlying these differences are continuous patterns that remain unchanged. We expect parents, as soon as they notice success, to add just enough new variation and challenge to maintain a state of active mindfulness in the child. The failure to do so results in static, repetitive and mindless interactions.

Finally, parents have to be aware of their emotional responses while participating with their child. When you are involved in a relationship, you experience success on an emotional, not a purely rational, level. For example, with Emma, I could feel that something had been established between us. We were relating in a smooth way and fully engaged. Our attentional resources were involved in figuring out how to maintain our interaction.

Feedback to Kendra

In my prior example, Kendra had a hard time noticing Philip's success. Philip was taking responsibility for regulating his own actions with hers Philip was using dynamic rather than static attention. He was rapidly shifting attention between self-regulation and co-regulation. There was no rule, or prompt advising him where to look and what to do. He had taken over responsibility for evaluating how and where he should focus. Yet, Kendra could not see Philip's success. She did not seek to provide new challenges for Philip, or to allow him to add variations.

At the end of the third trial of jumping towards one another, after Philip had been successful both prior times, he altered his actions. Instead of returning to the starting line, he moved a few feet farther away, then stopped and gazed at Kendra, awaiting her acknowledgement of his proposed elaboration. Kendra signaled to Philip that he must return to the starting line. He complied and they conducted another trial. After the fourth trial, Philip once again moved to the same place and awaited Kendra's response to his proposed enhancement. Once again she signaled that he must return to the starting line.

Kendra was not observing how Philip, after succeeding in their prior framework, was appropriately asking his mother both for greater challenge and to be allowed to function as a more active, contributing member of their partnership. Kendra was overly focused on the continuity part of their activity and not sufficiently on the other side of the balance, creating co-variation and new challenge. Ironically, at this moment, Philip, by offering to make simple enhancements and awaiting his mother's reply, was doing a better job of maintaining their Guided Participation Relationship than she was. His requested enhancements in no way disrupted the joint framework, nor did they deflect focus from the primary objective. Rather, his actions were a sign that Philip was becoming a more competent apprentice, trying, in an appropriate manner, to contribute more to the relationship.

In the work product that Kendra sent to her consultant David, she observed that Philip was doing a good job enacting his role. However, she wrote about being concerned that, after they had success, Philip continued to move away from the starting line. She wondered how she should handle this.

When David went on line to view Kendra's work analysis and accompanying video, he realized that she was having trouble seeing her son's newly emerging competence and was still overly worried about actions that did not strictly conform to the framework she created. This was not too surprising given Philip's history of spending years wandering aimlessly. Often, it is hard for parents to catch up with their child's new competence.

David wanted to support the great progress Kendra and Philip had made, but also wanted to help her re-frame Philip's actions as a sign of growth. He was concerned that if Kendra did not begin to acknowledge and encourage Philip's desire to contribute to their frameworks, he would become discouraged. He selected two short episodes from the larger clip that Kendra sent, to use as feedback. Then he added his own analysis and sent it to her.

David selected an initial segment in which Philip fluidly shifted his attention from self-regulation to co-regulation. He noted how well Kendra had done helping Philip learn to take responsibility in their relationship. He mentioned that this objective appeared to have been mastered, at least in this somewhat artificial setting, and recommended that they expand activities and settings. The second clip was also very short—about 30 seconds. It captured a few moments where Philip appropriately requested that they expand their framework. David commented that, in his opinion this was the most exciting part of the video and the clearest illustration of how much Kendra had facilitated her son's growth. Then, David asked Kendra to consider why she thought this might be so. You may wonder why David didn't just come out and tell Kendra something like, "The next time Philip tries to contribute something, you should encourage him to do so." The consultant's job is not to tell the guide-in-training how to think, or what to do. If consultant's acted in this way, there would be no opportunity for potential growth and parents would continue to remain dependent on their consultant. Parents would not be learning how to think for themselves, but only how to follow their guide's instructions.

As with any good guide, David wanted to present a small challenge for Kendra. He hoped that his feedback provided her with a moment of productive uncertainty, where she could observe her and Philip's actions in a new way.

Chapter Twelve

Guiding

Every human life is a journey into the unknown, often with guides, but rarely without taking risks and grasping opportunities.

—ALAN SROUFE

For children, the Guiding Stage represents entry into the main body of the curriculum, containing several hundred new objectives. The apprentice now has the opportunity to explore many dimensions of dynamic intelligence. During the prior child stages there was an extremely heavy emphasis on the social dimension of development, as the primary goal was to prepare the child to participate as an active apprentice. While many objectives continue to reflect social competence, we now begin to see a greater emphasis on dynamic cognitive and self development. New objectives explore concepts such as critical analysis, relative evaluation, functional equivalence, grey-area problem solving, multiple alternatives and improvisation, to name just a few. Some sample dynamic intelligence objectives are presented in Appendix D.

For parents, the Guiding Stage begins the gradual process of transferring essential tools of guided participation—framing, scaffolding and spotlighting—from consultant to parent.[51]

---

51   In an earlier chapter, Guided Participation: The Guide, I introduced the main tools employed by guides. Readers might wish to review these terms before tackling the contents of this section.

Framing is the process of analyzing and modifying any activity, to ensure that the apprentice has a legitimate role and that their attention and cognitive resources can be fully deployed to address a new challenge. Guides use their actions as scaffolds to gradually transfer both responsibility and ability for dynamic processes. Finally, guides spotlight critical moments of productive uncertainty and its resolution, so they are punctuated and have a better chance of standing out in memory as meaningful.

In this chapter, we add a fourth process I call elaboration. Parents learn to carefully determine how to start with initial prototypes and gradually embed, expand and evolve them so that they have far greater real-world applicability and sophistication.

FRAMING: A BRIEF REVIEW

As you may recall, framing is how we set limits and modify activities, determine the environment in which to undertake them and choose the partners who will participate. For instance, we may decide to cut down the variability in a task, without removing the potential for flexible response. We balance how much clarification we will provide, with how much uncertainty will remain. Later, in the section on elaboration, we will discuss how we may loosen the frame by, for example, moving from a more to a less predictable activity partner, such as from a familiar adult to a familiar peer.

Framing is contextually dependent. You may frame quite differently in a classroom than when the child is at home with parents.

Framing always begins by considering the objective that has been chosen. For example, if the objective is for the apprentice to become more proficient in kinesthetic awareness and conduct greater self-regulation, we might frame an activity, like learning how to ride a bike, to be conducted without training wheels, so the child would receive feedback about his balance. On the other hand, if our objective is for the child to take greater responsibility for social coordination, but the child has not yet mastered the self-regulatory ability to ride a bike and maintain his balance, we would frame the activity by providing training wheels. We would not want the child to use all of his resources to stay balanced and continuously worry about falling, when the primary objective has to do with regulating one's actions with others. Only later, once the child has acquired self-regulatory proficiency, would we remove the training wheels during a conjoint ride.

ACTIVITY LIMITS, ROLES AND MODIFICATIONS

Parents learn to set up clear, understandable but not static activity limits. They practice strategically managing time, space, amount of action, communication, materials and how changes and variations will be made. Necessary limits are thoughtfully balanced with creating as natural a context as possible.

Parents learn to modify activities so that there is minimal competition for the child's attention. The child's attentional resources are reserved for elements of the activity that relate to the selected objective, rather than some peripheral aspect.[52] This allows parents to maintain their selective focus on the challenge they want to introduce and ensures that the child has the resources to deal with the challenge. An example I used earlier, relating to my writing poetry in my second grade class, illustrates this concept. The teacher recognized that I would be unable to create poetry if my attention was absorbed by my handwriting. She temporarily re-framed poetry writing to eliminate the need for legible handwriting. This allowed me to concentrate on the authentic purpose of the lesson, the mental challenge of writing good poetry.[53]

The degree to which we reduce competition for a child's attention will differ and change over time. The point is not to take everything away and spend every day in a bare room. Parents should begin in their normal home setting, paying attention to not introduce too much chaos and noise. Working in a completely artificial setting

---

52   Often, learning to take on a new role can be peripheral if, for example, the objective is to use that role to learn about how to collaborate with a partner.

53   She also scaffolded the activity by temporarily agreeing to act as a compensation, by having me dictate my poems to her so that she could transcribe them with her legible handwriting.

severely restricts generalization. However, anyone's learning ability will break down if you add enough chaos and noise to the mix.

Peter's Typing Conversations

Peter is a thirteen-year-old young man with a severe auditory processing disorder. He has become a good apprentice and takes responsibility for co-regulating his actions when he is with another person. His non-verbal communication has become rich and reciprocal. It is time to address language-based conversation. The problem we face is that, due to his auditory processing difficulties, the moment that someone begins speaking to Peter he becomes very anxious and fearful that he will not be able to accurately retain and understand the speaker's words. Even when his comprehension is good, his anxiety usually leads to an impulsive rote, mindless response. When we eliminate spoken words and engage in non-verbal conversation or when we communicate through emails or letters, he is relaxed and competent.

In order to help Peter understand the prototype of a language-based conversation, I created a frame for having a conversation, by eliminating the auditory component, without removing the language or non verbal communication. Since Peter is a good keyboarder, we conversed while side-by-side in front of a computer, taking turns typing responses to each other.

Peter engaged in this new type of framed conversation without any anxiety. He communicated in a thoughtful and curious manner, something that would have not been possible, if the auditory component had not been temporarily eliminated. He continued to use his non-verbal communication in a rich manner. As Peter becomes more proficient, we will gradually re-introduce the auditory element. Hopefully, by then his anxiety related to conversation will have been significantly reduced. In the meantime, his brain will also have developed the neural integration required to manage the change in perspectives and the integration of self and other's subjective experiences that underlie any successful conversation.

FRAMING ELEMENTS

When activities are framed, new challenges introduced by the guide are made clearly distinguishable from those elements that are peripheral such as the instrumental activity goal. If a father and son are washing a car and working on establishing a regulatory pattern, you might see an emphasis on synchronized back and forth movement with less attention paid to the streaks on the window.

SCAFFOLDING

Scaffolding is a process in which dynamic responsibility and ability is gradually transferred from the mind of the more experienced guide to that of the less experienced apprentice. Guides deconstruct complex processes so that they can be transferred on a step-by-step basis and determine suitable prototypes that will build foundations for future development. They provide opportunities for the apprentice to observe the guide in action, including narration of decision-making and evaluative thinking. Guide's bridge the transfer process by taking on parts of it until the apprentice is gradually able to master more. They challenge and test whether mastery is really achieved.

DEMONSTRATING

You must learn from the mistakes of others. You can't possibly live long enough to make them all yourself.   —SAM LEVINSON

The first step in scaffolding is ensuring, through parent actions, that the child realizes he has to take responsibility for the mental process the parent would like to eventually transfer. Parents, through deliberate enactments, demonstrate the essential nature of the process that is about to be transferred. For example, we may be walking down the street together holding hands. To demonstrate the need for the child to take responsibility for staying side-by-side each time he gets ahead of me, I may stop abruptly thus providing him with the sensation of physical tension if he continued to walk farther ahead.

Transferring responsibility also requires communicating to the child that parents will no longer take on a specific part of their joint action they had previously been taking. The child must pick up the slack and his doing so is critical to the pair's joint success. Furthermore, if he does not take his role, no one will do it for him.

For instance, if a child is carrying a laundry basket full of clothes with his father and the child loses his grip, the father must not compensate by keeping the basket from falling. The child will need to see and feel the laundry fall to the floor.

The child needs to know that responsibility is a serious business even during play. For instance, a child and his mother may be playing a role-playing game they call "car dealership." She is buying a car and he is selling it. To sell the car he must pick up a pretend phone, call his mother and wait for her to pick up her phone and acknowledge him. Mother is clear that if her son tries to talk to her without dialing and waiting for her to come on the line, she will not respond to him. If he does not speak into the receiver, she will let him know through her own self dialogue ("Is there someone there?") that she cannot hear him.

As many of our examples illustrate, parents do not always have to model, or explain the child's responsibilities to him. Frequently, based upon the parents' enactment, the child will know what he has to do. However, this is not always the case. Therefore, the second step in this phase is what most people would think of as actual demonstration.

Because we are introducing a new, challenging way of thinking, we cannot simply tell the child what to do, or simply show him and have him imitate.[54] Rather, we encourage parents to model the gradual emergence of a new dynamic ability rather than the immediate mastery. For example, parents may begin their demonstration by narrating their own degree of confusion and anxiety, which they gradually overcome. During the demonstration, they use self talk to narrate how they cope with frustration and surmount problems they face. Having observed his parents' struggles and eventual triumph, the child hopefully gains confidence and is not discouraged when faced with his own difficulties.

Parents must remember to demonstrate simple enough versions of a new process.

---

54   There are certainly exceptions to this. For example, when we simply want to show the child elements of a new role action, we would demonstrate the action and clearly communicate that the child should imitate exactly what we do.

SELF TALK

Most adult mental processes are internalized, which means that we no longer communicate out loud about them and are often unaware that they are going on. These internal processes must be temporarily externalized and slowed down, if we want the child to be able to become aware of them and learn to employ them.

Parents learn to become mindful of their internal dialogues when engaged in solving problems, socially interacting, or managing their feelings. They learn to share these internal dialogues out loud by engaging in self-talk. This means using very simple language at a very slow pace.[55]

Self -talk should be clearly differentiated from external communication. The child has to recognize that his parent's speech is not actually being directed at him and is not being presented for a response. However, it is being made available for his benefit.

Think about cracking an egg and determining the right amount of force to use when doing so. Your goal, in this example, is not to teach the child how to crack an egg. Rather it is to demonstrate how you use your self-dialogue to evaluate and adjust your actions. You can conduct a self-dialogue, which may include something like, "Uh oh, I was too hard and the egg went everywhere. Maybe softer next time. Yeah, next time softer."

BRIDGING

Bridging is the process of temporarily taking joint responsibility for a new process that will eventually be completely taken over by the child. It is equivalent to saying, "I'm transferring a new responsibility to you, but I can't just throw it on you. I'm going to do part of it and you will do part and gradually you will do more and I'll do less."

Let me give you an example of a bridging scaffold I might use to help students in a classroom learn to shift their attention between independent work and periodically monitoring the classroom environment for new information. I construct a

---

55   Just as in demonstrating actions, there are times when parents need to use words to explain or instruct the child about his or her actions. However, we want to keep these moments to a bare minimum.

self-revolving power point presentation with each slide containing information that pertains to only one student and not others.[56] Each minute a new slide pops up that has a picture of a different student on it, along with information that may or may not be important for that student. The pictures pop-up at random so that students cannot predict when they will appear. Therefore, they must check every minute or so to see if they have appeared in the slide show and if they have, whether the information requires any actions on their part. Initially they might receive a cue—a tone—that indicates a new slide has appeared, to help them stop and check. Later the tone is faded out, as students are expected to take greater responsibility to monitor their environment. Eventually the slide show itself is phased out and replaced with increasingly more subtle information.

Philip Recycling with Patrick

Philip, aged five, and his father, Patrick, are holding hands while walking together towards two recycling bins at the curb, that they need to bring back to the house. After a couple of steps they stop holding one another's hand and walk side-by-side. Patrick is a big man, but very sensitive and careful in his scaffolding. He walks with slow, deliberate steps and Philip models him. After about eight steps Patrick suddenly stops to see if Philip is taking responsibility to monitor whether they are walking together. After getting one step ahead of Patrick, Philip suddenly stops and looks back towards his father. He takes the regulating action of reaching back to grasp Patrick's hand (perhaps thinking his father needs a bit more scaffolding) and they set off again for the curb. After approximately ten more steps, Patrick lets go and abruptly stops again. This time Philip stops too, looks back at his father, returns to him and tries to takes his hand. Patrick does not allow Philip to take his hand and off they go again, side-by-side, until they reach the recycle bins at the curb. Once there, dad lifts up a green bin and indicates in a wonderfully minimalist manner that the blue one is Philip's responsibility. Philip lifts up the blue one and they turn around and set off back down the driveway, towards the house.

---

56   Later you can include slides that pertain to some students and not others, or even some students some of the time and not all of the time.

The added attentional strain of carrying the bin is clearly making it more difficult for Philip to monitor the state of his coordination with his father. For the first time Philip gets ahead without Patrick doing anything, like stopping, to create the breakdown. Philip stops, not to coordinate, but to obtain a better grip on his bin. Patrick remains at the curb and doesn't try to obtain Philip's attention; he does not prompt or direct him in any manner. Philip sets off again. Patrick is still on the curb and Philip has taken about five steps back towards the house. At that moment, without any clues or additional information, Philip suddenly stops, turns, notices his father behind him and returns to where his father is standing. He reaches Patrick. Together they turn back towards the house and the two of them set off together carrying their bins side-by-side. Patrick's pace is even slower and more deliberate than when they were initially heading out to the curb. They reach the garage together and begin their recycling work.

Bridging for Paulie

Paulie, now aged five-and-a-half, and his father Dave are in their basement recreation room along with Paulie's younger sister, Cheryl. It is an informal setting. Paulie is sitting on a swing, hung from the ceiling, and is hanging out with his father. Cheryl is playing with different toys. Paulie, in a very natural manner, initiates the following conversation. Paulie's comments are in boldface:

*Okay … **But, you know what Cheryl's birthday is gonna be after? It will be after Thanksgiving.***

Right. This year she's going to be three years old.

Last year it was two … But it was same, because, because, because, and when she was two we went to Nana and Papa's house in Thanksgiving and then it was Cheryl's birthday and it was two years old. So, what will be look like at two [three] years old, right?

Yeah, it will be similar to last year.

Of two years old right. Right?

Yeah, we can go to the same restaurant this year.

You mean (pause while he thinks)… **the other restaurants, or the restaurant that has a train?**

Not the one with the train. The Chinese restaurant.

Oh!

Paulie spins around slowly and considers his father's reply.

But last year we go to the restaurant that had a train, right?

Yeah, but that wasn't Cheryl's birthday.

Paulie's face displays curiosity and some puzzlement. He is clearly considering Dave's statements, which have left him a bit uncertain. His father adds a bit of clarification.

"That was just near Nana and Papa's house."

Well that one is the restaurant that had a train in Georgia.

Right, Georgia.

And it had another … It isn't Thomas the train engine and there's another train that is Thomas the train engine, right?

Yeah. But for Cheryl's birthday we're going to go to a Chinese restaurant in North Carolina.

All right.

But I remember last year they had Sushi there.

Paulie is clearly more animated. His face appears more relaxed, as if he has figured something out.

And last year we go to the Sushi place!

And it had Sushi and other food too.

But last year we go to the Sushi place.

Well it was a Chinese place, but it still had Sushi.

But, but last year we go to the Chinese place.

Right.

So what will we say, like the other one?

It'll be the same restaurant this year.

Oh.

Paulie appears even more animated.

 Last year we go to a Chinese restaurant too daddy. And we saw Sushi there.

And I remember what you liked.

I like Asparagus too.

Yeah and I remember something else you liked.

I, I, Oh! At the restaurant I think we had jello too!

At this moment, it appears from Paulie's facial expression that he is fully re-experiencing last year's birthday.

We did! (Dad laughs) *I remember you liked it.*

Maybe, oh, the red jello I think!

Yeah it was red, and they might have had green too.

Yeah. They had green too.

Red and green jello.

We had red jello and green jello, but Chris (Paulie's neighborhood buddy) **just had green jello. Right?**

Really, I didn't see that. You know what? We can sing happy birthday to Cheryl when we go to the restaurant.

So after Thanksgiving we will go to Chinese restaurant for the birth of Cheryl's birthday.

It is quite exciting to realize that Paulie initiated this conversation completely on his own. Later, when I discuss the internalization process, you can look back on this as an important early indicator that Paulie was well on his way to taking ownership of his own mental development.

Paulie's intent was to have his father act as a reference point, specifically in the case of his sister's upcoming birthday. In the process of clarifying his confusion, Paulie and his father engage in a true reciprocal conversation. Paulie is very interested in what Dave has to say. He perceives his father as his mental guide, one who helps Paulie unravel his confusion about complex concepts, like how the past and future are inter-twined.

If you review Paulie's comments, you may be struck by how thoughtfully he communicates, how important he considers Dave's opinions and how much he desires his input. Also, you may be impressed that Paulie recognizes that his own memories are subjective and that there may be more than one perspective. He ends several of his statements with a "right?" He also uses the term "I think" to communicate that he is unsure of himself. This is a result of our focusing on the dynamic nature of communication, right from the very earliest stages of Paulie's communication development.

Dave is very careful with his scaffolding. He recognizes an opportunity to help Paulie elaborate his understanding of two emerging mental discoveries that the family had been focusing on in previous weeks. The first was the idea that things that have happened in the past may or may not predict what will happen in the future. The second was an elaboration of an earlier discovery, that two things can be both different and alike at the same time. We can see Paulie introducing this idea in his opening statement, "Last year it was two … but it was same." The application in this case is that the family can go to the same restaurant, even though Paulie's sister will be a year older.

An important part of learning to scaffold is realizing that you cannot focus on everything at once. Dave was not concerned at this moment about Paulie's grammar or syntax. He didn't correct Paulie when he said, "Cheryl is going to be two," because he realized what Paulie meant and wanted him to keep directing Paulie's resources to think about the future, not worry about specific words.

At a critical point in the conversation, Paulie becomes sidetracked. Dave has to be careful to redirect Paulie back to the main topic:

But last year we go to the restaurant that had a train, right?

Yeah, but that wasn't Cheryl's birthday.

Paulie's face is curious and a bit puzzled. He is clearly thinking again and a bit uncertain.

That was just near Nana and Papa's house.

Well that one is the restaurant that had a train in Georgia.

Right, Georgia.

And it had another ... It isn't Thomas the train engine and there's another train that is Thomas the train engine, right?

Dave realizes that he has to increase his scaffolding yet again. But he doesn't want to take ownership of the conversation away from Paulie. He is careful to "titrate" his scaffolding remarks to take as little ownership of the process as is necessary. He makes another refocusing statement:

Yeah. But for Cheryl's birthday we're going to go to a Chinese restaurant in North Carolina.

All right.

Dave now inserts a more concrete detail, in hopes of helping to trigger a meaningful personal memory:

But I remember last year they had Sushi there.

At this point Paulie appears more animated. He no longer wants to talk about trains. But it is not clear that Paulie is fully re-experiencing last year's birthday. Dad makes one more scaffolding comment to try and fully trigger Paulie's memory.

Yeah and I remember something else you liked.

I, I, Oh! At the restaurant I think we had jello too!

This seems to do the trick.

PERIPHERAL SUPPORT

The peripheral phase begins when guides realize that they have successfully transferred a new process, but are not sure the apprentice recognizes his new mastery. Parents learn to help the child realize that even though the parent is present, they are not responsible for the child's success. In some ways parents are spotlighting their non-scaffolding.

Think about teaching a child to ride a two-wheel bike. There is a time when the child can balance but doesn't yet have a complete sense of security. You may stand behind them, just close enough to communicate that you are there, but far enough away so that the child realizes you are not holding onto the bicycle. The child will often say, "I'm doing it. Look, I'm doing it." Typically, after a very short time, the child may tell you to go away. She wants do it on her own.

If you have a choice between framing a bit more and scaffolding, you always want to frame. Scaffolding inserts more of you into the episode and thus creates more dependency.

Paulie Cares for His Friend

Paulie, now six-years-old, is outside playing with his neighborhood friend Sam and Sam's older sister, Cara. Dave is present only because he wants to videotape how Paulie interacts with his peers. He is trying to remain as unobtrusive as possible. He is apparently successful, as none of the children pay any attention to him.

The two boys are on small cars and are rolling together from Paulie's garage, down the driveway which is on a small incline. Interestingly, Paulie does most of the work to make sure they are coordinated. He visually checks to see that Sam is ready. He also checks to see where they are, as they roll down the driveway. They both yell, "Yee haw" as they roll. They push their cars back to the top. Paulie arrives first and waits for Sam to be ready. When he is sure, he says, "Go" and the two boys take off again. They don't remain side-by-side while they role, but neither boy perceives this as important, or necessary.

A bit later the boys decide to ride bikes. They put on their helmets and get on the bikes. As they begin riding, they pass Cara. Paulie notices that she doesn't have a bike and as he approaches her he says, "***You can ride the baby bike***," (his sister's tricycle) "***if you want.***" Sam is oblivious to this interchange and continues to ride, getting somewhat ahead of Paulie.

A couple of minutes later the boys are at the bottom of the driveway. Paulie has gently, but firmly stated that he'd like to go back to rolling cars. Sam wants to continue riding bikes. Before the negotiation can proceed, Sam bursts into tears.

He leaves his bike, walks over to the grass, sits down, and continues to cry with his hands covering his face.

Paulie sighs, apparently unsure of what he should do. He stops and gazes at Sam, studying the situation with a puzzled and troubled expression on his face. Then, as if making up his mind, he gets onto his car and rolls up the driveway towards his father.

What happened to Sam, Paulie?

He's crying.

I wonder why?

Because he don't like to race.

I wonder if you could help make him feel better?

Paulie starts to get up off the car and says, "***Maybe a hug.***" He starts walking towards Sam, but turns briefly to his father to say, "***Hugs are good.***" Dave is careful to not indicate his approval or disapproval and simply says, "*Okay*" in a neutral manner.

Paulie heads back to Sam. He squats down facing Sam and puts his arms around him. He softly talks to Sam in a reassuring manner while gently patting him. He continues to gently comfort Sam with his face very close to Sam's, but not invasive in any way, until the moment that Sam first takes his hands away from his eyes. Sam looks to the side without crying. That is the moment when Paulie removes his arms, but remains in the same position carefully looking at his friend. Sam lifts his head up to gaze at Paulie. Paulie moves just a bit away and then starts to get up. Paulie is now on his feet, but he is continuing to direct all of his attention to his friend's emotional state. Still facing his friend, he takes a few steps back. He watches, while Sam gets back on his bike. He walks towards his own bike, still gazing at Sam. His gaze never turns away from his friend until the moment that Sam's feet touch the bicycle pedals (Sam is back in the saddle again!). Then, for the first time Paulie turns away. As he walks towards his bike he says, "***Okay***" in a matter-of-fact manner, to nobody in particular.

Dave's complete scaffolding contribution was five words. He served to remind Paulie that he was competent but he didn't take responsibility. Dave also did not offer emotional support. He was aware and purposeful of how little he should do.

Sometimes peripheral support is not the end of scaffolding. There are times when guides actively add an even greater degree of challenge in order to prepare the apprentice for a less predictable partner, such as a peer. Here is what might be going on in the guide's mind during such times, "I'm going to make it more challenging than it would normally be with you and me because I am preparing you for a world out there that doesn't include you and me. I want you to take more than half the responsibility because I am not preparing you to hang out with me, but with a future peer who will probably be less predictable than I am. I want you to be prepared for anyone, even someone who isn't taking their fair share of responsibility."

SPOTLIGHTING

The stream of thought flows on; but most of its segments fall into the bottomless abyss of oblivion. Of some, no memory survives the instant of their passage. Of others, it is confined to a few moments, hours or days. Others, again, leave vestiges which are indestructible, and by means of which they may be recalled as long as life endures.

—WILLIAM JAMES

Spotlighting is defined as setting psychological boundaries around specific critical periods within activities, based on the particular lesson we wish to impart. It is achieved by establishing contrast, making sure that specific piece moments stand out from the rest. We may also spotlight by making a noticeable change in an established pattern, or rhythm.

The goal of spotlighting is to enhance the potential for developing meaningful personal memories, making sure the apprentice remembers what they have discovered about themselves and their world, in a manner that will serve them in future situations.

When they began RDI, few ASD children have any memory of a relationship where, through the guidance of a family member or teacher, they learned to feel comfortable in situations of uncertainty. This is the first type of memory we wish to spotlight. Once this is established, we focus on memories in which the child encounters a challenge and eventually succeeds, initially through his mental efforts coupled with parental scaffolding and eventually through his own mental processes.

Successful spotlighting requires that the recipient of the spotlight encode memories containing three components which are essential for the formation of a personal memory: 1) moments of feeling challenged and uncertain, 2) connecting the uncertainty and challenge with its productive resolution through thoughtful actions taken by the apprentice, with or without help from the guide, and 3) connecting both of these with the apprentice's changed feelings, when he successfully resolves the challenge.

---

*Daniel Stern in his book, **The First Relationship**, discusses how parents intuitively spotlight their actions, when interacting with typically developing Infants, "They have more particularly marked behavioral rests or silences surrounding them. They are more slowly and exaggeratedly performed so that each separate presentation with its display is thrown into higher relief for the infant."*

PUNCTUATING CRITICAL MOMENTS

Guides spotlight critical moments during activities so that they are punctuated; they stand out more clearly in the apprentice's mind as meaningful. The critical moments are not the endpoint or result. Rather they are found during the process of managing the challenge. Spotlighting is not the same as praising, celebrating or providing rewards. In fact, these actions can often interfere with the formation of a productive personal memory. For example, a child can form a strong memory of parents being very excited when he was successful. However, if this memory does not include recalling how he initially felt when challenged by the problem and how he was able to alter his thinking to come to a successful resolution, then it has little value to the child in any future situation.

Spotlighting creates contrast, through pausing, stopping and prolonging, not getting louder or more amplified. Critical moments are more likely to be encoded into memory in a meaningful way when someone suddenly pauses, or stands still and becomes quiet, not when they are yelling and screaming.

We're Falling

Jack, a five-year-old with autism, and his father Paul are standing in their den. They have created a space where they can walk a few steps and fall onto a pile of beanbag chairs. Jack's comments are in boldface.

"Ready?" Paul says. ***"Okay!!"*** responds Jack. Paul instructs, "We're gonna fall on the beanbags. All right, this side." Jack says, ***"Okay. Here I go. Here I go!"*** Paul replies, "We're gonna fall together though." Paul moves them a few steps back. Jack is gazing at his father. Paul says, "We're gonna walk up and 'fa-a-a-ll' together." Jack gazes to Paul, and his dad says, "Ready." Father slowly lifts his leg and says, "Boom" as he lowers it.

Jack is carefully watching his dad while they move together. They approach and reach the beanbags as a single unit. Paul turns sideways to face his son and Jack turns to face his dad. Paul holds out his arms. Jack begins to fall prematurely. Paul says, "Uh, oh" and Jack returns to a standing position across from his father. Paul shouts out "Ahhhhh!" and leans in the opposite direction from the beanbags. Jack imitates and also leans away. Now Paul says, "Wowww" and leans forward, still holding his arms out. Jack has his arms out too and leans forward with his dad. Now the two of them return to their standing position, their arms still out. Paul leads them in leaning back again, away from the beanbags. Jack works hard to lean just as his father does. They lean forward again. Paul's voice is becoming higher pitched and Jack's excitement is also building to a crescendo. They lean backwards one more time, then forwards and then they begin a gradual completely synchronized fall onto the beanbags. Jack yells out, ***"Lets do it again!"***

What's in the Bag?

Rachel and her son Mark, aged six, are sitting on the bed with Rachel at a 90-degree angle from her son. Rachel is holding a small white paper shopping bag. She has one hand under the bag and one hand on the handle. She is slowly shaking the bag. Her shaking leads to Mark's shifting his attention between his mother's face and the bag. She stops shaking the bag and in a deliberate manner, shifts her gaze between the bag and her son. Rachel has not yet spoken a word or made a sound.

Mark says, ***"What's in there? Mommy, what's in there?"***

Rachel reaches a hand into the bag and keeps it there for a moment She removes her hand, moves the bag closer to her son and places his hand inside the bag along with hers. They both touch the object in the bag. Mark smiles and looks at Rachel. They share a smile. Rachel nods at her son and says her first word, "hard" prolonging the word. They continue to examine the object by touch, without being able to see it.

They both say "hmmm" at the same time. Mark's attention shifts between looking down at the bag as he feels what the object is and to his mother to share the experience of the moment. Mark says, ***"Take it out,"*** in a non-demanding way. Rachel prolongs the moment and says, "Hmmmmm" while they both continue to feel the object.

Rachel looks quizzically at Mark and says, "Stem?" They share a prolonged look. Clearly Mark is considering the impact of her last word. He says, ***"hmm"*** in a quizzical way. Now Rachel gives Mark another clue and says "Large, … with stem?" in a voice that gradually becomes a whisper. Mark's face suddenly becomes animated as he gazes at her with a big smile and says, ***"An apple!"***

Mark opens his mouth in an excited expression. He says, ***"Let's see."*** Rachel prolongs the moment just a bit more by saying, "Ready, set, pull it out," in a gradually louder and more excited voice. They pull the apple from the bag and laugh.

CREATING A MEANING BOUNDARY

A critical part of spotlighting is creating a consensually recognized meaning boundary around the critical elements embedded in a larger activity framework. The boundary can be drawn around certain moments that differentiate them from other moments, or certain attributes or patterns that differentiate them from others; for example, similar-but-different, or different-but-same.

Andrew and the Mailbox

Andrew, aged seven, and his mother, Vera, are conducting their daily trip to the mailbox to gather their mail. Andrew has already learned to take responsibility to remain coordinated with Vera while they walk together. Vera will insert her challenge when they reach their destination.

Andrew is not tall enough to reach the mailbox by himself, so the daily ritual entails Vera lifting Andrew up so he can open the box and remove the mail. However, today will be a bit different. Vera wants Andrew to discover that sometimes the people we depend upon may have difficulty completing their roles, or might take unexpected actions. So when the time comes to lift Andrew, Vera marks the beginning of a meaning boundary by suddenly slowing her movement and becoming much more deliberate. She goes to lift Andrew off the ground and with a groan of, "Oh no" she fails and slowly places him back on the ground. She says, "I didn't lift you. Let me try again." She makes another slow, determined effort and fails a second time. This is a brand new experience for Andrew. His face portrays some anxiety and he begins to turn away from Vera, taking a step backwards as if to withdraw.

Unlike previous times, Vera has been holding Andrew's hand through this process. She knows that when she increases the degree of challenge she typically has to temporarily "shrink" their zone of connection. Andrew moves as if to withdraw. Vera doesn't pull him back, but neither does she release his hand. Andrew stops and seems to re-group. After a moment, he smiles, moves closer and again faces Vera and they get ready for a third attempt. This time Vera is successful and Andrew is lifted high enough to retrieve the mail. However, before he can reach for the mail, Vera closes the meaning boundary. With Andrew in her arms, she turns away from the mailbox, looks at Andrew, smiles broadly and says, "We made it. We got you up." After a very brief celebration, Vera's expression again becomes neutral. She turns back towards the mailbox and allows Andrew to complete the task. She makes no comment after he successfully retrieves the mail. She wants to communicate that their success occurred when Andrew successfully managed his feelings to return and persevere with his mother, not when he reached to get mail.

Spotlighting Tips:

- Determine critical moments based on the specific objective or lesson.
- Create meaningful boundaries around moments where the apprentice experiences uncertainty and then productively manages it.
- Create contrast between critical and non-critical moments.
- Slow the pace of critical actions so they are easier to perceive and understand.
- Develop methods to facilitate awareness of feelings during critical moments.

Elaborating

Each time we celebrate a child's success in mastering a new ability, or taking on a new area of responsibility, we also must acknowledge that this is just one step out of many hundreds, if not thousands, on the road to eventual competence. Guides have to make sure that each small, but important achievement is translated into tools that will allow the child to achieve eventual real-world mastery in a complex, adult world. Elaboration, the term we use to describe this important process, is a strategic combination of modifying our framing and scaffolding to support taking discoveries out of the lab and into real world applications. Appendix E provides some sample elaborations. There are three important elements of elaboration: embedding, expanding and evolving.

Embedding involves making sure that new learning is integrated into current mental processes so that it can be used in a more functional, contextual manner. Embedding often relates to the question, "How does this relate to what I already know and how I already think?" It creates a stronger mental web of thinking.

Expanding relates to the question, "What is the point of this new discovery?" Through expansion, the child learns the broad ways that a new discovery can be applied in the real world with different partners, settings and problems. Additionally a simpler version of a mastered dynamic ability can be expanded, so that the ability has more value in a greater range of problems. The child also learns how new discoveries will expand prior ways of thinking about and categorizing his world.

Evolving entails adding greater complexity and sophistication to new learning so that over time previously mastered cognitive discoveries serve as springboards to more complex versions. An evolved objective might entail a new level of conceptual sophistication, a movement from understanding a single perspective to integrating multiple perspectives, or moving from an external to an internal version of a dynamic ability. For example, learning to reference oneself when uncertain, which is based on the earlier prototype of social referencing.

Brian's Ability is Evolving

Brian and his mother Jackie are in our clinic playroom participating in a periodic evaluation of his progress. Brian is now four and has been involved in RDI for about 20 months. He has become an excellent apprentice and is continuing to progress at a steady pace. Brian and Jackie are standing side-by-side at one end of the room facing a pile of five beanbag chairs at the other end. They are holding hands, counting together, "one, two, three, go!" running and then falling together onto the beanbags. Both are enjoying this immensely. Brian has a limited vocabulary, but this does not stop him from being an engaging, enthusiastic companion that anyone would want to play with. Brian takes excellent responsibility to make sure that he and mother start together. He checks by integrating visual and verbal channels to ensure his mother is ready. "Mommy ready?" he asks.

Jackie adds a bit more challenge to the task. As they return to their starting point, she no longer hold's Brian's hand. They begin their run in unison. However, Brian quickly gets ahead of her and jumps before she does. They try a second time and this time he slows down and keeps pace with her.

Now Jackie is ready to really challenge Brian to make a new discovery. They count to three and begin running together without holding hands. As they approach the beanbags, she abruptly stops a few feet away from the jumping off point and without warning freezes in place. Brian continues on and jumps onto the pile without her. As soon as he falls, he turns around and shifts his focus to his mother. He is engaged in studying the problem. After just a couple of seconds he says, "Oops. I'm sorry," a repair communication.

With these three words, along with the prosody, facial communication and postural shifts that accompany them, Brian is acknowledging that his responsibility was to stay with Jackie, even if she did not act in a predictable manner. She remains frozen in place and says, "What are you sorry about?" He does not have the words to explain, but he understands. Jackie says, "Come on. Let's try again." They return to the starting line and mom once again freezes at the exact spot as last time. Brian again runs past her, jumps on the beanbags and immediately gazes back to where she is standing to study the problem. Jackie says, "What happened?" Brian replies with, "One, two, three, go!" She says, "Did momma stop?" Brian responds with, "Yes." In a very matter-of-fact voice Jackie waves her arm back towards the starting point and says, "Let's try again." Brian happily joins her at the starting line.

Once again they are getting ready at the starting point. Brian does not seem anxious; he appears quite confident he will solve this problem. This time it is clear that something is different about his plan. First, Brian reaches out to try and hold his mother's hand. That is one way to manage the problem, but Jackie shrugs his hand off. By rejecting his bid for greater scaffolding, she is communicating her trust that he can master this challenge. Now Brian begins to count in a much more deliberate fashion, slowing the pace to give himself more time. His gaze is fixed on Jackie and not on the beanbag pile. If you stop the video just as they begin to run, you will see that Brian has modified his gaze. He has figured out that while they are running together, he has to fix his gaze about midway between his partner and the goal so he can more easily keep track of both. This third time, when she once again stops at the same place, Brian stops with her. They share a triumphant moment of joy. Without warning, Jackie takes off again and heads for the beanbags with Brian close by. When they reach the top of the pile, he jumps off the beanbags shouting, "One more time. One more time." He wants to prolong his moment of triumph.

Chapter Thirteen

Internalizing

Although we treat Guiding and Internalizing as two separate stages, the transition from one to the next is imperceptible. Internalizing has its roots in the Guiding Stage and evolves through a fluid, dynamic process.

For parents, internalizing means taking on more responsibility for framing, scaffolding, spotlighting and elaborating. It becomes easier to find opportunities throughout the day for guided participation. Parents learn to select appropriate objectives and actively participate in creating their own lessons and assignments. Face-to-face time with the consultant is reduced.

During this stage the child is engaging in a parallel internalization process. Now a fully participating apprentice, he is taking on increasing responsibility for problem-solving, self-regulation and social coordination. Children make their own discoveries during the course of the day and many objectives will be mastered without ever being formally addressed.

Teen and adult apprentices become part of the team, helping to choose their own objectives and lessons. Some are given their own assignments and produce their own work products.

Objectives increasingly focus on internal processes, such as reflection, imaginative creation and hypothetical thinking. Children explore their growing identity, through objectives that focus on different aspects of self-awareness. They become more capable, sophisticated collaborators, friends and family members.

Paulie—I'm a Brother

Paulie, age five, his father and his younger sister, Cara, are sitting next to one another at the dining room table, with Paulie in the middle. They are all drinking cups of "tea." This has become a daily family ritual, started because Dave liked to come home from work and de-pressurize by drinking a cup of tea. Paulie asked Dave if he could drink tea with him and once the ritual began Cara joined the tea drinkers club, although her cup is filled with soup as is Paulie's.

Lately, parents had been focusing on helping Paulie think about his role in the family. It had been hard for him to consider that his role shifted depending on the member of the family he was relating to. However, that is not on Dave's mind now. He is thinking about how the three of them are coordinating their actions and how this came about through no intention, or effort of his own.

Dave slowly lifts his cup. Then Paulie lifts his and usually, but not always, Cara lifts hers. They look a bit like a synchronized tea-drinking team, except that Cara, being a typical two-year-old, is a somewhat unpredictable member of the team and sometimes deliberately does what she wants to do just to see their reaction.

Cara is having trouble saying soup and has been saying "Sou." Paulie turns to his sister, moves his face close to hers and says, "Soup, soup," in a gentle voice. Then he gives her a big kiss on the lips and moves his head away. He enjoys this so much, that he leans over and gives her another kiss and then a third. Then he kisses Cara gently on the forehead, while she sips her soup. Now he nods his head and reaches over to pat her, with one hand around her back and the other on her tummy. He pats her very gently. But, Cara has had enough affection for the moment. She emits a "leave me alone" sound and Paulie immediately backs off. In a very sincere, convincing voice Paulie says, "I like you," to Cara, and she gazes towards her big brother.

The three return to synchronized tea drinking. They rhythmically and gently bang their cups down in quick succession—first dad, then Paulie and then Cara. Tea drinking progresses for another moment. Then Paulie puts his cup down and pauses as if thinking about something. He gazes over to Cara and says, "You're a sister. I'm the brother. I'm the brother, Cara." This is followed by resumption of their tea ceremony.

Going with the Flow

As the apprentice progresses, he is expected to thrive in increasingly complex, real-world settings, that demand resourcefulness. Apprentices display an internalized motivation, as they spontaneously take advantage of opportunities for challenge, competence and mastery. They demonstrate flexible problem solving, improvisation and resiliency. They present an attitude of being able to *go with the flow* with most anything that comes their way.

Brian—It's a Magic Trick!

Brian, now nine-years-old, is sitting at a table across from his friends, Ben and Aaron, who meet with him in a weekly group. In addition to this formal setting, they get together on their own fairly often. Ben is directly across from Brian, while Aaron is sitting at a 90-degree angle, a fourth group member is absent on this day. Dr. Sheely, the guide for the group, is sitting at her desk about six feet away from the boys, pretending to not pay attention to the group. The boys are fully involved with one another and generally do not attend to Dr. Sheely, unless she approaches their table.

Dr. Sheely has placed small waffle blocks on the boy's table before their arrival and has given no instructions for their use. She is not interested in what the boys actually do with the blocks, but has set up the framework to help them work toward mastery of managing both a foreground primary focus, along with a background secondary task. The boys have progressed enough so that almost any object will be treated as the background, while sharing their experiences, ideas and feelings remain in the foreground.

Brian has started to play a game he has just invented called, "What's inside the box." The other boys have agreed to play and the rules are very simple. One person builds a box from the waffle blocks. Then he places an object inside the box. Finally, he closes the box and holds it out for the others to guess what is inside.

When it is Ben's turn, he has trouble building the box. Brian patiently guides him to successfully construct his box. Finally, it is Brian's turn. He briefly turns away from his friends and places a small object inside his box. He makes sure they notice what he is doing . He places a waffle block on top to close the box, completing the cube and turns back towards his friends. Brian holds the box in front of them and shakes it so they can hear the object inside. He says, "Guess what it is!"

Before the game has a chance to progress, the bottom comes off Brian's box and the object he had placed inside falls to the floor. Only Brian notices this. He pauses briefly, to study this unexpected circumstance and determine how to manage it. Then he smiles and holds the box out further. The boys make their guesses. Brian smiles, like the cat that swallowed the canary and turns the box, so that the boys see there is nothing in it. He says, "Wrong. It's empty. It's a magic trick!"

FROM EXTERNAL TO INTERNAL

As children progress, objectives that were previously externalized require greater internal control. Social referencing is an external process in which the child responds to feelings of uncertainty, by using the emotional reactions of his guides as a reference point. In higher stages, social-referencing evolves into self-referencing. The child begins to rely more on his own personal memories to guide his actions when uncertain.

In a similar way monitoring external stimuli evolves into monitoring internal subjective states for greater self-regulation. As the following vignette illustrates, apprentices are also expected to become more proficient in self-spotlighting and creating their own personal memories.

Paulie—Cookie Memories

Paulie is now five-and-a-half years old. He and his family are baking Valentine cookies together. They carefully knead the dough and then shape their heart cookies, Dave, his father, takes periodic photographs. He is planning to place them into a memory book so that Paulie can practice narrating the memory to his younger sister Cara.

Paulie's mother, Barbara, turns to him and says, "You are such a good chef!" Paulie has developed his own sense of competence, and does not require praise, so he doesn't pay much attention. Instead, he is interested in the new concept his mother has introduced and asks, "What do chefs do?" Instead of answering in a simple, direct manner, Barbara decides to insert a bit of productive uncertainty into the dialogue. She responds with "You know what? Chefs cook. But, they also get to eat what they cook." Paulie considers this unexpected reply for a few seconds in a calm but curious manner. Then he says, "What? They eat too?" His mother nods. Paulie considers this for a few seconds and seems to have figured something out. He smiles and says, "We are all chefs, because chefs eat too!"

When the cookies are ready, they place them in the oven to bake. Finally, Barbara decides that the cookies are ready to come out of the oven. She opens the oven door and notices that the heat has unexpectedly caused all the carefully molded hearts to lose their shape. They look like blobs. Barbara is a professional chef and is clearly stunned. She shouts out, "Oh, no!" Hearing this outburst, Paulie breaks into hilarious laughter. He mimics his mother's "Oh, no" perfectly. (It is important to note that the tone of his voice is one of laughing *with*, not at his mother).

Paulie's assigned dynamic intelligence objective in the previous weeks has been to learn to expect and appreciate the unexpected. The family has deliberately framed many experiences, but they have also naturally punctuated other spontaneous moments, where things were expected to turn out one way but turned out differently.

At this moment, Paulie is creating a spotlight for the entire family. After hearing his "oh no" and laughter, Barbara's affect instantly changes from frustration to joyful absurdity. Paulie's little sister laughs along and also imitates her mother's words and voice, with her own version of, "Oh, no!" Dad asks, "What happened?" Paulie answers, "They got big." Dave says, "I wonder if we can still eat them?" Barbara hands Paulie a cookie. He takes a bite, "They're still good!" Cara takes a bite and says, "Good." The entire family giggles while they munch on cookies. Paulie turns to his mother to comfort her and says, "We'll try again tomorrow." But, he cannot really stop himself from giggling.

Transition to authentic friendships

While there is greater emphasis in later stages on the development of internal mental functioning, advanced objectives continue to provide new discoveries and elaborations in social-relational areas. For example, apprentices gradually prepare to become competent partners with their peers.

We do not recommend placing an ASD child in social training groups, until he has achieved a significant amount of competence.[57] It is hard for us to see the reasoning for placing a child who cannot yet function as an equal partner in a 1:1 relationship with a peer, into the exponentially more complex social environment of a group.

We also do not recommend the practice of deliberately buddying ASD children with peers who display significantly greater competence. If we enlist a typical peer as a social partner, we should assume that the more competent child is going to do all the work of maintaining the relationship. This may create a comforting illusion of a real reciprocal relationship. However, the typically developing child will be doing all the co-regulatory work, leaving the ASD child completely dependent and without opportunities to gradually become more of an equal partner.

The other problem with using more competent peers as social partners is that as their ability is so much greater than the ASD child, they may inadvertently leave the child feeling completely incompetent. Imagine that you are first learning how to play tennis and I tell you that you are now ready for a tennis partner. Now imagine that the first tennis partner I introduce you to is Venus Williams. How is that going to make you feel?

When children have learned to take sufficient collaborative responsibility with adults, we match them with a peer that is approximately at their level of mastery and competence. We want to find someone who is challenging, not someone who will unwittingly do all the work for you. We also do not want to create a match with a child who is much less competent.

---

57   We have no objection to children participating in any group setting, as long as we don't misconstrue the goal as developing social competence.

Brian and Ben

Brian and his buddy Ben, both ten-year-olds, are alone in one of our playrooms, which contains only a big stack of beanbag chairs. They are hanging out for a few minutes until Dr. Sheely arrives. It has been years since they have done anything with beanbags. However, that doesn't stop Ben from wanting to organize a massive construction project. Ben has been diagnosed with Asperger's Syndrome, while as a toddler Brian presented with classical autism. At this point, Brian's progress has exceeded Ben's, largely due to Brain's family's consistent insertion of RDI into their daily family life.

Ben still has some major obstacles to overcome in being a good friend, including the desire to be the boss. In contrast, when Brian is with a pal, the relationship far outweighs any particular outcome or object.

Ben gets the idea that they need to work together to build a huge tower out of the beanbags. Unbeknownst to Brian, Ben intends to climb to the top of the inevitably unstable structure when they are done. The boys work to stack the beanbags.

Ben: *"Put that one there."* (Happy in his boss role.)

Brian: *"I think this is not a good idea,"* (noticing how shaky the structure has become).

Ben: *"It will be a good idea if we just work together,"* (translated as, just do what I say). They continue to lift and stack. Brian works in a playful manner, while Ben is more serious.

Ben: *"Lift. Lift. Hold it,"* (back to work mode).

Brian: *"King of the world. Now my foot's stuck. Good. Now we're done."* (Maybe we can stop now?)

Ben: *"Not all the way done. We want to make it higher right?"*

Brian: *"Okay,"* (oh well, who cares).

The tower continues to grow. Brian notices that Ben is having trouble. He rushes over while saying, "I'll help you," and helps Ben lift the beanbag to an even higher place.

Brian: *"Man. It's almost touching the ceiling!"* (Maybe now he will see that it is enough.)

Ben: *"Yeah. Let's just put that very last beanbag on top of the red."*

Brian: *"And THEN it will be Mt. Everest!"* (Maybe that will impress Ben.)

Ben works doggedly to place one more beanbag on top, while Brian races back and forth to assess the structural integrity of the mountain. He notices that Ben's efforts are about to topple the structure. He races to the other side to support the structure while saying, *"Uhhh. I'll keep it steady. You just put it up there. I'll keep it steady."* Ben is so determined to get one more beanbag on top he is toppling the structure. But Brian compensates for his actions to keep it steady. Finally, with extensive assistance from Brian, they get the green beanbag on top. Now Ben is ready to start climbing to the top of what is clearly a completely unstable structure. It is only staying up through Brian's supportive efforts. Without letting the mountain fall, Brian keeps changing his position to see what Ben is up to.

Finally, Ben says, *"I'm almost at the top."* Brian uses a higher pitched voice to express his surprise and says, *"You're trying to get to the top?"* Ben reaches the top and says, *"I made it."*

Ben seems oblivious to the fact that the only reason he is not falling off is because Brian is using his strength to support the beanbags from toppling over. Brian, who is facing Ben with both hands holding up the mountain, now sees a wonderful opportunity to tease his friend. He temporarily lets go of his grip and the mountain starts to topple. He says, *"Okay, we need to do something."* At the last second he keeps mountain and friend from falling. They both scream and laugh. Ben still laughing says, *"That was close. Brian are you crazy?"* Brian replies, *"What am I going to do. Just stand right here for the rest of my life?"* As he says these words Brian turns his back to Ben, supporting the mountain with his back. He crosses his arms in mock anger. His voice tone is a perfect blend of humor and feigned annoyance. Brian turns towards his friend once again. Ben says, *"Just keep the beanbag up."* Brian turns away again. This time he crosses his legs and turns his face away. He is supporting the structure with one hand and has placed his other hand on his hip. All in all it is a perfect nonverbal, nonchalant communication.

Suddenly an adult walks into the room, spots the situation and in a casual voice asks, *"Need some help?"* Brian responds in a slightly higher toned, milder voice portraying a hint of sarcasm. He says, *"No thank you. I'm just fine."* He is now communicating that he has Ben up in the air at his mercy.

Brian realizes that he has to find a way to end this project as Ben would likely have it go on forever. He wants to get it over with, but also make it fun for both of them. He decides to have a countdown during which he will gradually allow the mountain to come down. Brian says *"Okay, Now you're going to blow up in 10, 9..."* Both boys laugh hilariously as the mountain comes tumbling down.

Chapter Fourteen

Conclusion

At the time of this book's publication, RDI has been available as a systematic program for approximately eight years. During this time, it has undergone such significant growth and revision, that those reading my original book, ***Solving the Relationship Puzzle,*** might have difficulty recognizing it. Nevertheless, the roots of the current version of RDI are present even in that earliest prototype. Through the incredible contributions of hundreds of professionals and families, we have made substantive strides from those developmental foundations. What was back then mainly a group of concepts and general principles, has evolved into a sophisticated, comprehensive program.

Thousands of families currently participate in RDI. While the program has not been available long enough to track the development of young children into adulthood, we have been able to gather preliminary results for children who have been involved in the program for several years.

The vast majority of families participating in RDI report meaningful changes in the following areas:

- *Children are significantly more motivated to accept guidance.*
- *Children value time interacting with parents over other activities and objects.*
- *Children are more interested in how parents and other family members feel.*
- *Children show a strong desire to take greater responsibility in their daily lives.*

- *Parents perceive their children as engaging more in planned, thoughtful actions and see a significant increase in their ability to generate productive creative ideas and responses.*
- *Parents feel more hopeful and less fearful about what the future holds.*
- *Parents feel a decreased need to act as a buffer and advocate for the child.*

In a paper published in 2007,[58] we presented the results of a research study conducted with children ages five to nine, who had been involved in RDI for an average of 2 ½ years. We found that only15% of children were still in special education classes, compared to over 90% prior to RDI. Parents reported an increase in age-appropriate flexibility and adaptation from 16% to over 70% of the time. While over 90% of children were rated in the autism range of the ADOS[59] prior to RDI, only two of the 16 children we followed received the autism rating at their follow up period. More research is currently underway at the world renowned Tavistock Institute in London, under the guidance of Jessica and Peter Hobson.

RDI has resulted in dramatic change for the majority of our families. For example, of the 18 children we are following into adolescence in a current study, eleven have made such impressive gains that I have no doubt about their ability to attain a high quality of life as adults.

However, the picture isn't completely rosy. For example, four of the children we are following have made significant progress, but are not yet functioning at the level where I can be confident that they will be independent and attain a normal life.

Progress for a third group of three teenagers we are following is even more limited. Parents have seen gains. Family life has undoubtedly improved. Guided participation is beginning to function. However, prognosis for completely independent life remains poor. These three children have multiple, severe neurological impairments in addition to their ASD. In these cases the classic signs of autism are overshadowed by their other neurological problems.

---

58   Gutstein, Burgess and Montfort (2007).
59   The Autism Diagnostic Observation Schedules—the most widely used diagnostic instrument in the ASD field.

Individuals with ASD are an amazingly diverse group, with some who clearly suffer from a much more severe degree of neural dysfunction than others. The pathway leading to the breakdown of the GPR can be reached in many ways. Rather than thinking of this third group as just falling over the edge based on the confluence of dysfunction, the strength of their disabilities should be thought of as providing a strong shove.

RDI is not a miracle. It cannot move children beyond their structural neurological limitations. What we try to do is to restore the Guided Participation Relationship and the desire for growth and expansion inherent in every child, so that they can develop to their full potential.

We have to accept that the severity of the problems that led to the autism in the first place may, for certain children, function as a limiting factor in the child's prognosis. We may think of this as a second threshold. Whereas the first threshold can be seen as a degree of dysfunction sufficient to thwart the development of the GPR and resulting in ASD, the second threshold represents a situation where the degree of neurological dysfunction is so severe, that even with the resumption of the GPR, the prospects for higher level mental development are more limited.

I have emphasized the importance of taking a bio-psycho-social approach to intervention. There is certainly a relationship between attaining physical health and improving prospects for remediation. Additionally, I have discussed how the high degree of co-occurring and secondary disorders necessitates the involvement of an inter-disciplinary team, especially during the Readiness Stages of the program. From a bio-psycho-social perspective, there is no reason why RDI cannot encompass the use of different levels of analysis to obtain optimal results. For example, we might want to take a behavioral point of view in treating a child's phobia. If a child is suffering from allergies, a biomedical perspective will be most helpful. Still at other times we may want to focus on the sensory-motor or perceptual system of the child. And there are clearly times when a family and larger systems perspective will be most fruitful.

WHAT OF THE FUTURE?

What does the future hold for RDI? The program has gone through much change and will continue to evolve as we learn what is most effective in helping our families and children to attain a quality of life.

My greatest hope is that RDI continues to evolve into a worldwide community united by a common mission: developing increasingly effective ways for families to resume their natural function as guides to their children, when the relationship has not developed, or has gone awry. We are gratified to see the expansion of RDI over the world. At the time of publication of this book, almost 400 RDI consultants and consultants-in-training are based in 20 different countries. We feel that the feedback from these talented professionals provides a rich broadening tapestry of the Guided Participation Relationship, as it is enacted in diverse cultures.

We envision the growth, over the coming years, of the RDI Learning System as a thriving Community of Practice. Thousands of professionals, parents and teachers are learning a common terminology, methodology and format for documenting progress. This provides a consensual framework for individuals from diverse cultural and professional backgrounds to communicate.[60] We believe that such a committed, mission-driven community can make enormous contributions to the development of RDI methodology.

CHILDREN AND FAMILIES

We are seeing many of our children turning into thriving teenagers. They are reaching out into the larger world and inward into their own internal beings. But, this is clearly not the case for many children with neuro-developmental disorders, who have not had the opportunity for RDI. Despite decades of dramatically increased awareness, advocacy and funding, children with neuro-developmental differences often remain marginalized in society. We believe that most of these children have the potential to accomplish much more. However, research and our

---

60   To meet the increasing demand for RDI in many different countries, we hope to provide multilanguage translations of the curriculum on the learning system in the near future.

own experience tells us that they will fail if they do not learn to analyze, evaluate and rapidly adjust to the dynamic currents of our modern society. Most schools and intervention programs inadequately prepare these children for successful life in our ever-changing, rarely predictable world. They do not turn on the drive for competence that every human being is born with. They do not provide the thrill of facing challenges and overcoming them through resilience, or of slowly developing mastery through dedication and hard work. Our expectations are much too low! Most methods are geared to survival not success! We can and will do much better.

We see the RDI movement as continuing to advocate for balancing dynamic intelligence and the concomitant construction of neural integration, alongside more traditional academic and self-help objectives, whether they are structured for typical students, or those with special needs. We no longer believe RDI is limited to individuals with ASD. There are a variety of parents and children with other diagnoses who, for various reasons, have lost the capacity to optimally carry out the Guided Participation Relationship. While the loss of guided participation and the failure to develop dynamic intelligence is universal to ASD, it is not unique to this disorder. Consultants are finding success working with many families of children diagnosed with Reactive Attachment Disorder, ADHD, Tourette's Syndrome, Bipolar Illness, Seizure disorders and a host of lesser known neurological syndromes.

We are also seeing an expansion in the age of children involved in RDI. It is now quite common for our consultants to be working with ASD adults who may seek RDI themselves, or along with their family members. As I stated earlier, we do not observe any age limitations, or critical periods, after which remediation cannot be productive. The greatest obstacle is the motivation of the ASD adult to participate in the process.

Finally, one of the most gratifying experiences we have had, comes from the number of parents, both mothers and fathers, who have decided that they wish to make a career change and become RDI Consultants. Our rule is that they cannot begin training until they have made significant progress with their own child. However, we see the unique strengths they bring to the program, through their ability to provide hope through sharing their own personal journeys.

RECOMMENDED READING

While I have included an extensive reference section, for those wishing to explore the foundations of RDI, I am providing a short list of references which I believe represent a good starting point.

Charman, C. (2003). Why is joint attention a pivotal skill in autism? *Philosophical Transactions of the Royal Society of London* (358), 315-324.

Collins, A., Brown, J., Holum, A. (1991). Cognitive Apprenticeship: Making thinking visible. *American Educator*, winter, 1-18.

Damasio, A. (1994). *Descartes Error: Emotion, Reason and the Human Brain.* New York: Harpercollins Books.

Fogel, A. (1993). *Developing Through Relationships: Origins of Communication, Self, and Culture.* Chicago: University of Chicago Press.

Hobson, P. (2002). *The Cradle of Thought: Exploring the Origins of Thinking.* London, UK: Macmillan.

Kaye, K. (1982). *The Mental and Social Life of Babies: How Parents Create Persons.* Chicago, Illinois: The Harvester Press.

Klin, A., Jones, W., Schultz, R., Volkmar, F. (2003). The enactive mind, or from actions to cognition: Lessons from autism. *Philosophical Transactions of the Royal Society of London* B (358), 345-360.

Lehrer, J. (2009). *How We Decide.* Boston: Houghton Mifflin Harcourt.

Minshew, N., Williams, D. (2007). The new neurobiology of Autism: Cortex, Connectivity and Neural Organization. *Archives of Neurology* (64), 945-950.

Rogoff, B. (1990). *Apprenticeship in Thinking: Cognitive development in social context.* New York, NY: Oxford University Press.

Siegel, D. (1999). *The Developing Mind: How Relationships and the Brain Interact to Shape Who We Are.* New York, NY: Guilford Press.

Sroufe, A. (1996). *Emotional Development: The Organization of Emotional Life in the Early Years.* Cambridge: Cambridge University Press.

Tomasello, M. (2007). Cooperation and communication in the 2nd year of life. *Child Development Perspectives* (1), 8-12.

Tronick, E. (1989). Emotions and emotional communication in infants. *American Psychologist* (44), 112-119.

REFERENCES BY CHAPTER

Introduction

Alliance, 2. C. (2000). *Building America's 21st Century Workforce: National Alliance of Business and US Department of Labor.* Retrieved from 21st Century Workforce Commission: http://www.21stcenturylearningalliance.com.

Barnard, J., Harvey, V., Potter,D., Prior, A. (2001). *Ignored or ineligible? The reality for adults with autism spectrum disorders.* The National Autistic Society report for Autism Awareness Week. London: NAS Publications.

Bruner, J. S. (1983). Education as social invention. *Journal of Social Issues* (39), 129-14.

Busse, R. (1992). The new basics: Today's employers want the three R's and so much more. *Vocational Education Journal* (67), 24-25.

Conference Board of Canada. (2000, January 17). *Employability skills 2000+.* Retrieved 2001, from http://www.conferenceboard.ca/nbec/pdf/esp2000.pdf.

Courchesne E, P. K. (2005). Why the frontal cortex in autism might be talking only to itself: Local over-connectivity but long-distance disconnection. *Current Opinion in Neurobiology* (15), 225-230.

Edelson, MG. (2006). Are the Majority of Children With Autism Mentally Retarded? A Systematic Evaluation of the Data. *Focus on Autism and Other Developmental Disabilities* (21), 66-83.

Farraly, M. (2001). What happens after school? Outcome for individuals with Asperger's syndrome/high functioning autism. *Frontline of Learning Disability, 47*(online).

Fogel, A. (1993). *Developing Through Relationships: Origins of Communication, Self, and Culture.* Chicago: University of Chicago Press.

Hobson, P. (1993). *Autism and the Development of Mind.* Mahwah, NJ: Lawrence Erlbaum.

Hobson, P. (2002). *The Cradle of Thought: Exploring the Origins of Thinking.* London, UK: Macmillan.

Howlin, P. (2003). Outcome in high-functioning adults with autism with and without early language delays: Implications for the differentiation between autism and Asperger syndrome. *Journal of Autism and Developmental Disorders* (33), 3-13.

Kanner, L. (1943). Autistic disturbances of affective contact. *Nervous Child* (2), 217-250.

Kanner, L. (1968). Follow-up study of eleven children originally reported in 1943. *Acta Paedopsychiatrica* (35), 100-136.

Lankard, B. (1990). Employability—The Fifth Basic Skill. *ERIC Digest , ED 325 659* (104).

Rogoff, B. (1990). *Apprenticeship in Thinking: Cognitive Development in Social Context.* New York, NY: Oxford University Press.

Seltzer, M., Krauss, M. (2002). *Adolescents and Adults with Autism: A Profile of Adolescents and Adults with Autistic Spectrum Disorder.* National Institute on Aging. AAA.

Sigman M, Dijamco A, Gratier M, Rozga A. (2004). Early Detection of Core Deficits in Autism. *Mental Retardation and Developmental Disabilities Research Reviews* (10), 221-233.

Sroufe, A. (1996). *Emotional Development: The Organization of Emotional Life in the Early Years.* Cambridge: Cambridge University Press.

Chapter 1: Dynamic Brains

Bauman ML, Kempter, TL. (2007). The neuroanatomy of the brain in autism: Current thoughts and future directions. In G. P. Perez JM, *New developments in autism: The future is today* (pp. 259-267). London: Jessica Kingsley Publisher.

Belmonte MK., Allen, G., Beckel-Mitchener, A., Boulanger, LM., Carper, R., Webb, SG. (2004). Autism and Abnormal Development of Brain Connectivity. *Journal of Neuroscience* (24), 9228-9231.

Belmonte, MK., Cook, EH., Anderson, GM., Rubenstein, JLR., Greenough, WT., Beckel-Mitchener, A., Courchesne, E., Boulange, LM., Powell, SB., Levitt, PR., Perry, EK., Jiang YH., DeLorey, TM., Tierney, E. (2004). Autism as a disorder of neural information processing: Directions for research and targets for therapy. *Molecular Psychiatry* (9), 646-663.

Bransford, JD., Brown, AL., Cocking, R. (Eds.) (2000). *How People Learn.* Commission on Behavioral and Social Sciences and Education, The National Research Council and the National Academy of Sciences (NAS), The Committee on Development in the Science of Learning. Washington, D.C.: National Academy Press.

Cherkassky, VL, Kana, RK., Keller, TA., Just, MA. (2006). Functional connectivity in a baseline resting-state network in autism. *Neuroreport: For Rapid Communication of Neuroscience Research* (17), 1687-1690.

Courchesne E, Pierce K. (2005). Why the frontal cortex in autism might be talking only to itself: Local over-connectivity but long-distance disconnection. *Current Opinion in Neurobiology* (15), 225-230.

Courchesne, E., Pierce, K.(2005). Brain overgrowth in autism during a critical time in development: Implications for frontal pyramidal neuron and interneuron development and connectivity. *International Journal of Developmental Neuroscience* (23), 153-170.

Henderson, L., Yoder, P., McDuffie, A. (2002). Getting the point: Electrophysiological correlates of protodeclarative pointing. *International Journal of Developmental Neuroscience* (20), 449-458.

Huether, G. (1998). Stress and the adaptive self-organization of neuronal connectivity during early childhood. *International Journal of Developmental Neuroscience, 16* (3-4), 297-306.

Just M., Cherkassky V., Keller T., Minshew N. (2004). Cortical activation and synchronization during sentence comprehension in high-functioning autism: Evidence of underconnectivity. Brain. *A Journal of Neurology* (127), 1811-1821.

Minshew, NJ., Webb, SJ., Williams, DL., Dawson, G. (2006). Neuropsychology and Neurophysiology of autism Spectrum Disorders. In R. J. Modin SO, *Understanding autism: From basic neuroscience to treatment.* (pp. 379-415). Boca Raton, Florida: CRC Press.

Siegel, D. (1999). *The Developing Mind: How Relationships and the Brain Interact to Shape Who We Are.* New York, NY: Guilford Press.

Chapter 2: Dynamic Intelligence

Allal, L., Ducrey, G.P. (2000). Assessment of-or-in the zone of proximal development. *Learning and Instruction.* 10(2), 137-152.

Baker-Sennett, J. Matusov, E., Rogoff, B. (1993). Planning as developmental process. H. Reese (Ed.), *Advances in Child Development and Behavior,* Vol. 24. (pp. 253-281). San Diego, Academic Press, Inc.

Fabio, R. A. (2005). Dynamic Assessment of Intelligence is a better reply to adaptive behavior and cognitive plasticity. *Journal of General Psychology* (132), 41-64.

Gardner, H. (1999). *Reframing Intelligence.* New York: Basic Books.

Grigorenko, L., Sternberg, R. (1998). Dynamic Testing. *Psychological Bulletin* (124), 75-111.

Haywood, H.C., Lidz, C.S. (2007). *Dynamic assessment in practice: Clinical and educational applications.* New York, New York: Cambridge University Press.

Lehrer, J. (2009). *How We Decide.* New York: Houghton Mifflin.

Lidz, C.S., Elliott, J.G. (Eds.). (2000). *Dynamic assessment: Prevailing models and applications.* Amsterdam: JAI/Elsevier Science.

Sternberg, R. (1985). *Beyond IQ: A triarchic theory of human intelligence.* New York, NY: Cambridge University Press.

Sternberg, R., Grigorenko, E. (2002). *Dynamic Testing: The Nature and Measurement of Learning Potentia.* Cambridge: Cambridge University Press.

Sternberg, R. (1986). *Intelligence Applied.* San Diego, CA: Harcourt.

Thelen, E., Smith, L, (1994). *A Dynamic Systems Approach to the Development of Cognition and Action.* Cambridge, MA: MIT Press.

Tzuriel, D. (2001). *Dynamic Assessment of Young Children.* Kluwer Academic/Plenum Publishers.

Chapter 3: Dynamic Communication

Camaioni, L. (1997). The emergence of intentional communication in ontogeny, phylogeny and pathology. *European Psychologist* (2), 216-225.

Carpenter, M., Akhtar, N., Tomasello, M. (1998). Social cognition, joint attention, and communicative competence from 9 to 15 months of age. *Monographs of the Society for Research in Child Development , 63* (4).

Fogel, A. (1993). *Developing Through Relationships: Origins of Communication, Self, and Culture.* Chicago: University of Chicago Press.

Frick, R. (1985). Communicating emotion: The role of prosodic features. *Psychological Bulletin* (97), 412-429.

Harding, C. G., Weissmann, L., Kromelow, S., Stilson, S. R. (1997). Shared minds: How mothers and infants co-construct early patterns of choice within intentional communication partnerships. *Infant Mental Health Journal* (18), 24-39.

Kriegstein, K., Kleinschmidt, A., Sterzerr, P., Giraud, A. (2005). Interaction of face and voice areas during speaker recognition. *Journal of Cognitive Neuroscience* (17), 367-376.

MacWhinney, B. (1998). Models of the emergence of language. *Annual Review of Psychology*, (49), 199-227.

Papousek, M. (2007). Communication in early infancy: An arena of intersubjective learning. *Infant Behavior and Development* (30), 258-266.

Tomasello, M., Carpenter, M. (2005, March). The Emergence of Social Cognition in Three Young Chimpanzees. *Monographs of the Society for Research in Child Development*, 70 (1), 1 136.

Walker-Andrews, A. (1997). Infants' perception of expressive behaviors: Differentiation of multimodal information. *Psychological Bulletin* (121), 437-456.

Warneken, F., Chen, F., Tomasello, M. (2006). Cooperative Activities in Young Children and Chimpanzees. *Child Development*, 77 (3), 640-663.

Chapter 4: Dynamic Departures

Adrien J, Martineau J, Barthelemy C, Bruneau N. (2005). Disorders of regulation of cognitive activity in autistic children. *Journal of Autism and Developmental Disorders* (25), 249-263.

Bachevalier, J., Loveland, KA., (2003). Early orbitofrontal-limbic dysfunction and autism. In: Cicchetti, D., Walker, E. eds. *Neurodevelopmental mechanisms in psychopathology.* New York, NY: Cambridge University Press; 215-236.

Bacon, A., Fein, D., Morris, R., Waterhouse, L., Allen, D. The responses of autistic children to the distress of others. *Journal of Autism and Developmental Disorders* (28), 129-142.

Baron-Cohen, S., Baldwin, D., Crowson M. (1997). Do children with autism use the speaker's direction of gaze strategy to crack the code of language? *Child Development* (68), 48-57.

Bauman ML, Kempter, TL. (2007). The neuroanatonomy of the brain in autism: Current thoughts and future directions. In G. P. Perez JM, *New developments in autism: The future is today* (pp. 259-267). London: Jessica Kingsley Publisher.

Belmonte MK., Allen, G., Beckel-Mitchener, A., Boulanger, LM., Carper, R., Webb, SG. (2004). Autism and Abnormal Development of Brain Connectivity. *Journal of Neuroscience* (24), 9228-9231.

Belmonte, MK., Cook, EH., Anderson, GM., Rubenstein, JLR., Greenough, WT., Beckel-Mitchener, A., Courchesne, E., Boulange, LM., Powell, SB., Levitt, PR., Perry, EK., Jiang YH., DeLorey, TM., Tierney, E. (2004). Autism as a disorder of neural information processing: Directions for research and targets for therapy. *Molecular Psychiatry* (9), 646-663.

Berger, H., Van, S., Kare,l P., Horstink, M., Buytenhuijs, E. (1993). Cognitive shifting as a predictor of progress in social understanding in high-functioning adolescents with autism: A prospective study. *Journal of Autism and Developmental Disorders.* (23), 341-359.

Boucher, J. (2007). Memory and generativity in very high functioning autism: A firsthand account, and an interpretation. *Autism* (11), 255-264.

Bowler, D., Gardiner, J., Grice, S. (2000). Episodic Memory and Remembering in Adults with Asperger Syndrome. *Journal of Autism and Developmental Disorders.* 30, (4)

Bowler, D., Gardiner, J., Berthollier, N. (2004.) Source Memory in Adolescents and Adults with Asperger's Syndrome. *Journal of Autism and Developmental Disorders* (34), 533-542.

Bowler, D. Autism: Specific cognitive deficit or emergent endpoint of multiple interacting systems? (2001). In: Burack, J., Charman, T., Yirmiya, N., Zelazo, P. eds. *The development of autism: Perspectives from theory and research.* (pp. 219-235). Mahwah, NJ: Lawrence Erlbaum.

Brosnan, M., Scott, F., Fox, S., Pye, J. (2004). Gestalt processing in autism: Failure to process perceptual relationships and the implications for contextual understanding. *Journal of Child Psychology and Psychiatry* (45), 459-469.

Bruck, M., London, K., Landa, R., Goodman, J. (2007) Autobiographical memory and suggestibility in children with autism spectrum disorder. *Development and Psychopathology* (19), 73-95.

Burack, J. (1994) Selective attention deficits in persons with autism: Preliminary evidence of an inefficient attentional lens. *Journal of Abnormal Psychology* (103), 535-543.

Carpenter, M., Pennington, B., Rogers, S. (2001) Understanding of others' intentions in children with autism. *Journal of Autism and Developmental Disorders* (31), 589-599.

Channon, S., Charman, T., Heap, J., Crawford, S., Rios, P. (2001) Real-life-type problem-solving in Asperger's syndrome. *Journal of Autism and Developmental Disorders* (31), 461-469.

Cherkassky, VL, Kana, RK., Keller, TA., Just, MA. (2006). Functional connectivity in a baseline resting-state network in autism. *Neuroreport: For Rapid Communication of Neuroscience Research* (17), 1687-1690.

Courchesne E, Pierce K. (2005). Why the frontal cortex in autism might be talking only to itself: Local over-connectivity but long-distance disconnection. *Current Opinion in Neurobiology* (15), 225-230.

Craig, J., Baron-Cohen, S. (1999). Creativity and imagination in Autism and Asperger Syndrome. *Journal of Autism and Developmental Disorders* (29), 319-326.

Dawson, G., Munson, J., Webb, S., Nalty, T., Abbott, R., Toth, K. (2007). Rate of Head Growth Decelerates and Symptoms Worsen in the Second Year of Life in Autism. *Biological Psychiatry* (61), 458-464.

Dawson, G., Toth, K., Abbott, R., Osterling, J., Munson, J., Estes, A., Liaw, J. (2004). Early Social Attention Impairments in Autism: Social Orienting, Joint Attention, and Attention to Distress. *Developmental Psychology* (40), 271-283.

Downs, A., Smith, T. (2004). Emotional understanding, cooperation, and social behavior in high-functioning children with Autism. *Journal of Autism and Developmental Disorders* (34), 625-635.

Edelson, MG. (2006). Are the Majority of Children With Autism Mentally Retarded? A Systematic Evaluation of the Data. *Focus on Autism and Other Developmental Disabilities* (21), 66-83.

Emerich, D., Creaghead, N., Grether, S., Murray, D., Grasha, C. (2003). The Comprehension of Humorous Materials by Adolescents with High-Functioning Autism and Asperger's Syndrome. *Journal of Autism and Developmental Disorders* (33), 253-257.

Fogel, A. (1995). Development and relationships: A dynamic model of communication. *Advances in the study of behavior* (24), 259-290.

Geller, E. (1998). An investigation of communication breakdowns and repairs in verbal autistic children. *British Journal of Developmental Disabilities* (87), 71-85.

Hobson, P. (1993). *Autism and the Development of Mind.* Mahwah, NJ: Lawrence Erlbaum.

Hoeksma, M., Kemner, C., Verbaten, M., Van Engeland, H. (2004). Processing Capacity in Children and Adolescents with Pervasive Developmental Disorders. *Journal of Autism and Developmental Disorders* (34),341-354.

Hughes, C., Russell, J., Robbins, T. (1994). Evidence for executive dysfunction in autism. *Neuropsychologia* (32), 477-492.

Hughes, C., Russell, J. (1993). Autistic children's difficulty with mental disengagement from an object: Its implications for theories of autism. *Developmental Psychology* (29), 498-510.

Hughes, C. (2001). Executive dysfunction in autism: Its nature and implications for the everyday problems experienced by individuals with autism. In J. C. Burack, *The development of autism: Perspectives from theory and research.* (pp. 255-271).

Jarrold, C., Boucher, J., Smith, P. (1996). Generativity defects in pretend play in autism. *British Journal of Developmental Psychology* (14), 275-300.

Just M., Cherkassky V., Keller T., Minshew N. (2004). Cortical activation and synchronization during sentence comprehension in high-functioning autism: Evidence of under-connectivity. Brain. *A Journal of Neurology* (127), 1811-1821.

Keen, D. (2005). The use of non-verbal repair strategies by children with autism. *Research in Developmental Disabilities* (26), 243-254.

Laing, R.D. (1967). *The Politics of Experience.* New York: Pantheon Books.

Luna, B., Doll, SK., Hegedus, S., Minshew, N., Sweeney, J. (2007). Maturation of Executive Function in Autism. *Biological Psychiatry* (61), 474-481.

Millward, C., Powell, S., Messer, D., Jordan, R. (2000). Recall for Self and Other in Autism: Children's Memory for Events Experienced by Themselves and Their Peers. *Journal of Autism and Developmental Disorders*(30), 15-28.

Minshew, N., Meyer, J., Goldstein, G. (2002). Abstract reasoning in autism: A disassociation between concept formation and concept identification. *Neuropsychology* (16), 327-334.

Minshew, NJ., Webb, SJ., Williams, DL., Dawson, G. (2006). Neuropsychology and Neuro-physiology of autism Spectrum Disorders. In R. J. Modin SO, *Understanding autism: From basic neuroscience to treatment.* (pp. 379-415). Boca Raton, Florida: CRC Press.

Minshew, N., Williams, D., Goldstein, G. (2004a). A further characterization of complex cognitive abilities in high functioning autism. *Paper presented at the International Meeting for Autism Research, Sacramento California: 2004.*

Nair, J. (2004). Knowing Me, Knowing You: Self-Awareness in Asperger's and Autism. In: Beitman, B., Nair, J, eds. *Self-awareness deficits in psychiatric patients: Neurobiology, assessment, and treatment.* New York, NY: W. W. Norton and Co.

Ozonoff, S., South, M., Provencal, S. (2007). Executive functions in autism: Theory and practice. In G. P. Pérez JM, *New Developments in Autism: The Future is Today* (pp. 185-213). London, UK: Jessica Kingsley.

Papousek, M. (2007). Communication in early infancy: An arena of intersubjective learning. *Infant Behavior and Development* (30), 258-266.

Rajendran, G., Mitchell, P. (2007). Cognitive theories of autism. *Developmental Review* (27), 224-260.

Sternberg, RJ., Pretz, JE. (2005). *Cognition and Intelligence: Identifying the mechanisms of the mind.* New York, NY: Cambridge University Press.

Toichi, M., Kamio, Y., Okada, T., Sakihama, M., Youngstrom, A., Findling, L., Yamamoto K. (2002). A lack of self-consciousness in autism. *American Journal of Psychiatry* (159),1422-1424.

Tomasello, M. (1999). *The Cultural Origins of Human Cognition.* Cambridge, MA: Harvard University Press.

Whitehouse, A., Maybery, M., Durkin, K. (2006). Inner speech impairments in autism. *Journal of Child Psychology and Psychiatry* (47), 857-865.

Chapter 5: The Guided Participation Relationship

Rogoff, B. (1990). *Apprenticeship in Thinking: Cognitive development in social context.* New York, NY: Oxford University Press.

Vygotsky, L. (1978). *Mind in Society: The Development of Higher Psychological Processes.* Cambridge, MA: Harvard University Press.

Chapter 6: Guided Participation - The Guide

Bruner, J., (1961). The act of discovery. *Harvard Educational Review* (31), 2132.

Collins, A. (1991). Cognitive apprenticeship and instructional technology. In L. Idol, B.F. Jones (Eds.), *Educational values and cognitive instruction: Implication for reform* (pp. 121-138). Hillsdale, NJ: Lawrence Erlbaum Associates.

Collins, A., Brown, J., Holum, A. (1991). Cognitive Apprenticeship: Making thinking visible. *American Educator*, winter, 1-18.

Collins, A., Brown, J., Newman, S. E. (1989). Cognitive apprenticeship: Teaching the craft of reading, writing, and mathematics. In L. B. Resnick (Ed.), *Knowing, learning, and instruction: Essays in honor of Robert Glaser* (pp. 453-494). Hillsdale, NJ: Lawrence Erlbaum Associates.

Dorn, Linda., Soffos, Carla, (2001). *Scaffolding Young Writers: A Writers' Workshop Approach*. Portland, Maine: Stenhouse Publishing.

Rogoff, B. (1990). *Apprenticeship in Thinking: Cognitive development in social context*. New York, NY: Oxford University Press.

Shunk, D. (2000). *Learning theories: An educational perspective (3rd ed)*. Upper Saddle River, NJ: Prentice Hall.

Vygotsky, L. (1978). *Mind in Society: The Development of Higher Psychological Processes*. Cambridge, MA: Harvard University Press.

Chapter 7: Guided Participation - The Apprentice

Bakerman, R., Adamson, L. (1984). Coordinating Attention to people and objects in mother-infant and peer-infant interactions. *Child Development* (55), 1278-1289.

Baldwin, D., Moses, L. (1996). The ontogeny of social information gathering. *Child Development* (67), 1915–1939.

Bates, E., Benigni, L., Bretheront, I., Camaioni, L., Volterra, V. (1979). *The Emergence of Symbols: Cognition and Communication in Infancy*. New York, New York: Academic Press.

Bates, E., Camaioni, L., Volterra, V. (1975). The acquisition of performatives prior to speech. *Merrill-Palmer Quarterly* (21), 205-226.

Bazhenova, O., Plonskaia, O., Porges, S. (2001). Vagal reactivity and affective adjustment in infants during interaction challenge. *Child Development* (72), 1314-1326.

Bellagamba, F., Tomasello, M. (1999). Re-enacting intended acts: Comparing 12-and 18-month-old. *Infant Behavior and Development* (22), 277-282.

Bigelow, A. (1999). Infants' sensitivity to imperfect contingency in social interaction. In P. R. (Ed.), *Early Social Cognition.* HIllsdale, NJ: Erlbaum.

Bruner, J., Sherwood, V. (1976). Peek-a-boo and the learning of rule structures. In A. J. J. Bruner, *Play.* New York: Basic Books.

Buss, K., Kiel, E. (2004). Comparison of sadness, anger and fear facial expressions when toddlers look at their mothers. *Child Development* (75), 1761-1773.

Camaioni, L. (1997). The emergence of intentional communication in ontogeny, phylogeny and pathology. *European Psychologist* (2), 216-225.

Camaioni, L., Perucchini, P., Bellagamba, F., Colonnesi, C. (2004). The Role of Declarative Pointing in Developing a Theory of Mind. *Infancy* (5), 291-308.

Campos, J., Sternber, C. Perception, appraisal, and emotion: The onset of social referencing . In. M. Lamb., L. Sherrod (Eds.), *Infant Social Cognition: Empirical and Theoretical Considerations.* Hillsdale, NJ: Erlbaum.

Carpenter, M., Akhtar, N., Tomasello, M. (1998). Fourteen-to-18-month-old infants differentially imitate intentional and accidental actions. *Infant Behavior and Development,* 21, 315–330.

Carpenter, M., Akhtar, N., Tomasello, M. (1998). Social cognition, joint attention, and communicative competence from 9 to 15 months of age. *Monographs of the Society for Research in Child Development ,* 63 (4).

Cohn, J., Tronick, E. (1987). Mother-infant face-to-face interaction: The sequence of dyadic states at 3, 6, and 9 months. *Developmental Psychology* (23), 68-77.

Eckerman, C, Didow, S. (1996). Nonverbal imitation and toddler's mastery of verbal means of achieving coordinated action. *Developmental Psychology* (32), 141-152.

Feldman, R. (2006). From biological rhythms to social rhythms: Physiological precursors of mother-infant synchrony. *Developmental Psychology* (42), 175-188.

Fernald, A. (1985). Four-month-old infants prefer to listen to motherese. *Infant Behavior and Development* (8), 181-195.

Fogel, A. (1993). *Developing Through Relationships: Origins of Communication, Self, and Culture.* Chicago: University of Chicago Press.

Greenfield, P. (1972). Playing peek-a-boo with a four-month-old: A study of the role of speech and non-speech sounds in the formation of a visual schema. *Journal of Psychology* (82), 287-298.

Harding, C. G., Weissmann, L., Kromelow, S., Stilson, S. R. (1997). Shared minds: How mothers and infants co-construct early patterns of choice within intentional communication partnerships. *Infant Mental Health Journal* (18), 24-39.

Henderson, L., Yoder, P., McDuffie, A. (2002). Getting the point: Electrophysiological correlates of protodeclarative pointing. *International Journal of Developmental Neuroscience* (20), 449-458.

Hobson, P. (2002). *The Cradle of Thought: Exploring the Origins of Thinking.* London, UK: Macmillan.

Jaffe, J., Beebe, B., Feldstein, S., Crown, C., Jasnow, M. (2001). Rhythms of dialogue in Infancy. *Monographs of the Society for Research in Child Development* (66).

Kaye, K. (1982). *The Mental and Social Life of Babies: How Parents Create Persons.* Chicago, Illinois: The Harvester Press.

Klinnert, M., Emde, R., Butterfield, P., Campos, J. (1986). Social referencing: The infant's use of emotional signals from a friendly adult with mother present. *Developmental Psychology* (22), 427-432.

Kokkinaki, T. (2003). A longitudinal, naturalistic and cross-cultural study on emotions in early infant-parent imitative interactions. *British Journal of Developmental Psychology, 21* (2), 243-258.

Louis J., Baldwin, D., Rosicky, J., Tidball, G. (2001). Evidence for referential understanding in the emotions domain at twelve and eighteen months. *Child Development, 72* (3), 718-735.

Mandler, J. (1992). How to build a baby II: Conceptual Primitives. *Psychological Review* (99), 587-604.

Mayes, L., Carter, A. (1990). Emerging social regulatory capacities as seen in the still-face situation. *Child Development* (61), 754-763.

Meltzoff, A. (1995). Understanding the intentions of others: Re-enactment of intended acts by 18-month-old children. *Developmental Psychology* (31), 838-850.

Moore, G., Calkins, S. (2004). Infants' Vagal regulation in the still-face paradigm is related to dyadic coordination of mother-infant interaction. *Developmental Psychology* (40), 1068-1080.

Morales, M., Mundy, P., Delgado, C. E. F., Yale, M., Messinger, D., Neal, R .(2000). Responding to joint attention across the 6- through 24-month age period and early language acquisition. *Journal of Applied Developmental Psychology* (21), 283-298.

Nielson, M. (2006). Copying actions and copying outcomes: Social learning through the second year. *Developmental Psychology* (42), 555-565.

Porter, C. (2003). Co-regulation in mother-infant dyads: Links to infants' cardiac Vagal tone. *Psychological Reports* (92), 307-319.

Reddy, V., Hay, D., Murry, L., Trevarthen, C. (1997). Communication in infancy: Mutual regulation of affect and attention. In A. S. G. Bremner, *Infant Development: Recent Advances.* Hove, UK: Psychological Press.

Repacholi, B., Gopnik, A.(1997). Early understanding of desires: Evidence from 14 and 18-month-olds. *Developmental Psychology* (33), 12-21.

Rochat, P. (2001). *The Infant's World.* Cambridge, MA: Harvard University Press.

Rochat, P., Querido, J., Striano, T. (1999). Emerging sensitivity to the timing and structure of proto-conversation in early infancy. *Developmental Psychology, 35* (4), 950-957.

Rochat, P., Striano, T. (1999). Social cognitive development in the first year. In P. R. (Ed.), *Early Social Cognition.* Hillsdale, NJ: Erlbaum.

Sander, L. (1977). The regulation of exchange in the infant-caretaker system and some aspects of the context-content relationship. In M. L. (Eds.), *Interaction, Conversation and the Development of Language.* New York, NY: Wiley.

Scherer, K., Zentner, M., Stern, D. (2004). Beyond Surprise: The puzzle of infants' expressive reactions to expectancy violation. *Emotion* (4), 389-402.

Schwartz, G., Izard, C., Ansul, S. (1985). The 5-month-old's ability to discriminate facial expressions of emotion. *Infant Behavior and Development* (8), 65-77.

Siegel, D. (1999). *The Developing Mind: How Relationships and the Brain Interact to Shape Who We Are.* New York, NY: Guilford Press.

Sroufe, A. (1996). *Emotional Development: The Organization of Emotional Life in the Early Years.* Cambridge: Cambridge University Press.

Stern, D. (1977). *The First Relationship: Infant and Mother*. Cambridge, MA: Harvard University Press.

Stern, D. (1985). *The Interpersonal World of the Infant*. New York, NY: Basic Books.

Striano, T., Rochat, P.(2000). Emergence of selective social referencing in infancy. *Infancy* (1), 253-264.

Tomasello, M. (2007). Cooperation and communication in the 2nd year of life. *Child Development Perspectives* (1), 8-12.

Tomasello, M. (1995). Joint attention as social cognition. In C. M. (Eds.), *Joint Attention: Its Origins and Role in Development*. Hillsdale, NJ: Erlbaum.

Tomasello, M., Max, K. (2003). Understanding attention: 12 and 18-month-olds know what is new for other persons. *Developmental Psychology*, 39 (5), 906-912.

Trevarthen, C., Aitken, KJ. (2001). Infant intersubjectivity: Research, theory, and clinical applications. *Journal of Child Psychology and Psychiatry* (42), 3-48.

Tronick, E. (1989). Emotions and emotional communication in infants. *American Psychologist* (44), 112-119.

Tronick, E., Gianino, A. (1986). Interactive mismatch and repair: Challenges to the coping infant. *Zero to Three*, 6 (3), 1-6.

Warneken, F., Chen, F., Tomasello, M. (2006). Cooperative Activities in Young Children and Chimpanzees. *Child Development*, 77 (3), 640-663.

Yale, M., Messinger, D., Cobo-Lewis, A., Delgado, C. (2003). The temporal coordination of early infant communication. *Developmental Psychology* (39), 815-824.

Chapter 8: The Breaking Point

Bacon, A., Fein, D., Morris, R., Waterhouse, L., and Allen, D. The responses of autistic children to the distress of others. *Journal of Autism and Developmental Disorders* (28), 129-142.

Baron-Cohen, S. (1989). Joint-attention deficits in autism: Towards a cognitive analysis. *Development and Psychopathology* (1), 185-189.

Baron-Cohen, S. (1989). Perceptual role taking and protodeclarative pointing in autism. *British Journal of Developmental Psychology* (7), 113-127.

Belmonte, MK., Cook, EH., Anderson, GM., Rubenstein, JLR., Greenough, WT., Beckel-Mitchener, A., Courchesne, E., Boulange, LM., Powell, SB., Levitt, PR., Perry, EK., Jiang YH., DeLorey, TM., Tierney, E. (2004). Autism as a disorder of neural information processing: Directions for research and targets for therapy. *Molecular Psychiatry* (9), 646-663.

Berger, M. (2006). A model of preverbal social development and its application to social dysfunctions in autism. *Journal of Child Psychology and Psychiatry, 47,* 338-371.

Bieberich, A., Morgan, S. (1998). Affective expression in children with autism or downs syndrome. *Journal of Autism and Developmental Disorders , 28* (4), 333-338.

Bono, M., Daley, T., Sigman, M. (2004). Relations among joint attention, amount of intervention and language gain in Autism. *Journal of Autism and Developmental Disorders* (34), 495-505.

Camaioni, L., Perucchini, P., Muratori, F., Parrini, B., Cesari, A. (2003). The communicative use of pointing in autism: Developmental profile and factors related to change. *European Psychiatry* (18), 6-12.

Capps, L., Kehres, J., Sigman, M. (1998). Conversational abilities among children with autism and children with developmental delays. *Autism* (2), 325-344.

Carpenter, M., Pennington, B., Rogers, S. (2002). Interrelations among social-cognitive skills in young children with autism. *Journal of Autism and Developmental Disorders* (32), 91-106.

Charman, C. (2003). Why is joint attention a pivotal skill in autism?. *Philosophical Transactions of the Royal Society of London* (358), 315-324.

Charman, T., Swettenham, J., Baron-Cohen, S., Cox, A., Baird, G., Drew, A. (1997). Infants with autism: An investigation of empathy, pretend play, joint attention, and imitation. *Developmental Psychology* (5), 782-789.

Charman, T., Taylor, E., Drew, A., Cockerill, H., Brown, J. A., Baird, G. (2005). Outcome at 7 years of children diagnosed with autism at age 2: Predictive validity of assessments conducted at 2 and 3 years of age and pattern of symptom change over time. *Journal of Child Psychology and Psychiatry* (46), 500-513.

Dawson, G., Carver, L., Meltzoff, A., Panagiotides, H., McPartland, J., Webb, S. (2002). Neural correlates of face and object recognition in young children with autism spectrum disorder, developmental delay and typical development. *Child Development,* (73), 700-717.

Dawson, G., Hill, D., Spencer, A., Galpert, L., Watson, L. (1990). Affective exchanges between young autistic children and their mothers. *Journal of Abnormal Child Psychology* (18), 335-345.

Dawson, G., Toth, K., Abbott, R., Osterling, J., Munson, J., Estes, A., Liaw, J. (2004). Early social attention impairments in autism: Social orienting, joint attention and attention to distress. *Developmental Psychology* (40(2)), 271-283.

Geller, E. (1998). An investigation of communication breakdowns and repairs in verbal autistic children. *British Journal of Developmental Disabilities* (87), 71-85.

Gipps, R. (2004). Autism and intersubjectivity: Beyond cognitivism and the theory of mind. *Philosophy, Psychiatry, and Psychology* (11), 195-198.

Goodhart, F., Baron-Cohen, S. (1993). How many ways can the point be made? Evidence from children with and without autism. *First Language* (13), 225-233.

Hale, C., Tager-Flusberg, H. (2005). Social communication in children with autism: The relationship between theory of mind and discourse development. *Autism* (9), 157-178.

Hauck, M., Fein, D., Waterhouse, L.,Feinstein, C. (1995). Social initiations by autistic children to adults and other children. *Journal of Autism and Developmental Disorders* (6), 579-595.

Hobson, P. (1989). On sharing experiences. *Development and Psychopathology* (1), 197-203. Mahwah, NJ: Lawrence Erlbaum.

Hobson, P. (1993). *Autism and the development of mind.* Mahwah, NJ: Lawrence Erlbaum.

Hobson, P. (2002). *The Cradle of Thought: Exploring the Origins of Thinking.* London, UK: Macmillan.

Hobson, P. (2007). On being moved in thought and feeling: An approach to autism. In J. G. Pérez, *New developments in autism: The future is today* (pp. 139-154). London, UK: Jessic Kingsley.

Hobson, R., Bishop M. The pathogenesis of autism: Insights from congenital blindness. In H. E. Frith U, *Autism: Mind and Brain* (pp. 109-126). New York, New York: Oxford University Press.

Hobson, P., Lee, A. (1998). Hello and goodbye: A study of social engagement in autism. *Journal of Autism and Developmental Disorders* (28).

Hughes, C. (2001). Executive dysfunction in autism: Its nature and implications for the everyday problems experienced by individuals with autism. In J. C. Burack, *The development of autism: Perspectives from theory and research.* (pp. 255-271).

Kanner, L. (1943). Autistic disturbances of affective contact. *Nervous Child* (2), 217-250.

Kasari, C., Sigman, M., Baumgartner, P., Stipek, D. (1993). Pride and mastery in children with autism. *Journal of Child Psychology and Psychiatry and Allied Disciplines* (34), 353-362.

Kasari, C., Sigman, M., Mundy, P., Yirmiya, N. (1990). Affective sharing in the context of joint attention interactions of normal, autistic and mentally retarded children. *Journal of Autism and Development Disorders* (20), 87-100.

Keen, D. (2005). The use of non-verbal repair strategies by children with autism. *Research in Developmental Disabilities* (26), 243-254.

Loddo, S. (2003). The understanding of actions and intentions in autism. *Journal of Autism and Developmental Disorders* (33), 545-546.

Maestro S, Muratori F, Barbieri F, Casella C, Cattaneo V, Cavallaro M, Cesari A, Milone A, Rizzo L, Viglione V, Stern D, Palacio-Espasa F. (2001). Early Behavioral Development in Autistic Children: The First 2 Years of Life through Home Movies. *Psychopathology* (34), 147-152.

Maestro, S., Muratori, F., Cavallaro, MC., Pecini, C., Cesari, A., Paziente, A., Stern, D., Golse, B., Palacio, E., Francisco. (2005) How Young Children Treat Objects and People: An Empirical Study of the First Year of Life in Autism. *Child Psychiatry and Human Development.* (35), 383-396.

Mayes, S., Dickerson, Calhoun S, L. (2001). Non-significance of early speech delay in children with autism and normal intelligence and implications for DSM-IV Asperger's disorder. *Autism* (5), 81-94.

McGovern, C., Sigman, M.(2005). Continuity and change from early childhood to adolescence in autism. *Journal of Child Psychology and Psychiatry* (46), 401-408.

Mundy, P., Crowson, M. (1997). Joint attention and early social communication: Implications for research on interventions with autism. *Journal of Autism and Developmental Disorders* (6), 653-676.

Mundy, P., Kasari, C., Sigman, M. (1992). Nonverbal communication, affective sharing and intersubjectivity. *Infant Behavioral Development* (15), 377-381.

Mundy, P., Kasari, C., Sigman, M., Ruskin, E. (1995). Nonverbal communication and early language acquisition in children with Down syndrome and in normally developing children. *Journal of Speech and Hearing Research* (38), 157-167.

Mundy, P., Sigman, M., Ksari, C. (1990). A longitudinal study of joint attention and language development in autistic children. *Journal of Autism and Developmental Disorders* (20), 115-128.

Mundy, P., Thorp, D. (2007). Joint attention and autism: Theory, assessment and neurodevelopment. In G. P. Pérez JM, *New Developments in Autism: The Future is Today* (pp. 104-138). London, UK: Jessica Kingsley.

Osterling, J., Dawson, G. (1994). Early recognition of children with autism: A study of first birthday home videotapes. *Journal of Autism and Developmental Disorders* (24), 247-257.

Osterling, J., Dawson, G., Munson, J. (2002). Early recognition of 1-year-old infants with autism spectrum disorder versus mental retardation. *Development and Psychopathology* (14), 239-251.

Peterson, C., Wellman, H., Liu, D. (2005). Steps in Theory-of-Mind Development for Children with Deafness or Autism. *Child Development* (76), 502-517.

Philips, W., Baron-Cohen, S., Rutter, M. (1998). Understanding intention in normal development and in autism. *British Journal of Developmental Psychology* (16), 337-348.

Recchia, S. L. (1997). Establishing intersubjective experience: Developmental challenges for young children with congenital blindness and autism and their caregivers. 116-129.

Reddy, V., Williams, E., Vaughan, A. (2002). Sharing humour and laughter in autism and Down's syndrome. *British Journal of Psychology* (93), 219-242.

Robertson, J., Tanguay, P., L'Ecuyer, S., Sims, A., Waltrip, C. (1999). Domains of social communication handicap in autism spectrum disorder. *Journal of the American Academy of Child and Adolescent Psychiatry*, *38* (6), 738-745.

Rutherford, M., Baron-Cohen, S., Wheelwright, S. (2002). Reading the mind in the voice: A study with normal adults and adults with Asperger syndrome and high functioning autism. *Journal of Autism and Developmental Disorders* (32), 189-194.

Shriberg, L., Paul, R., McSweeny, J., Klin, A., Cohen, D. (2001). Speech and prosody characteristics of adolescents and adults with high-functioning autism and Asperger syndrome. *Journal of Speech, Language, and Hearing Research* (44), 1097-1115.

Sigman M, Dijamco A, Gratier M, Rozga A. (2004). Early Detection of Core Deficits in Autism. *Mental Retardation and Developmental Disabilities Research Reviews* (10), 221-233.

Sigman, M., Dissanayake, C., Corona, R., Espinosa, M. (2003). Social and cardiac responses of young children with autism. *Autism* (7), 205-216.

Sigman, M., McGovern, C. (2005). Improvement in cognitive and language skills from preschool to adolescence in autism. *Journal of Autism and Developmental Disorders* (35), 15-23.

Stahl, L., Pry, R. (2002). Joint attention and set shifting in young children with autism. *Autism* (6), 383-396.

Stone, W., Ousley, O., Yoder, P., Hogan, K., Hepburn, S. (1997). Nonverbal communication in two- and three-year-old children with autism. *Journal of Autism and Developmental Disorders* (27), 677-696.

Stone, W., Yoder, P. (2001). Predicting spoken language level in children with autism spectrum disorders. *Autism* (5), 341-361.

Tanguay, P., Robertson, J., Derrick, A. (1998). A dimensional classification of autism spectrum disorder by social communication domains. *Journal of the American Academy of Child and Adolescent Psychiatry* (37), 271-277.

Travis, L., Sigman, M. (1998). Social deficits and interpersonal relationships in autism. *Mental Retardation and Developmental Disabilities Research Reviews* (2), 65-72.

Travis, L., Sigman, M., Ruskin, E. (2001). Links between social understanding and social behavior in verbally able children with autism. *Journal of Autism and Developmental Disorders, 31* (2), 119-130.

Trevarthen, C., Aitken, K., Papoudi, D., Robarts, J. (1996). *Where development of the communicating mind goes astray: Children with Autism.* London, UK: Jessica Kingsley.

Trevarthen, C., Daniel, S. (2005). Disorganized rhythm and synchrony: Early signs of autism and Rett syndrome. *Brain and Development* (27), 525-534.

Tronick, E., Gianino, A. (1986). Interactive mismatch and repair: Challenges to the coping infant. *Zero to Three, 6* (3), 1-6.

Warreyn, P., Roeyers, H., De Groote, I. (2005). Early social communicative behaviors of preschoolers with autism spectrum disorder during interaction with their mothers. *Autism* (9), 342-361.

Williams J., Nash, S. (2000). Are infants with autism socially engaged? A study of recent retrospective parental reports. *Journal of Autism and Developmental Disorders* (30), 525-536.

Chapter 10: Readiness

Baker E, B. M. (2005). Stress levels and adaptability in parents of toddlers with and without autism spectrum disorders. *Research and Practice for Persons with Severe Disabilities* (30), 194-204.

Bitsika, V., Sharpley, CF. (2004). Stress, Anxiety and Depression Among Parents of Children With Autism Spectrum Disorder. *Australian Journal of Guidance and Counseling* (14), 151-161.

Boyd, B. (2002). Examining the relationship between stress and lack of social support in mothers of children with autism. *Focus on Autism and Other Developmental Disabilities* (17), 208-215.

Gottman, J. (1999). *The Seven Principles for Making Marriage Work.* New York: Three Rivers Press.

Gutstein, S. (In Press). Empowering families through Relationship Development Intervention: An important part of the bio-psycho-social management of Autism Spectrum Disorders. *Annals of Clinical Psychiatry.*

Leyfer, OT., Folstein, SE., Bacalman, S., Davis, NO., Dinh, E., Morgan, J., Tager, F., Lainhart, JE. (2006). Comorbid Psychiatric Disorders in Children with Autism: Interview Development and Rates of Disorders. *Journal of Autism and Developmental Disorders* (36), 849-861.

Pisula, E. (2007). A comparative study of stress profiles in mothers of children with autism and those of children with Down's syndrome. *Journal of Applied Research in Intellectual Disabilities* (20), 274-278.

Tonge, B., Brereton, A., Gray, K., Einfeld, S. (1999). Behavioral and emotional disturbance in high-functioning autism and Asperger syndrome. *Autism* (3), 117-130.

REFERENCES BY AUTHOR

Acosta, M.,Pearl, P. (2003). *The neurobiology of autism: new pieces of the puzzle.* Current Neurological Neuroscience Reports.

Alliance, 2. C. (2000). *Building America's 21st Century Workforce: National Alliance of Business and US Department of Labor.* Retrieved from 21st Century Workforce Commission: http://www.21stcenturylearningalliance.com.

Bacon, A., Fein, D., Morris, R., Waterhouse, L., and Allen, D. The responses of autistic children to the distress of others. *Journal of Autism and Developmental Disorders* (28), 129-142.

Baker E, B. M. (2005). Stress levels and adaptability in parents of toddlers with and without autism spectrum disorders. *Research and Practice for Persons with Severe Disabilities* (30), 194-204.

Bakerman, R., Adamson, L. (1984). Coordinating Attention to people and objects in mother-infant and peer-infant interactions. *Child Development* (55), 1278-1289.

Barnard, J., Harvey, V., Potter, D., Prior, A. (2001). *Ignored or ineligible? The reality for adults with autism spectrum disorders.* The National Autistic Society report for Autism Awareness Week. London: NAS Publications.

Baron-Cohen, S. (1989). Joint-attention deficits in autism: Towards a cognitive analysis. *Development and Psychopathology* (1), 185-189.

Baron-Cohen, S. (1989). Perceptual role taking and protodeclarative pointing in autism. *British Journal of Developmental Psychology* (7), 113-127.

Bates, E., Benigni, L., Bretheront, I., Camaioni, L., Volterra, V. (1979). *The Emergence of Symbols: Cognition and Communication in Infancy.* New York, New York: Academic Press.

Bates, E., Camaioni, L., Volterra, V. (1975). The acquisition of performatives prior to speech. *Merrill-Palmer Quarterly* (21), 205-226.

Bauman ML, Kempter, TL. (2007). The neuroanatomy of the brain in autism: Current thoughts and future directions. In G. P. Perez JM, *New developments in autism: The future is today* (pp. 259-267). London: Jessica Kingsley Publisher.

Bazhenova, O., Plonskaia, O., Porges, S. (2001). Vagal reactivity and affective adjustment in infants during interaction challenge. *Child Development* (72), 1314-1326.

Bellagamba, F., Tomasello, M. (1999). Re-enacting intended acts: Comparing 12-and 18-month-old. *Infant Behavior and Development* (22), 277-282.

Belmonte MK., Allen, G., Beckel-Mitchener, A., Boulanger, LM., Carper, R., Webb, SG. (2004). Autism and Abnormal Development of Brain Connectivity. *Journal of Neuroscience* (24), 9228-9231.

Belmonte, MK., Cook, EH., Anderson, GM., Rubenstein, JLR., Greenough, WT., Beckel-Mitchener, A., Courchesne, E., Boulange, LM., Powell, SB., Levitt, PR., Perry, EK., Jiang YH., DeLorey, TM., Tierney, E. (2004). Autism as a disorder of neural information processing: Directions for research and targets for therapy. *Molecular Psychiatry* (9), 646-663.

Berger, M. (2006). A model of preverbal social development and its application to social dysfunctions in autism. *Journal of Child Psychology and Psychiatry, 47,* 338-371.

Bieberich, A., Morgan, S. (1998). Affective expression in children with autism or downs syndrome. *Journal of Autism and Developmental Disorders , 28* (4), 333-338.

Bigelow, A. (1999). Infants' sensitivity to imperfect contingency in social interaction. In P. R. (Ed.), *Early Social Cognition.* HIllsdale, NJ: Erlbaum.

Bitsika, V., Sharpley, CF. (2004). Stress, Anxiety and Depression Among Parents of Children With Autism Spectrum Disorder. *Australian Journal of Guidance and Counseling* (14), 151-161.

Bono, M., Daley, T., Sigman, M. (2004). Relations among joint attention, amount of intervention and language gain in Autism. *Journal of Autism and Developmental Disorders* (34), 495-505.

Boyd, B. (2002). Examining the relationship between stress and lack of social support in mothers of children with autism. *Focus on Autism and Other Developmental Disabilities* (17), 208-215.

Bransford, JD., Brown, AL., Cocking, R. (Eds.) (2000). *How People Learn*. Commission on Behavioral and Social Sciences and Education, The National Research Council and the National Academy of Sciences (NAS), The Committee on Development in the Science of Learning. Washington, D.C.: National Academy Press.

Bruner, J., (1961). The act of discovery. *Harvard Educational Review* (31), 2132.

Bruner, J. S. (1983). Education as social invention. *Journal of Social Issues* (39), 129-14.

Bruner, J., Sherwood, V. (1976). Peek-a-boo and the learning of rule structures. In A. J. J. Bruner, *Play*. New York: Basic Books.

Bunge, S., Dudukovic, N., Thomason, M., Vaidya, C., Gabrieli, J. (2002). Immature frontal lobe contributions to cognitive control in children: Evidence from fMRI. *Neuron* (33), 301-311.

Buss, K., Kiel, E. (2004). Comparison of sadness, anger and fear facial expressions when toddlers look at their mothers. *Child Development* (75), 1761-1773.

Busse, R. (1992). The new basics: Today's employers want the three R's and so much more. *Vocational Education Journal* (67), 24-25.

Camaioni, L. (1997). The emergence of intentional communication in ontogeny, phylogeny and pathology. *European Psychologist* (2), 216-225.

Camaioni, L., Perucchini, P., Bellagamba, F., Colonnesi, C. (2004). The Role of Declarative Pointing in Developing a Theory of Mind. *Infancy* (5), 291-308.

Camaioni, L., Perucchini, P., Muratori, F., Parrini, B., Cesari, A. (2003). The communicative use of pointing in autism: Developmental profile and factors related to change. *European Psychiatry* (18), 6-12.

Campione, J., Brown, A., Ferrara, R., Bryant, N. (1984). The zone of proximal development: Implications for individual differences and learning. In B. Rogoff., J. Wertsch (Eds.), *Children's Learning in the Zone of Proximal Development*. San Francisco: Jossey-Bass.

Campos, J., Sternber, C. Perception, appraisal, and emotion: The onset of social referencing . In M. Lamb., L. Sherrod (Eds.), *Infant Social Cognition: Empirical and Theoretical Considerations*. Hillsdale, NJ: Erlbaum.

Capps, L., Kehres, J., Sigman, M. (1998). Conversational abilities among children with autism and children with developmental delays. *Autism* (2), 325-344.

Carpenter, M., Akhtar, N., Tomasello, M. (1998). Fourteen-to-18-month-old infants differentially imitate intentional and accidental actions. *Infant Behavior and Development*, 21, 315–330.

Carpenter, M., Akhtar, N., Tomasello, M. (1998). Social cognition, joint attention, and communicative competence from 9 to 15 months of age. *Monographs of the Society for Research in Child Development*, 63 (4).

Carpenter, M., Pennington, B., Rogers, S. (2002). Interrelations among social-cognitive skills in young children with autism. *Journal of Autism and Developmental Disorders* (32), 91-106.

Charman, C. (2003). Why is joint attention a pivotal skill in autism? *Philosophical Transactions of the Royal Society of London* (358), 315-324.

Charman, T., Swettenham, J., Baron-Cohen, S., Cox, A., Baird, G., Drew, A. (1997). Infants with autism: An investigation of empathy, pretend play, joint attention, and imitation. *Developmental Psychology* (5), 782-789.

Charman, T., Taylor, E., Drew, A., Cockerill, H., Brown, J. A., Baird, G. (2005). Outcome at 7 years of children diagnosed with autism at age 2: Predictive validity of assessments conducted at 2 and 3 years of age and pattern of symptom change over time. *Journal of Child Psychology and Psychiatry* (46), 500-513.

Cherkassky, VL., Kana, RK., Keller, TA., Just, MA. (2006). Functional connectivity in a baseline resting-state network in autism. *Neuroreport: For Rapid Communication of Neuroscience Research* (17), 1687-1690.

Cohn, J., Elmore, M. (1988). Effect of contingent changes in mothers' affective expression on the organization of behavior in 3-month-old infants. *Infant Behavior and Development* (11), 493-505.

Cohn, J., Tronick, E. (1987). Mother-infant face-to-face interaction: The sequence of dyadic states at 3, 6, and 9 months. *Developmental Psychology* (23), 68-77.

Collins, A., Brown, J., Holum, A. (1991). Cognitive Apprenticeship: Making thinking visible. *American Educator, winter*, 1-18.

Conference Board of Canada. (2000, January 17). *Employability skills 2000+*. Retrieved 2001, from http://www.conferenceboard.ca/nbec/pdf/esp2000.pdf

Courchesne E, P. K. (2005). Why the frontal cortex in autism might be talking only to itself: Local over-connectivity but long-distance disconnection. *Current Opinion in Neurobiology* (15), 225-230.

Courchesne, E., Pierce, K.(2005). Brain overgrowth in autism during a critical time in development: Implications for frontal pyramidal neuron and interneuron development and connectivity. *International Journal of Developmental Neuroscience* (23), 153-170.

Courchesne E, Pierce K. (2005). Why the frontal cortex in autism might be talking only to itself: Local over-connectivity but long-distance disconnection. *Current Opinion in Neurobiology* (15), 225-230.

Dawson, G., Carver, L., Meltzoff, A., Panagiotides, H., McPartland, J., Webb, S. (2002). Neural correlates of face and object recognition in young children with autism spectrum disorder, developmental delay and typical development. *Child Development*, (73), 700-717.

Dawson. G., Hill, D., Spencer, A., Galpert, L., Watson, L. (1990). Affective exchanges between young autistic children and their mothers. *Journal of Abnormal Child Psychology* (18),335-345.

Dawson, G., Toth, K., Abbott, R., Osterling, J., Munson, J., Estes, A., Liaw, J. (2004). Early social attention impairments in autism: Social orienting, joint attention and attention to distress. *Developmental Psychology* (40(2)), 271-283.

Diaz, R., Neal, C., Vachio, A. (1991). Maternal teaching in the zone of proximal development: A comparison of low and high-risk dyads. *Merrill Palmer Quarterly* (37), 83-107.

Downs, A., Smith, T. (2004). Emotional understanding, cooperation, and social behavior in high-functioning children with Autism. *Journal of Autism and Developmental Disorders* (34), 625-635.

Eckerman, C, Didow, S. (1996). Nonverbal imitation and toddler's mastery of verbal means of achieving coordinated action. *Developmental Psychology* (32), 141-152.

Edelson, MG. (2006). Are the Majority of Children With Autism Mentally Retarded? A Systematic Evaluation of the Data. *Focus on Autism and Other Developmental Disabilities* (21), 66-83.

Engstrom I., Ekstrom, L., Emilsson, B. (2003). Psycho-social functioning in Swedish adults with Asperger's syndrome or high-functioning autism. *Autism* (7), 99-110.

Fabio, R. A. (2005). Dynamic Assessment of Intelligence is a better reply to adaptive behavior and cognitive plasticity. *Journal of General Psychology* (132), 41-64.

Farraly, M. (2001). What happens after school? Outcome for individuals with Asperger's syndrome/high functioning autism. *Frontline of Learning Disability* , 47 (online).

Feldman, R. (2006). From biological rhythms to social rhythms: Physiological precursors of mother-infant synchrony. *Developmental Psychology* (42), 175-188.

Fernald, A. (1985). Four-month-old infants prefer to listen to motherese. *Infant Behavior and Development* (8), 181-195.

Feuerstein, R., Feuerstein S.(1991). Mediated learning experience: A theoretical review. In P. K. R. Feuerstein, *Mediated learning experience (MLE): Theoretical, psychosocial, and learning implications* (pp. 3-51). London: Freund Publishing House, LTD.

Fogel, A. (1993). *Developing Through Relationships: Origins of Communication, Self, and Culture.* Chicago: University of Chicago Press.

Fogel, A., Stevenson, M., Messinger, D. (1992). A comparison of the parent-child relationship in Japan and the United States. In J. R. (Eds.), *Parent-Child Relations in Diverse Cultural Settings.* Norwood, NJ: Ablex Publishing.

Fogel, A., Thelen, E. (1987). Development of early expressive and communicative action: Reinterpreting the evidence from a dynamic systems perspective. *Developmental Psychology* (23), 747-761.

Frick, R. (1985). Communicating emotion: The role of prosodic features. *Psychological Bulletin* (97), 412-429.

Friedman, S., Shaw, D., Artru, A., Richards, T., Gardner, J., Dawson, G., Posse, S., Dager, S. (2003). Regional brain chemical alterations in young children with autism spectrum disorder. *Neurology* (60), 100-110.

Gardner, H. (1999). *Reframing Intelligence.* New York: Basic Books.

Gardner, H. (1995). *The Unschooled Mind: How Children Think and How Schools Should Teach.* New York: Basic Books.

Gaussen, T. (2001). Dynamic systems theory: Revolutionizing developmental psychology. *Irish Journal of Psychology* , 22 (3-4), 160-175.

Geller, E. (1998). An investigation of communication breakdowns and repairs in verbal autistic children. *British Journal of Developmental Disabilities* (87), 71-85.

Giedd, J. (2004). Structural magnetic resonance imaging of the adolescent brain. *Annals of the New York Academy of Sciences* (1021), 77-85.

Giedd J., Blumenthal, J., Jeffries, N. (1999). Brain development during childhood and adolescence: a longitudinal MRI study. *Nature Neuroscience* , 2 (10), 861-863.

Gipps, R. (2004). Autism and intersubjectivity: Beyond cognitivism and the theory of mind. *Philosophy, Psychiatry, and Psychology* (11), 195-198.

Goldapple, K., Segal, Z., Garson, C., Lau, M., Bieling, P., Kennedy, S. and Mayberg, H. (2004). Modulation of cortical-limbic pathways in major depression: treatment-specific effects of cognitive behavior therapy. *Archives of General Psychiatry* (61), 34-41.

Goodhart, F., Baron-Cohen, S. (1993). How many ways can the point be made? Evidence from children with and without autism. *First Language* (13), 225-233.

Gottman, J. (1999). *The Seven Principles for Making Marriage Work*. New York: Three Rivers Press.

Greenfield, P. (1972). Playing peek-a-boo with a four-month-old: A study of the role of speech and non-speech sounds in the formation of a visual schema. *Journal of Psychology* (82), 287-298.

Grigorenko, L., Sternberg, R. (1998). Dynamic Testing. *Psychological Bulletin* (124), 75-111.

Gruber, O., Goschke, T. (2004). Executive control emerging from dynamic interactions between brain systems mediating language, working memory and attentional processes. *Acta Psychologica, 155* (2-3), 105-121.

Guterman, E. (2002). Toward a dynamic assessment of reading: Applying metacognitive awareness guidance to reading assessment tasks. *Journal of Research in Reading* (25), 283-298.

Gutstein, S. (2000). *Solving the Relationship Puzzle*. Arlington, Texas: Future Horizons.

Gutstein, S. (2005). Relationship Development Intervention: Developing a treatment program to address the unique social and emotional deficits of autism spectrum disorders. *Autism Spectrum Quarterly* (Winter).

Gutstein, S. (In Press). Empowering families through Relationship Development Intervention: An important part of the bio-psycho-social management of Autism Spectrum Disorders. *Annals of Clinical Psychiatry* .

Gutstein, S., Burgess, A., Montfort, K. (2007). Evaluation of the Relationship Development Intervention Program. *Autism* (11), 397-411.

Gutstein, S., Gutstein, H., Baird, C. Eds.(2006). *My Baby Can Dance: Stories of Autism, Asperger's and Success Through the Relationship Development Intervention Program*. Houston, Texas: Connections Center Publishing.

Gutstein, S., Gutstein, H., Baird, C. Eds. (2007). *The Relationship Development Intervention Program and Education.* Houston, Texas: Connections Center Publications.

Gutstein, S., Sheely, R. (2002). *Relationship Development Intervention with Adolescents and Adults: Social and Emotional Development Activities for Asperger's Syndrome, Autism, PDD and NLD.* London, UK: Jessica Kingsley.

Gutstein S., Sheely, R. (2002). *Relationship Development Intervention with young children: Social and emotional development activities for Asperger Syndrome, autism, PDD and NLD.* London, UK: Jessica Kingsley.

Gutstein, S., Whitney, T. (2002). Asperger syndrome and the development of social competence. *Focus on Autism and Other Developmental Disabilities* (17), 161-171.

Hadwin, J., Baron-Cohen, S., Howlin, P., Hill, K. (1996). Can we teach children with autism to understand emotions, belief, or pretence? *Development and Psychopathology* (8), 345-365.

Hale, C., Tager-Flusberg, H. (2005). Social communication in children with autism: The relationship between theory of mind and discourse development. *Autism* (9), 157-178.

Harding, C. G., Weissmann, L., Kromelow, S., Stilson, S. R. (1997). Shared minds: How mothers and infants co-construct early patterns of choice within intentional communication partnerships. *Infant Mental Health Journal* (18), 24-39.

Hauck, M., Fein, D., Waterhouse, L.,Feinstein, C. (1995). Social initiations by autistic children to adults and other children. *Journal of Autism and Developmental Disorders* (6), 579-595.

Hay, D. (1979). Cooperative interactions and sharing between very young children and their parents. *Developmental Psychology* (15), 647-657.

Haywood, H.C., Lidz, C.S. (2007). *Dynamic assessment in practice: Clinical and educational applications.* New York, New York: Cambridge University Press.

Heckhausen, J. (1987). How do mothers know? Infants' chronological age or infants' performance as determinants of adaptation in maternal instruction? *Journal of Experimental Child Psychology* (43), 212-226.

Henderson, L., Yoder, P., McDuffie, A. (2002). Getting the point: Electrophysiological correlates of protodeclarative pointing. *International Journal of Developmental Neuroscience* (20), 449-458.

Herschkowitz, N. (2000). Neurological bases of behavioral development in infancy. *Brain Development* (22), 411-416.

Hobson, P. (1989). On sharing experiences. *Development and Psychopathology* (1), 197-203. Mahwah, NJ: Lawrence Erlbaum.

Hobson, P. (1993). *Autism and the Development of Mind.* Mahwah, NJ: Lawrence Erlbaum.

Hobson, P. (2002). *The Cradle of Thought: Exploring the Origins of Thinking.* London, UK: Macmillan.

Hobson, P. (2007). On being moved in thought and feeling: An approach to autism. In J. G. Pérez, *New developments in autism: The future is today* (pp. 139-154). London, UK: Jessic Kingsley.

Hobson, R., Bishop M. The pathogenesis of autism: Insights from congenital blindness. In H. E. Frith U, *Autism: Mind and Brain* (pp. 109-126). New York, New York: Oxford University Press.

Hobson, P., Lee, A. (1998). Hello and goodbye: A study of social engagement in autism. *Journal of Autism and Developmental Disorders* (28).

Hodapp, R., Goldfield, E., Boyatzis, C. (1984). The use and effectiveness of maternal scaffolding in mother-infant games. *Child Development* (55), 772-781.

Howlin, P. (2003). Outcome in high-functioning adults with autism with and without early language delays: Implications for the differentiation between autism and Asperger syndrome. *Journal of Autism and Developmental Disorders* (33), 3-13.

Howlin, P., Goodes, S. (2000). Outcome in adult life for people with autism and Asperger's syndrome. *Autism , 4* (1), 63-83.

Huether, G. (1998). Stress and the adaptive self-organization of neuronal connectivity during early childhood. *International Journal of Developmental Neuroscience, 16* (3-4), 297-306.

Hughes, C. (2001). Executive dysfunction in autism: Its nature and implications for the everyday problems experienced by individuals with autism. In J. C. Burack, *The development of autism: Perspectives from theory and research.* (pp. 255-271).

Ito, M. (2004). Nurturing the brain' as an emerging research field involving child neurology. *Brain,* (26),429-433.

Jaffe, J., Beebe, B., Feldstein, S., Crown, C., Jasnow, M. (2001). Rhythms of dialogue in Infancy. *Monographs of the Society for Research in Child Development* (66).

Just M., Cherkassky V., Keller T., Minshew N. (2004). Cortical activation and synchronization during sentence comprehension in high-functioning autism: Evidence of under-connectivity. Brain. *A Journal of Neurology* (127), 1811-1821.

Kagan, J. (1981). *The Second Year: The Emergence of Self-Awareness*. Cambridge, MA: Harvard University Press.

Kanner, L. (1968). Follow-up study of eleven children originally reported in 1943. *Acta Paedopsychiatrica* (35), 100-136.

Kanner, L. (1943). Autistic disturbances of affective contact. *Nervous Child* (2), 217-250.

Karpov, Y., Haywood, H. (1998). Two ways to elaborate Vygotsky's concept of mediation: Implications for instruction. *American Psychologist* (53), 27-36.

Kasari, C., Sigman, M., Baumgartner, P., Stipek, D. (1993). Pride and mastery in children with autism. *Journal of Child Psychology and Psychiatry and Allied Disciplines* (34), 353-362.

Kasari, C., Sigman, M., Mundy, P., Yirmiya, N. (1990). Affective sharing in the context of joint attention interactions of normal, autistic and mentally retarded children. *Journal of Autism and Development Disorders* (20), 87-100.

Kaye, K. (1977). Infants' effects upon their mothers' teaching strategies. In J. C. (Ed.), *The Social Context of Learning and Development*. New York, New York: Gardner.

Kaye, K. (1982). *The Mental and Social Life of Babies: How Parents Create Persons*. Chicago, Illinois: The Harvester Press.

Keen, D. (2005). The use of non-verbal repair strategies by children with autism. *Research in Developmental Disabilities* (26), 243-254.

Klin, A., Jones, W., Schultz, R., Volkmar, F. (2003). The enactive mind, or from actions to cognition: Lessons from autism. *Philosophical Transactions of the Royal Society of London B* (358), 345-360.

Klinnert, M., Emde, R., Butterfield, P., Campos, J. (1986). Social referencing: The infant's use of emotional signals from a friendly adult with mother present. *Developmental Psychology* (22), 427-432.

Kochanska, G., Aksan, N. (2004). Development of mutual responsiveness between parents and their young children. *Child Development* (75), 1657-1676.

Kokkinaki, T. (2003). A longitudinal, naturalistic and cross-cultural study on emotions in early infant-parent imitative interactions. *British Journal of Developmental Psychology*, *21* (2), 243-258.

Koshino, H., Carpenter, P., Minshew, N., Cherkassky, T., Just, M. (2004). Functional connectivity in an fMRI working memory task in high functioning autism. *23* (online).

Kriegstein, K., Kleinschmidt, A., Sterzerr, P., Giraud, A. (2005). Interaction of face and voice areas during speaker recognition. *Journal of Cognitive Neuroscience* (17), 367-376.

Kunnen, E., Saskia, B., Harke, A. (2000). Development of meaning making: A dynamic systems approach. *New Ideas in Psychology* (18), 57-82.

Laing, R.D. (1967). *The Politics of Experience*. New York: Pantheon Books.

Lankard, B. (1990). Employability - The Fifth Basic Skill. *ERIC Digest*, *ED 325 659* (104).

Lehrer, J. (2009). *How We Decide*. New York: Houghton Mifflin.

Levitt, J., O'Neill, J., Blanton, R., Smalley, S., Fadale, D., McCracken, J., Guthrie, D., Toga, A., Alger, J. (2003). Proton magnetic resonance spectroscopic imaging of the brain in childhood autism. *Biological Psychiatry* (54), 1355-1366.

Lewis, D., Tamminga, C. (2004). Structure of the human prefrontal cortex. *American Journal of Psychiatry*, *161* (8), 1366-1368.

Lewis, M. (2000). The promise of dynamic systems approaches for an integrated account of human development. *Child Development* (71), 36-43.

Leyfer, OT., Folstein, SE., Bacalman, S., Davis, NO., Dinh, E., Morgan, J., Tager, F., Lainhart, JE. (2006). Comorbid Psychiatric Disorders in Children with Autism: Interview Development and Rates of Disorders. *Journal of Autism and Developmental Disorders* (36), 849-861.

Lidz, C.S., Elliott, J.G. (Eds.). (2000). *Dynamic assessment: Prevailing models and applications*. Amsterdam: JAI/Elsevier Science.

Loddo, S. (2003). The understanding of actions and intentions in autism. *Journal of Autism and Developmental Disorders* (33), 545-546.

Louis J., Baldwin, D., Rosicky, J., Tidball, G. (2001). Evidence for referential understanding in the emotions domain at twelve and eighteen months. *Child Development, 72* (3), 718-735.

Luna, B., Minshew, N., Garver, K., Lazar, N., Thulborn, K., Eddy, W. and Sweeney, J. (2002). Neocortical system abnormalities in autism: An fMRI study of spatial working memory. *Neurology* (59), 834-840.

MacWhinney, B. (1998). Models of the emergence of language. *Annual Review of Psychology*, (49), 199-227.

Maestro, S., Muratori, F., Barbieri, F., Casella, C., Cattaneo, V., Cavallaro, M., Cesari, A., Milone, A., Rizzo, L., Viglione, V., Stern, D., Palacio-Espasa, F. (2001). Early Behavioral Development in Autistic Children: The First 2 Years of Life through Home Movies. *Psychopathology* (34), 147-152.

Maestro, S., Muratori, F., Cavallaro, MC., Pecini, C., Cesari, A., Paziente, A., Stern, D., Golse, B., Palacio, E., Francisco. (2005) How Young Children Treat Objects and People: An Empirical Study of the First Year of Life in Autism. *Child Psychiatry and Human Development*. (35),383-396.

Mandler, J. (1992). How to build a baby II: Conceptual Primitives. *Psychological Review* (99), 587-604.

Matusov, E., Bell, N., Rogoff, B. (2002). Schooling as cultural process: Working together and guidance by children from schools differing in collaborative practices. (R. K. Reese, Ed.) *Advances in child development and behavior , 29.*

Mayes, L., Carter, A. (1990). Emerging social regulatory capacities as seen in the still-face situation. *Child Development* (61), 754-763.

Mayes, S., Dickerson, Calhoun S, L. (2001). Non-significance of early speech delay in children with autism and normal intelligence and implications for DSM-IV Asperger's disorder. *Autism* (5), 81-94.

McGovern, C., Sigman, M.(2005). Continuity and change from early childhood to adolescence in autism. *Journal of Child Psychology and Psychiatry* (46), 401-408.

Meltzoff, A. (1995). Understanding the intentions of others: Re-enactment of intended acts by 18-month-old children. *Developmental Psychology* (31), 838-850.

Miller, A., Chretien, K. (2007). *The Miller Method: Developing the Capacities of Children on the Autism Spectrum.* London, UK: Jessica Kingsley.

Minshew, NJ., Webb, SJ., Williams, DL., Dawson, G. (2006). Neuropsychology and Neuro-physiology of autism Spectrum Disorders. In R. J. Modin SO, *Understanding autism: From basic neuroscience to treatment.* (pp. 379-415). Boca Raton, Florida: CRC Press.

Minshew, NJ., Williams, DL. (2007). The new neurobiology of Autism: Cortex, Connectivity and Neural Organization. *Archives of Neurology* (64), 945-950.

Moore, G., Calkins, S. (2004). Infants' Vagal regulation in the still-face paradigm is related to dyadic coordination of mother-infant interaction. *Developmental Psychology* (40), 1068-1080.

Morales, M., Mundy, P., Delgado, C. E. F., Yale, M., Messinger, D., Neal, R .(2000). Responding to joint attention across the 6- through 24-month age period and early language acquisition. *Journal of Applied Developmental Psychology* (21), 283-298.

Mosier, C., Rogoff, B. (2003). Privileged treatment of toddlers: Cultural aspects of individual choice and responsibility. *Developmental Psychology* , 39 (6), 1047-1060.

Mundy, P. (2003). The neural basis of social impairments in autism: the role of the dorsal medial-frontal cortex and anterior cingulated system. *Journal of Child Psychology and Psychiatry* (44), 1-17.

Mundy, P., Crowson, M. (1997). Joint attention and early social communication: Implications for research on interventions with autism. *Journal of Autism and Developmental Disorders* (6), 653-676.

Mundy, P., Kasari, C., Sigman, M. (1992). Nonverbal communication, affective sharing and intersubjectivity. *Infant Behavioral Development* (15), 377-381.

Mundy, P., Kasari, C., Sigman, M., Ruskin, E. (1995). Nonverbal communication and early language acquisition in children with Down syndrome and in normally developing children. *Journal of Speech and Hearing Research* (38), 157-167.

Mundy, P., Sigman, M., Ksari, C. (1990). A longitudinal study of joint attention and language development in autistic children. *Journal of Autism and Developmental Disorders* (20), 115-128.

Mundy, P., Thorp, D. (2007). Joint attention and autism: Theory, assessment and neurodevelopment. In G. P. Pérez JM, *New Developments in Autism: The Future is Today* (pp. 104-138). London, UK: Jessica Kingsley.

Neitzel, C., Stright, AD. (2003). Mothers' scaffolding of children's problem solving: Establishing a foundation of academic self-regulatory competence. *Journal of Family Psychology* (17), 147-159.

Nielson, M. (2006). Copying actions and copying outcomes: Social learning through the second year. *Developmental Psychology* (42), 555-565.

Osterling, J., Dawson, G. (1994). Early recognition of children with autism: A study of first birthday home videotapes. *Journal of Autism and Developmental Disorders* (24), 247-257.

Osterling, J., Dawson, G., Munson, J. (2002). Early recognition of 1-year-old infants with autism spectrum disorder versus mental retardation. *Development and Psychopathology* (14), 239-251.

Papousek, M. (2007). Communication in early infancy: An arena of intersubjective learning. *Infant Behavior and Development* (30), 258-266.

Peterson, C., Wellman, H., Liu, D. (2005). Steps in Theory-of-Mind Development for Children with Deafness or Autism. *Child Development* (76), 502-517.

Philips, W., Baron-Cohen, S., Rutter, M. (1998). Understanding intention in normal development and in autism. *British Journal of Developmental Psychology* (16), 337-348.

Pisula, E. (2007). A comparative study of stress profiles in mothers of children with autism and those of children with Down's syndrome. *Journal of Applied Research in Intellectual Disabilities* (20), 274-278.

Porter, C. (2003). Co-regulation in mother-infant dyads: Links to infants' cardiac Vagal tone. *Psychological Reports* (92), 307-319.

Recchia, S. L. (1997). Establishing intersubjective experience: Developmental challenges for young children with congenital blindness and autism and their caregivers. 116-129.

Reddy, V., Hay, D., Murry, L., Trevarthen, C. (1997). Communication in infancy: Mutual regulation of affect and attention. In A. S. G. Bremner, *Infant Development: Recent Advances*. Hove, UK: Psychological Press.

Reddy, V., Williams, E., Vaughan, A. (2002). Sharing humour and laughter in autism and Down's syndrome. *British Journal of Psychology* (93), 219-242.

Repacholi, B., Gopnik, A.(1997). Early understanding of desires: Evidence from 14 and 18-month-olds. *Developmental Psychology* (33), 12-21.

Robertson, J., Tanguay, P., L'Ecuyer, S., Sims, A., Waltrip, C. (1999). Domains of social communication handicap in autism spectrum disorder. *Journal of the American Academy of Child and Adolescent Psychiatry* , *38* (6), 738-745.

Rochat, P. (2001). *The Infant's World*. Cambridge, MA: Harvard University Press.

Rochat, P., Querido, J., Striano, T. (1999). Emerging sensitivity to the timing and structure of proto-conversation in early infancy. *Developmental Psychology, 35* (4), 950-957.

Rochat, P., Striano, T. (1999). Social cognitive development in the first year. In P. R. (Ed.), *Early Social Cognition*. Hillsdale, NJ: Erlbaum.

Rogoff, B. (1990). *Apprenticeship in Thinking: Cognitive development in social context*. New York, NY: Oxford University Press.

Rogoff, B. (1993). Children's guided participation and participatory appropriation in socio-cultural activity. In R. W. (Eds.), *Development in context: Acting and Thinking in Specific Environments*. Hillsdale, NJ: Lawrence Erlbaum.

Rogoff, B. (1995). Observing sociocultural activity on three planes: Participatory appropriation, guided participation, and apprenticeship. In P. d. J. Wertsch, *Sociocultural Studies of Mind* (pp. 139-164). New York, NY: Cambridge University Press.

Rogoff, B. (2003). *The Cultural Nature of Human Development*. New York, NY: Oxford University Press.

Rogoff, B., Baker-Sennett, J., Matusov, E. (1994). Considering the concept of planning. In M. H. (Eds.), *The Development of Future-oriented Processes*. Chicago, IL: University of Chicago Press.

Rogoff, B., Lave, J. (1984). *Everyday Cognition: Development in Social Context*. Cambridge, MA: Harvard University Press.

Rutherford, M., Baron-Cohen, S., Wheelwright, S. (2002). Reading the mind in the voice: A study with normal adults and adults with Asperger syndrome and high functioning autism. *Journal of Autism and Developmental Disorders* (32), 189-194.

Sander, L. (1977). The regulation of exchange in the infant-caretaker system and some aspects of the context-content relationship. In M. L. (Eds.), *Interaction, Conversation and the Development of Language*. New York, NY: Wiley.

Scherer, K., Zentner, M., Stern, D. (2004). Beyond Surprise: The puzzle of infants' expressive reactions to expectancy violation. *Emotion* (4), 389-402.

Schwartz, G., Izard, C., Ansul, S. (1985). The 5-month-old's ability to discriminate facial expressions of emotion. *Infant Behavior and Development* (8), 65-77.

Schwartz, J. (1998). Neuroanatomical aspects of cognitive-behavioural therapy response in obsessive-compulsive disorder: An evolving perspective on brain and behaviour. *British Journal of Psychiatry*, *173* (35), 38-44.

Seltzer, M., Krauss, M. (2002). *Adolescents and Adults with Autism: A Profile of Adolescents and Adults with Autistic Spectrum Disorder.* National Institute on Aging. AAA.

Seltzer, M., Shattuck, P., Abbeduto, L., Greenberg, J. (2004). Trajectory of Development in Adolescents and Adults with Autism. *Mental Retardation and Developmental Disabilities Research Reviews* (10), 234-247.

Shastri, L. (2002). Episodic memory and cortico-hippocampal interactions. *Trends in Cognitive Sciences* (6), 162-168.

Shriberg, L., Paul, R., McSweeny, J., Klin, A., Cohen, D. (2001). Speech and prosody characteristics of adolescents and adults with high-functioning autism and Asperger syndrome. *Journal of Speech, Language, and Hearing Research* (44), 1097-1115.

Siegel, D. (1999). *The Developing Mind: How Relationships and the Brain Interact to Shape Who We Are.* New York, NY: Guilford Press.

Sigman M, Dijamco A, Gratier M, Rozga A. (2004). Early Detection of Core Deficits in Autism. *Mental Retardation and Developmental Disabilities Research Reviews* (10), 221-233.

Sigman, M., Dissanayake, C., Corona, R., Espinosa, M. (2003). Social and cardiac responses of young children with autism. *Autism* (7), 205-216.

Sigman, M., McGovern, C. (2005). Improvement in cognitive and language skills from preschool to adolescence in autism. *Journal of Autism and Developmental Disorders* (35), 15-23.

Sowell E., Thompson P., Holmes C. (1999). In vitro evidence for post-adolescent brain maturation in frontal and striatal regions. *Nature Neuroscience* (2), 859-861.

Sroufe, A. (1996). *Emotional Development: The Organization of Emotional Life in the Early Years.* Cambridge: Cambridge University Press.

Stahl, L., Pry, R. (2002). Joint attention and set shifting in young children with autism. *Autism* (6), 383-396.

Stern, D. (1977). *The First Relationship: Infant and Mother.* Cambridge, MA: Harvard University Press.

Stern, D. (1985). *The Interpersonal World of the Infant.* New York, NY: Basic Books.

Sternberg, R. (1985). *Beyond IQ: A triarchic theory of human intelligence.* New York, NY: Cambridge University Press.

Sternberg, R. (1986). *Intelligence Applied.* San Diego, CA: Harcourt.

Sternberg, R. (2000). *Practical Intelligence in Everyday Life.* New York, NY: Cambridge University Press.

Sternberg, R., Grigorenko, E. (2002). *Dynamic Testing: The Nature and Measurement of Learning Potentia.* Cambridge: Cambridge University Press.

Sternberg, RJ., Pretz, JE. (2005). *Cognition and Intelligence: Identifying the mechanisms of the mind.* New York, NY: Cambridge University Press.

Stone, W., Ousley, O., Yoder, P., Hogan, K., Hepburn, S. (1997). Nonverbal communication in two- and three-year-old children with autism. *Journal of Autism and Developmental Disorders* (27), 677-696.

Stone, W., Yoder, P. (2001). Predicting spoken language level in children with autism spectrum disorders. *Autism* (5), 341-361.

Striano, T., Rochat, P.(2000). Emergence of selective social referencing in infancy. *Infancy* (1), 253-264.

Tanguay, P., Robertson, J., Derrick, A. (1998). A dimensional classification of autism spectrum disorder by social communication domains. *Journal of the American Academy of Child and Adolescent Psychiatry* (37), 271-277.

Thelen, E., Smith, L, (1994). *A Dynamic Systems Approach to the Development of Cognition and Action.* Cambridge, MA: MIT Press.

Thornton, S. (1999). Creating the conditions for cognitive change: The interaction between task structures and specific strategies. *Child Development* (70), 588-603.

Tomasello, M. (1995). Joint attention as social cognition. In C. M. (Eds.), *Joint Attention: Its Origins and Role in Development.* Hillsdale, NJ: Erlbaum.

Tomasello, M. (2007). Cooperation and communication in the 2nd year of life. *Child Development Perspectives* (1), 8-12.

Tomasello, M., Carpenter, M. (2005, March). The Emergence of Social Cognition in Three Young Chimpanzees. *Monographs of the Society for Research in Child Development* , *70* (1), pp. 1-136.

Tomasello, M., Max, K. (2003). Understanding attention: 12 and 18-month-olds know what is new for other persons. *Developmental Psychology* , *39* (5), 906-912.

Tonge, B., Brereton, A., Gray, K., Einfeld, S. (1999). Behavioral and emotional disturbance in high-functioning autism and Asperger syndrome. *Autism* (3), 117-130.

Travis, L., Sigman, M. (1998). Social deficits and interpersonal relationships in autism. *Mental Retardation and Developmental Disabilities Research Reviews* (2), 65-72.

Travis, L., Sigman, M., Ruskin, E. (2001). Links between social understanding and social behavior in verbally able children with autism. *Journal of Autism and Developmental Disorders* , *31* (2), 119-130.

Trevarthen, C., Aitken, KJ. (2001). Infant intersubjectivity: Research, theory, and clinical applications. *Journal of Child Psychology and Psychiatry* (42), 3-48.

Trevarthen, C., Aitken, K., Papoudi, D., Robarts, J. (1996). *Where development of the communicating mind goes astray: Children with Autism.* London, UK: Jessica Kingsley.

Trevarthen, C., Daniel, S. (2005). Disorganized rhythm and synchrony: Early signs of autism and Rett syndrome. *Brain and Development* (27), 525-534.

Tronick, E. (1989). Emotions and emotional communication in infants. *American Psychologist* (44), 112-119.

Tronick, E., Gianino, A. (1986). Interactive mismatch and repair: Challenges to the coping infant. *Zero to Three* , *6* (3), 1-6.

Tzuriel, D. (2001). *Dynamic Assessment of Young Children.* Kluwer Academic/Plenum Publishers.

Vygotsky, L. (1978). *Mind in Society: The Development of Higher Psychological Processes.* Cambridge, MA: Harvard University Press.

Walker-Andrews, A. (1997). Infants' perception of expressive behaviors: Differentiation of multimodal information. *Psychological Bulletin* (121), 437-456.

Warneken, F., Chen, F., Tomasello, M. (2006). Cooperative Activities in Young Children and Chimpanzees. *Child Development* , *77* (3), 640-663.

Warreyn, P., Roeyers, H., De Groote, I. (2005). Early social communicative behaviors of preschoolers with autism spectrum disorder during interaction with their mothers. *Autism* (9), 342-361.

Williams J., Nash, S. (2000). Are infants with autism socially engaged? A study of recent retrospective parental reports. *Journal of Autism and Developmental Disorders* (30), 525-536.

Wood, C. (1999). *Changing the Pace of School.* Turners Falls, MA: Northeast Foundation for Children.

Yale, M., Messinger, D., Cobo-Lewis, A., Delgado, C. (2003). The temporal coordination of early infant communication. *Developmental Psychology* (39), 815-824.

Appendix A:

MENTAL PROCESSES

Anticipating: We anticipate, when we focus our attention, thought and emotion on predicting and experiencing potential future circumstances. We try to **predict** whether partners will approve of our actions before we take them, or what subsequent reading passages will be about, based on what we have read up to that point. We **mentally preview** how we will feel when we reach a goal, to serve as a powerful motivation to persist. We pre-experience a potential negative consequence to **emotionally inoculate** ourselves, just in case the worst happens. We consider what might go wrong during a future event and **mentally rehearse** different ways that we will cope with it. We make **contingency plans** based upon different possible future circumstances.

Appraising describes the manner in which we subjectively "pre-evaluate" a situation, problem, or interaction and determine its personal meaning, safety, value and importance. The goal of appraisal is to keep us safe and aid us in decision-making, particularly resource distribution and prioritization. Appraisal is an active, integrated perceptual, cognitive and emotional process. **Valuation** is a form of appraisal defined as subjectively determining the personal worth, significance, or status of something or someone. We learn that sometimes what is valuable to one person may be worthless to another. Similarly, we learn that our prior experience with objects, places, or persons impacts the degree to which we may place value. We also learn that our current needs will partly determine the degree to which we value something (e.g. If you are dying of thirst, a cup of water is more valuable to you than a cup of diamonds). Prioritization entails appraising personal needs and goals, as well as external demands, to create a sequential order of tasks and problems to be solved. We conduct **readiness appraisal** when we have been preparing for an upcoming task or event and wish to determine if we are sufficiently ready. We engage in **risk appraisal** to determine the level of risk in relation to reward, of a potential action, setting, problem or persons. **Resources appraisal** includes pre-evaluating time availability, space limitations, budgetary considerations and competition for needed resources. We engage in **task appraisal** when we base our analysis of task difficulty, on our appraisal of our strengths and limitations in relation to the task. When uncertain about how to appraise something new or different, we engage in **studying**; focusing attention on uncertain or ambiguous stimuli in order to gain greater understanding.

<u>Assimilating:</u> We assimilate by finding ways to link new information and discoveries to what we already know and understand. **Embedding** is making sure that new learning is meaningfully integrated into a larger context of your prior understanding. **Extension finding** involves looking for possible extensions of what you already understand and perceive (e.g. "How does this fit with what I already know?").

<u>Attributing</u> is commonly referred to as **reasoning**. Attributions are our personal theories about why things happened in a certain manner; why we think, feel and act the way we do. Based on our belief of what things are conditionally and causally related, we develop **generalized expectations** that guide us in anticipating and predicting our world. *Examples:* attributing feelings to prior actions of oneself and others, explaining why success or failure was achieved, interpreting ones degree of effort (desire), attributing responsibility (blame, credit).

<u>Contextual Processing</u> involves learning that the meaning and significance of any specific element can only be determined through that elements' unique relationship to a specific reference point. Information has no absolute meaning or value on its own. Rather, certain critical factors are temporarily seen as determining and/or altering its meaning. For example, we learn that any action we take may have different consequences depending on where and when it is taken. Similarly, we learn that information presented along with changed non-verbal communication (e.g. tone of voice) can dramatically alter the

meaning of our words. **Critical analysis** is a contextual process where we determine the **central** features of actions, emotions patterns, modifications, changes and relationships and distinguish them from **peripheral**, non-essential features. **Complexity analysis** entails recognizing that we can analyze any problem, setting, living thing or idea on a number of different levels, for example from superficial to highly sophisticated conceptually, with greater or lesser specificity, or from macro to micro depending on the situation or problem. **Perspective taking** involves examining, observing or thinking about something from multiple perspectives in order to have a more flexible range of response to it. Quantitative comparisons are not meaningful unless we engage in **contextual referencing** (e.g. a 20 story office building in NYC is considered small). **Performance analysis** involves determining good enough performance criteria based upon different factors (e.g. evaluating mistakes in a rough vs. final draft).

Deconstructing: To deconstruct is to begin with a more complex process and take it apart so that its component parts are revealed. De-construction involves determining both the parts involved in a larger ability or entity and the unique way that the components are organized, and relate to one another.

Discriminating: To discriminate is to distinguish by exposing differences, especially from another like element, by making finer and subtler distinctions between elements. **Divergent analysis** is a form of discrimination where we determine how two entities are in the process of becoming increasingly different from one-another in one or more attributes (e.g. marriages that are heading for divorce). *Examples:* making distinctions, dividing subjective states into degrees of experience, differentiating different emotions, differentiating oneself from others, differentiating degrees of attributes, differentiating subjective reactions, determining how things that may appear alike on one level are actually different when analyzed from another perspective (similar-but-different), finding unique attributes that distinguish one member of a species from another.

Evaluating: We evaluate by determining the quality of a response or performance based upon its relationship to some pre-determined goal or objective. The term is used both in the context of evaluating the meaning and value of external events, as well as evaluating personal actions taken in relation to some goal or reference point. We can evaluate on a quantitative or qualitative basis. We can evaluate on a relative (improvement from where I was before) or absolute basis. We can employ personally meaningful-subjective or consensual-objective criteria.

<u>Expanding:</u> One form of expanding is **broadening**, which is the process of translating, or transferring some mental discovery into multiple modalities, settings, problems and encounters. We develop a fuller understanding of concepts by connecting them with different ways of thinking, perceiving and feeling. It can also be defined as adapting what we already know in one setting to generate strategies, solutions or perspectives that are put into successful use in a variety of others. **Cross-modal transfer** is a form of expansion in which a pattern is translated from one sensory modality into another. **Strategizing** consists of transferring solutions that have proven successful in one type of task or problem to others that share critical similarities. **Elaborating** involves finding previously unperceived elements of settings, problems and persons that expand their meaning, as well as adding new elements of complexity. **Evolving** is a specific type of expansion, where a simpler prototype may gradually evolve into an entirely new more sophisticated version.

<u>Fuzzy Thinking:</u> Fuzzy thinking pertains to problem solving, where the solutions are unclear and problems are somewhat ambiguous. **Grey-area problem-solving** involves managing situations where striving for the correct response can only lead to frustration and failure. For example two person's involved in conversation can never expect to understand one another with 100% accuracy. Instead they perceive comprehension in a grey-area manner, by assuming certain levels of misunderstanding. When misunderstandings reach some subjective threshold they attempt to gain clarification. The opposite of grey-area thinking is black-and-white thinking in which there are absolute answers and right/wrong distinctions. Examples of black-and-white thinking are: If it's not sure he's innocent then he must be guilty. If things aren't perfect, then they must be horrible. If your child isn't brilliant then he must be stupid. If you're not fascinating then you must be boring.

Band-Aid thinking involves managing problems that must be dealt with but that may not be solvable in more than a band-aid or temporary basis. **Improvising** is a form of fuzzy thinking, where we try to make-do with whatever resources are at hand.

Inferencing is the act of determining meaning and making deductions without having all of the information. It involves knowing when you have sufficient information to reliably predict or deduce. Inferencing consists of deriving a general conception or principle from particulars, drawing a general conclusion from specific instances, or determining when there is sufficient similarity to consider one thing the equivalent of another (e.g. "If it works for this one, it will probably work as well for the other one, as they are quite similar in all but superficial ways."). In science, we engage in inferencing when we construct likely hypotheses to fit our observations. **Hypothetical thinking** is a form of inferencing, in which we consider how some future event might be different, if a specific variable were to change.

Innovating is defined as acting on ideas in a creative manner to make some specific and productive difference. When we innovate, we bring our novel thinking to life and practice. We take ideas, objects, information and past experiences and use them in a new and productive manner to aid us in managing our lives. We may find new uses for familiar objects and ideas. We engage in **Outside-the-box thinking**, where we search for unusual and unexpected relationships. **Speculating** involves going beyond available information to wonder about possible relationships and events. **Brainstorming** involves collaborating with others to produce associations that might help to provide new insights to problems and solutions. Innovation typically involves a bit of risk-taking, as well as the desire to experiment.

Integrating is defined as the combining of diverse conceptions into a coherent whole. **Broadband communication** involves integrating various communication channels (facial, gestural, vocal and language) into single packets of meaning. We integrate concepts, ideas, feelings, reading passages and actions. **Memory linking** involves connecting together different episodes in your life in a common classification. **Perspective sharing** entails taking on another person's subjective state to understand something from their point-of-view, as well as your own. **Co-creating** involves integrating the mental contributions of collaborative partners to create something that is a unique product of the collaborative entity. Reminiscing entails integrating you and your partners' memories of a shared event

<u>**Internalizing**</u> involves the elaboration and evolution of processes that originated from an external source, so that they can function as internal mental events (e.g. moving from a parent prompting a child to change his behavior, to the child monitoring his own actions). Internalizing encompasses the ways that we communicate with ourselves to regulate our internal world. Language becomes internalized when we use it to adjust our own actions in a private manner. We employ internalized language when **self-instructing** and **self-soothing**. We engage in **Self-questioning** when we recognize that we can easily be confused and think we understand when we do not. We may also engage in a form of self-questioning to more fully embed what we are reading into our existing understanding. **Mentally translating** communication in oral or written form, involves actively processing the information to determine its personal, subjective meaning. **Imagining** is an amalgam of internalization, a representation where we form a mental image of something not present to the senses, or never before wholly perceived in reality. **Pretending** is a form of imagining where we make-believe that something has properties it does not possess. **Previewing** or pre-experiencing is a critical integration of internalizing and anticipating, where we create powerful episodic experiences, referred to as prospective memories, of future outcomes and events. **Visualizing**, a product of internalizing and representing, entails creating internal representations of external things, as well as making "movies" in your mind of things that have happened in the past, or might happen in the future. **Introspecting** is a type of internal dialogue that is considered a meta process, in that we engage in *thinking about our thinking*. It is deliberately inspecting mental activity to determine what is most salient in our conscious experience. It can be considered as an internal equivalent of studying an external object or task when unsure, conducted when one is uncertain about ones subjective state. **Social referencing** is an early prototype of internalizing. When uncertain about what to do, we expand our range of options by us-

ing another person's reactions to a shared stimulus for a reference point. It later evolves into **self referencing** or **personal reflection**. **Identification** is a type of internalizing that entails adopting the subjective experience of another as one's own. This is similar to "trying on" their point of view, their subjective stance, to aid one in problem-solving and increased competence. **Empathy** is a more advanced form of identification.

Monitoring is a basic dynamic process involving shifting attention between background factors and primary foreground activities to determine whether attention re-distribution and specific actions are warranted. Monitoring has four components: 1) observation over time, 2)attention shifting, 3) reference-point selection and 4) evaluation for resource re-allocation. **Self monitoring** involves tracking your actions, feelings and internal states, such as distraction, frustration or physical sensation. **Communication monitoring** involves scanning mutual comprehension to determine if sufficient mutual understanding has been achieved. **Vigilance** is heightened monitoring for some external stimulus, whose occurrence is seen as critically important.

Postponing is the ability to subjectively move a planned action into a later time than originally intended. **Constraining** is defined as checking one's true feelings and impulses when dealing with others. **Inhibiting** requires not responding to immediate internal impulses and desires along with environmental "pulls," in the service of reaching future goals (e.g. delaying gratification). It also requires the understanding that one can carry out actions at a later period of time. Examples include: stopping yourself to think about what the other person has said, before responding to them and searching for all possible solutions, rather than settling on the first one.

Reflecting is a form of re-experiencing prior events. **Self-referencing** is the integration of reflecting and internalizing, where we retrieve past experiences to help us manage currently uncertain situations. **Re-framing** is a form of reflecting, where we find some new way of understanding the meaning of familiar activities, settings, actions and past experiences that have previously been understood in a different manner. When we re-frame we question our typical attributions and explanations and look at a prior event from another point of view. **Re-fueling** involves reflecting on past successful experiences, to aid you manage current setbacks and failures. **Troubleshooting** is looking back on a problem or situations where a successful outcome was not reached, in order to determine mistakes that can be prevented in the future. Reflection assumes the development of personal (autobiographic) memory.

Representing: We engage in representing, when we act towards a symbolic substitution of something, as if it were the actual object, person or event. **Symbolizing** is a form of representing where something is allowed to stand for or suggest something else, by reason of relationship, association, convention, or accidental resemblance; especially a visible sign of something invisible. For example, a drawing, a written word, or a spoken word comes to be understood as representing a real dog. Representation is typically developed in creative play, wherein checkers are cookies, papers are dishes, a box is the table, and so on. There are many examples of representation. These include, **labeling, pretending, role-laying, virtualizing, quantifying, diagramming, graphing, journaling, mapping, photographing, videotaping, story-telling, charting, drawing and painting.**

Summarizing involves creating some representation of information, events or problems that succinctly addresses the critical elements in a coherent, organized manner. **Thematic analysis** is a form of summarizing where we seek to find the underlying theme of a work of art or literature. **Critical analysis** involves determining essential information and characteristics. **Condensing** is a form of summarizing where we squeeze greater information into a more concise version without losing the basic meaning, (e.g. Getting to the point). When we **narrate** experiences for those who were not present, we are expected to present relevant summaries that skip the peripheral details. **Spotlighting** is a form of summarizing in which we select some critical elements of our experience and create a summarized representation of its salience to be stored in our memory. When we spotlight, we create clear boundaries around a critical moment in an activity, causing that moment to stand out from its temporal neighbors and thus representing the experience in the memory we are forming.

Synthesizing is an analytic process where the specific attributes of two or more stimuli are compared in relation to how they can be perceived as alike, or becoming more alike. Synthesis implies seeking to find similarities amidst differences (e.g. different-but-same). It is also related to searching for patterns and regularities. **Equivalence analysis** seeks to determine if two objects or stimuli can be treated as functional equivalents. Intersubjectivity consists of comparing different subjective states to create temporary "you-me" experiences. Intersubjectivity requires holding onto ones own subjective interpretations, ideas and feelings, alongside those of another person for purposes of comparison. Intersubjectivity additionally requires the individual to first have developed some awareness of his own subjective state and to maintain that state while temporarily appropriating that of a social partner. **Classifying** is a form of synthesis that consists of the conceptual act of determining the membership of any element in a larger category, based upon one of more properties of the element. Classification elements include: **functional classification, cross-classification, conditional classification**, in which we determine the degree to which any element should be considered a member of a specific class and **hierarchical classification. Pattern analysis** involves studying the basic underlying patterns inherent in any stimulus. It includes identifying the pattern itself, along with determining the patterns stability, predictability and occurrence over time and space. **Trend analysis** involves finding events, persons and objects that are not yet similar, but are increasing in their similarity, or converging on some common point over time. *Examples:* finding common features of things that, at first glance, might appear different, determining whether you can use different objects and tools as functional equivalents, finding commonalities in two different authors, recognizing that you and a friend are becoming emotionally closer to one another.

Appendix B:

SPECIFIC RDI GOALS

1. COLLABORATION

Contributing as a capable partner, group and team member to formulate and attain common goals. Collaboratively negotiating roles and organizing role-relations, time constraints, resource needs and project plans. Taking responsibility to synchronize actions, intentions, interpretations and roles with partners.

Making sure communication is mutually understood. Adapting communication contextually based on partners' understanding, expertise and interest. Effectively using and interpreting multiple non-verbal communication channels. Finding common ground for sharing and integrating perspectives, ideas, memories and feelings.

Balancing personal needs with larger group goals. Respecting established lines of authority and responsibility. Using effective methods for managing interpersonal conflict through negotiation and compromise. Monitoring emotional coordination with partners. Maintaining mutual respect and fairness.

2. DELIBERATION

Operating thoughtfully and carefully in unfamiliar, novel environments. Approaching problems in an analytic manner. Determining main points, critical information and appropriate levels of analysis. Determining necessary resources, as well as degree of care, accuracy and thoroughness required by problems. Reflecting upon, seeking out and evaluating different approaches and perspectives before selecting optimal strategies.

Anticipating possible consequences of your actions. Postponing actions that are inappropriate in current settings. Thinking carefully about the impact of your words, before speaking.

Preparing for future problems and challenges. Planning for contingencies. Developing realistic expectations. Mentally rehearsing possible scenarios and options, including less-than-optimal outcomes.

3. FLEXIBILITY

Monitoring, evaluating and adjusting actions, attention and thinking on an ongoing basis, to reflect feedback from your prior actions, new information and altered circumstances.

Managing real-world grey-area problems with no right or wrong solutions. Making-do and improvising with what is available. Working effectively with limited resources and time. Determining good-enough performance criteria.

Solving problems in an imaginative, novel manner. Thinking outside the box. Creating and perceiving new, unusual combinations, connections and relationships, Thinking in speculative and divergent ways, Perceiving things at multiple levels and from different perspectives.

4. FLUENCY

Selecting and using optimal reading strategies based on the type of media (e.g. newspapers, novels, technical books, websites) and ones' immediate goals (e.g. critical analysis, pleasure, finding information). Monitoring reading for comprehension. Effectively summarizing and synthesizing information. Analyzing information from many different levels (e.g. detail, thematic, objective, subjective). Writing in a coherent, organized manner. Writing with good enough syntax, spelling and clarity, depending on the task and audience (e.g. note taking vs. job applications). Understanding, selecting and effectively implementing optimal writing strategies based on goals.

Determining and efficiently obtaining necessary information from a variety of sources, including on line and written reference materials. Demonstrating proficiency using important tools of analysis and inquiry, such as quantitative analysis, charts, maps and graphs. Understanding basic economics, historical reflection and scientific inquiry, methods and procedures. Demonstrating competent technical skills in the use of computers, software, video cameras and other tools and equipment necessary for 21st century employability.

Possessing the skills and tools to effectively access, organize and communicate experiences and information in a variety of media (e.g. art, rhetoric, narrative), for both experience sharing and influence.

5. FRIENDSHIP

Maintaining ongoing relationships based on shared positive experiences, common attributes and interests, emotional coordination and mutual concern. Demonstrating loyalty as an ally. Placing close friends needs above ones' own. Maintaining an overall balance of emotional give-and-take.

Developing a shared memory bank of common bonding experiences, that include overcoming challenges together, mutual enjoyment, empathy, mutual caregiving and trust. Successfully repairing inevitable conflicts and misunderstandings. Projecting the relationship into the future. Differentiating degrees of friendship based on history of trust and awareness of relationship strengths and limitations.

6. INITIATIVE

Acting autonomously to begin projects or tasks, when things need to get done. Getting the job done as needed, even if it means going beyond initial expectations of effort and finding alternate ways to succeed.

Expressing curiosity and desire to explore new ideas, skills, places and persons. Not always taking the safe and easy route. Seeking out unfamiliar, but potentially rewarding experiences. Perceiving challenges as opportunities for learning and growth. Maintaining a lifelong desire for competence and mastery.

Taking responsibility for setting, tracking and attaining personal goals, even when there is no immediate, or tangible payoff. Possessing a generalized desire to improve and master areas of weakness as well as of strength.

7. RESPONSIBILITY

Acting with honesty, integrity and mutuality. Taking responsibility for negative as well as positive outcomes. Considering and respecting others' feelings and needs along with your own. Respecting commitments and promises. Being seen as reliable and trustworthy.

Taking appropriate role actions to care for and contribute to the well being of family members, neighbors, classmates teammates, workmates and pets. Recognizing responsibilities of team, club and community membership. Taking good care of things that have value to yourself and others.

8. SELF MANAGEMENT

Possessing personal habits necessary for health maintenance (e.g. diet, sleep, hygiene). Managing time effectively, including monitoring time for background tasks (e.g. time to stop watching T.V. to get to an appointment).

Establishing and maintaining routines related to independent living (e.g. paying bills on time,). Understanding and complying with cultural norms in regards to hygiene, dress and behavior (e.g. showering, table manners, social expectations). Possessing tools and procedures needed for autonomous living (e.g. managing transportation, grocery shopping, laundry, house cleaning). Making and following daily schedules.

Developing a storehouse of personal memories used for productive reflection. Regularly engaging in reflection, to review prior events and extract personally meaningful information for future use. Learning from setbacks and successes.

Troubleshooting problems. Reflecting to manage fears, new situations and challenging problems and tasks.

Realistically evaluating personal strengths, limitations and motivations in relation to goals. Understanding personal preferences and opinions. Developing thoughtful, reasoned beliefs and values. Developing a personal moral and ethical code.

Maintaining a longer-term perspective of personal development. Appreciating how progress and change unfold over time. Making productive appraisals of personal value, meaning and importance.

Managing internal states to maintain productive functioning and well-being (e.g. fatigue, focus, frustration). Managing emotions in a productive manner to maintain personal equilibrium. Coping with stress through self soothing and appropriate support. Managing frustration, anxiety, disappointment, rejection, loneliness and loss. Functioning with emotional resilience to bounce back from obstacles and setbacks. Using emotions as tools to understand oneself and ones' relationships.

Appendix C:

SOME POTENTIAL CHILD OBSTACLES TO APPRENTICESHIP

- Anxiety and phobias

- Arousal disorders (under or over-arousal)

- Attachment Disorders

- Attention Deficit Disorder

- Avoidant Disorder

- Bi-polar Disorder

- Depression

- Eating Disorders

- G.I. Disorders

- General emotional irritability

- Hearing problems

- "Hyper-verbia" (over-speaking)

- Immune System Disorders

- Imitation and observational learning deficits

- Impulsivity and Disinhibition

- Language processing and speech disorders, Apraxia and Aphasia

- Memory dysfunction (associative, recognition, sequential, semantic)

- Narcissistic Personality Disorder

- Obsessive Compulsive Disorder

- Oppositional-Defiant Disorder

- Extreme passivity

- Respiratory problems

- Seizures

- Sensory processing problems

- Sleep disorders

- Tourette's Syndrome

- Vision problems

- Visual and Auditory perceptual problems

- Visual organization problems (e.g. pattern recognition)

Appendix D:

SAMPLE EARLY DYNAMIC INTELLIGENCE DISCOVERIES THAT PARALLEL THE PARENT GUIDING STAGE

You check to see if you your partners are available for communication and interaction, even when they are nearby. This objective presents a critical step in developing communication responsibility. The child realizes that communication is only possible if both parties first agree to be available. The child discovers that just because partners are physically in the same area, that does not mean that they are available for communication.

You check to see if you correctly understand what your partners are communicating. The child discovers that he may not always correctly interpret his partner's communication. This is coupled with the discovery that such misinterpretations are common and universal, so the discovery is also made that everyone else will frequently misunderstand as well. This sets the stage for the child developing motivation to monitor communicative understanding

You compare your actions to your guides', to make sure that the accuracy and care of your actions matches theirs. The child discovers that, to function as a competent apprentice, she must compare her actions to those of her guides on a continuous process basis.

You discover that sometimes there is more than one right way to do something, or more than one correct answer to a question or problem. The child learns that many problems have more than one right or good answer or solution. He recognizes the value and feelings of competence one obtains from generating multiple solutions and trying them out.

You recognize that the same actions can be interpreted one way in one setting and another way in a different setting. The child discovers the prototype of contextual evaluation. She learns that the same actions she takes can be evaluated in different ways in different settings. For example, the same action can be considered dangerous and/or inappropriate in one place and safe and/or appropriate in another.

You regularly pause what you are doing, to check on what is happening around you. This objective serves as a prototype for environmental monitoring. The child discovers that he may be primarily involved with a task that requires concentration. Yet, at the same time he has to make sure he is not oblivious to important changes occurring around him. This is a special type of attention shifting that we refer to as monitoring.

You discover that you can deliberately stop to consider taking actions, without actually taking them first. This lesson develops yet another major prototype for internal language. Here, the child discovers that she can generate self-instructions to deliberately short-circuit a sequence of actions.

You discover that you can experience degrees of a feeling. This objective introduces the child to the dynamic nature of internal events. Here, she discovers that emotional states are not yes-or-no events but occur on a continuum.

You discover that when working on tasks, everyone will make mistakes. This lesson focuses on developing realistic expectations for performance for oneself as well as others. The child discovers that making mistakes, while working on challenging tasks and in the normal course of daily life is normal (inevitability of making mistakes).

You have discovered that certain things will change and then go back to the way they were and some will not. In this lesson we want the child to experiment with the concept of reversibility. We would like her to learn that some things may be reversible and others may not. Some things more easily go back to the way they were before, while others may return to an earlier state, but require a great deal of effort to do so.

You discover that some things get associated by accident or coincidence and other things are more permanently connected. The child explores the concept of degrees of connection between things. This is an important discovery that sets the stage for understanding the special relationships, like friendships that bind people together, as opposed to more transient or accidental encounters.

You determine how good-enough different parts of your performance should be, in order to consider yourself finished with them. The child discovers the concept of good enough performance criteria: He understands and accepts that guides can establish and demonstrate good-enough stopping points as representations of desirable end-points. Eventually we want him to be able to carry out this process on his own.

Appendix E:

SAMPLE ELABORATIONS

1. Increase partner complexity
   a. From one to two adults
   b. From one adult to one familiar peer
   c. From a familiar to an unfamiliar peer
   d. From a single peer to two or more peers
2. Increase setting complexity
   a. From indoor to outdoor settings
   b. From home to school
   c. From familiar to unfamiliar settings
   d. From quieter to noisier settings
3. Introduce objects that serve as a competition for attention
4. Increase frequency and unpredictability of variations
5. Allow mutual variations (co-variation)
6. Increase the need for continuous monitoring and regulating
7. Increase the demand for rapidity of processing
8. Require greater degrees of discrimination (e.g. finer distinctions)
9. Introduce more ambiguous information
10. Require greater integration of communication channels
11. Require greater contextual awareness

GRAPHICS INDEX

INDEX

A

activities
  modify 49, 58, 168, 173, 178, 196, 242, 243
  modifying 114, 177, 179, 191, 242, 261
  selecting 84, 198, 333, 334
adaptation 42, 57, 83, 129, 276, 310
agency 126, 144
anticipating 49, 17, 323, 324, 328, 334
appraising 49, 323
apprentice 93–157
apprenticeship 207–240
assignment 60, 173, 174, 176, 177, 178, 265
assimilating 49, 324
assimilation 83
attributing 49, 324
attunement 130, 131, 171, 193, 212
avoidance 44, 162, 183, 190, 214, 218

B

balanced planning 200, 203, 243
bandwidth 69, 71
basal ganglia 40
batting .300 example 191, 192
bio-psycho-social 27, 200, 201, 203, 277, 302, 309
brain-based learning 44
bridging 122, 123, 124, 247, 249
broadband 327
broadening 128, 278, 326

C

cognitive apprentice 26, 126, 128, 207
collaboration 23, 24, 26, 28, 40, 79, 80, 83, 87, 104, 124, 128, 129, 148, 149, 167, 175, 176, 197, 224, 225, 333
communication bandwidth 69, 71
compensation 200, 205, 243
competence 28, 84, 90, 96, 102, 108, 109, 111, 126, 129, 137, 140, 153, 155, 161, 163, 171, 172, 173, 182, 212, 214, 215, 235, 236, 238, 241, 261, 267, 269, 270, 279, 286, 293, 306, 310, 315, 329, 336, 341
competing 43, 51, 190
competition for attention 113
complexity 15, 42, 72, 122, 128, 129, 149, 159, 162, 188, 216, 224, 230, 262, 325, 326, 345
compression 71, 72
condensing 330
connectivity 23, 36, 39, 41, 44, 281, 283, 284, 285, 288, 289, 304, 306, 307, 311, 313, 315
contextual processing 49, 324
continuous process 127, 341
conversation 58, 61, 68, 69, 70, 74, 75, 76, 80, 120, 175, 205, 229, 244, 249, 251, 252, 253, 295, 317, 326
co-occurring 20, 21, 169, 200, 201, 202, 277
coordination 18, 72, 106, 107, 128, 133, 134, 142, 144, 155, 172, 176, 191, 209, 218, 224, 225, 228, 229, 230, 232, 235, 236,

Q

quality of life 13, 14, 15, 20, 21, 22, 81, 82, 83, 84, 167, 169, 196, 276, 278
quieting 182, 183, 184, 194, 196, 212

R

RDI Consultant 172
  consultant training 27
RDI Learning System 28, 174, 175, 177, 178, 278
RDILS 15, 174, 175
reactive disorders 20, 179, 182, 202
readiness 179–207
reflecting 47, 49, 103, 329, 330, 333, 337
re-framing 329
regulation 44, 54, 73, 105, 136, 138, 144, 155, 171, 176, 218, 221, 224, 227, 229, 237, 238, 242, 265, 268, 287, 295, 315, 316, 317
remediation 26, 167, 168, 169, 195, 196, 200, 202, 203, 204, 277, 279
reminiscing 328
representing 49, 155, 169, 328, 330
resilience 135, 279, 337
resonance 131, 212, 226, 308, 313
responsibility, transferring 118, 245

S

scaffolding 111, 114, 118, 119, 122, 123, 136, 213, 226, 227, 232, 236, 241, 245, 248, 252, 253, 254, 256, 257, 261, 263, 265, 292, 311, 315
school 20, 321, 355
self awareness 72, 73
self referencing 176, 329
self regulation 73
self talk 108, 246
similar-but-different 140, 214, 260, 325
simultaneous processing 70

social referencing 26, 129, 147, 155, 160, 171, 176, 205, 212, 262, 268, 293, 294, 296, 305, 312, 319, 328
social skills 18, 216
spotlighting 111, 124, 125, 241, 253, 256, 257, 258, 260, 261, 265, 268, 330
stages 176
staging 14, 103, 109, 123, 203
static intelligence 23, 48, 82, 85
static neural processing 67
still face (developmental phenomena) 130
studying 43, 44, 51, 77, 121, 129, 141, 146, 149, 153, 171, 255, 263, 324, 328, 331
summarizing 49, 330, 334
sympathetic nervous system 130, 131
synthesizing 49, 331, 334

T

threshold 60, 102, 152, 168, 277, 326
top-down processing 43, 74, 232
transfer 71, 98, 106, 110, 111, 118, 173, 195, 242, 245, 326
troubleshooting 177, 330, 337
trust 55, 79, 104, 109, 129, 135, 140, 141, 162, 173, 181, 186, 193, 204, 207, 208, 214, 225, 263, 335

U

underconnectivity 36, 285, 290, 312

V

visualizing 105, 328

W

webinars 174
work products 177, 265

Z

ABOUT DR. GUTSTEIN

Dr. Steven Gutstein earned his Ph.D. in Clinical Psychology from Case Western Reserve University and conducted his Internship and Post-Doctoral work at Rutgers Medical School. Between 1979 and 1987, he served as an Assistant Professor of Psychiatry and Pediatrics at Baylor College of Medicine and the University of Texas Medical School. During this tenure, Dr. Gutstein also served as the Director of Psychology for Texas Children's Hospital and Director of Family Therapy Training for the Baylor College of Medicine.

Prior to focusing his efforts on remediating Autism Spectrum Disorders, Dr. Gutstein was recognized as a nationally renowned developer of innovative clinical programs for children and teens with high-risk conditions. In 1983, he received the largest grant ever awarded by the Hogg Foundation for Mental Health, to develop family-based intervention programs for severely suicidal youth. He has developed innovative, family-based programs for children with various medical conditions and Attention Deficit Hyperactivity Disorders. He has also developed school programs for children with problems related to Executive Functioning.

Since 1995 Steve and his wife, Dr. Rachelle Sheely, have served as the co-directors of RDIconnect Inc., in Houston, Texas, which provides training and support to thousands of professionals and families around the world.